SERPENTS AND APPLES:

Emotional, Spiritual, and Physical Well-Being for Working Women

By Karen Barrie and Kathleen Cain

New Win Publishing, Inc.

Copyright © 1992 by Karen Barrie and Kathleen Cain

All rights reserved. No part of this book may be used or reproduced in any manner whatsoever without prior written permission from the publisher except in the case of brief quotations embodied in critical reviews and articles. All inquiries should be addressed to NEW WIN PUBLISHING, INC., P.O. Box 5159, Clinton, NJ 08809

Library of Congress Cataloging-in-Publication Data

Barrie, Karen.
   Serpents & apples : emotional, spiritual & physical well-being for working women / Karen Barrie & Kathleen Cain.
     p.   cm.
   Includes bibliographical references.
   ISBN 0-8329-0469-4 : $17.95
   1. Women — United States — Psychology. 2. Women — Employment — United States — Psychological aspects. 3. Job stress — United States.
I. Cain, Kathleen. II. Title. III. Title: Serpents and apples.
HQ1206.B273 1992
305.42'0973 — dc20
                                                               92-41695
                                                                             CIP

Dedication

To my mother, who confronts life's limitations with courage, caring and great energy; my sister, as we learn together; and to my children, another generation searching to transcend what went before.

Karen

With love and gratitude to the women in my family . . .
    My mother, in honor of her quiet strength and courage
    My sister, for her love and support
    My daughter, who brought new meaning to my life
    My grandmothers, two very special women.

Kathy

Table of Contents

Introduction		ix
PART I	YOUR EMOTIONAL SELF	
Chapter 1	It's A Jungle In Here	1
2	Turning Wounds Into Wonders	33
3	Resolving Inner Conflicts	49
4	Savvy Systemic Solutions	67
5	A Word on Communication	97
PART II	YOUR SPIRITUAL SELF	
6	Divine Discontent	113
7	The Spiritual Bottom Line	129
PART III	YOUR PHYSICAL SELF	
8	Your Well-Working Body	175
9	Weeding Your Garden of Eden	223
10	Hormonal Rites of Passage At Work	237
Appendix I	Self-Massage Techniques	253
Appendix II	Work Moves	257
Appendix III	Affirmation and Question Cards	266
Appendix IV	Resources and Further Reading	273
	Notes	289
	Bibliography	292
	Index	294

Acknowledgments

KAREN'S

With gratitude, I acknowledge the women — great women — who have blessed my life with their love, companionship, and example. The honesty with which they have disclosed their satisfactions and pains, unsuccessful and successful experiments in living as strong women, has expanded what I know and impelled me to write about women's wellness. Special thanks to Carol Moran, who asks the best questions, even of herself. What a gift!

And the men — they, too, have taught me about women's wellness by the ache of their own search in counterpoint to mine, and in the variety of their love and friendship. Particularly Jack, my partner, who sees the flaws (and tells me!) and still wouldn't change a thing about me.

KATHY'S

Although this book is for and about women, I give thanks with affection to the man in my life, Bill, for tolerating hours of absence and months of seclusion while I wrote. His love and support never faltered. To the hundreds of women, young and old, who have been in my various classes, I have learned so much from your celebrations and struggles. I will forever be grateful to my yoga instructor, Judy Landecker, a gifted person who has taught me so much about myself, life, and how to teach others. And finally, a very special thanks to my mother, Virginia Thompson, who is the real writer in the family!

Co-Acknowledgments

With many things, in life, "two heads are better than one." Being co-authors, we toast each other. We never could have brought *Serpents and Apples* to life without our solid friendship. We have each other's talent, support, and sense of humor to thank.

As we delved deeper into the heart of the book "many heads" made contributions which helped to strengthen this book. *9 to 5*, National Association of Working Women, was a great resource to us. Diana Roose, Research Director of *9 to 5*, has a wealth of knowledge of women and the work place which she graciously shared. She also reviewed part of our manuscript and made valuable comments. We also salute *9 to 5* for granting us permission to reprint "A Model VDT Work Station." We greatly appreciate the Boston Women's Health Book Collective for giving us permission to reprint *Rights of Pregnant Workers* from their booklet, "Our Jobs, Our Health."

A special thanks to Dr. Mary Lang Carney and Dr. Linda Hughey Holt for taking the time to review the chapter "Hormonal Rights of Passage," and for their helpful comments.

We appreciate the many professionals who are cited throughout the book for their willingness to share their knowledge. And, we are extremely grateful for the numerous organizations listed in the Resource section that are devoted to women's issues and needs. Due to the lack of space and abundance of organizations, we regret we couldn't list more.

Introduction

Are working women liberated or imprisoned? The Biblical creation account has it that humans had to leave Paradise and lead lives of labor all because of Eve, who was tempted by a serpent to eat from the Tree of Knowledge of Good and Evil. Sounds pretty black and white, doesn't it? But it's not that simple. When we understand that everything in life can be either good or bad, depending on what we make of it, then sometimes serpents don't seem so awful and apples don't seem so great. When we have knowledge of the good and bad, we are empowered to make wise choices and to bring Paradise a little closer to home. That's what this book is all about.

Work can be a blessing or a curse; what each woman does with her workday determines whether or not she will be healthy, wealthy, and wise. When it comes to work, what are the temptations and what are the true fruits of our labor? This book answers this question by helping each woman create her own Garden of Eden on the job.

Eve was no fool. Put yourself in her place. Here you are in the Garden of Eden, perfectly content (as far as you know) with everything around you. To the best of your knowledge, all of your needs are met.

Then . . .

Along comes new information, some data you didn't have before. It's good here, all right. Very good. But . . . it could be even better, complete, perfect. The sudden knowledge that you don't yet have it all disrupts your peace, and you are unsettled. Dissatisfied. Unblessed. You perceive two choices. Either try to pretend you don't know what you already know (sort of like telling the jury to disregard what they've just heard, as if striking evidence from the record turns back the hands of time), or act on the new data with the hope that you will be, once again, content. What to do?

Well, you haven't yet bitten the apple, but already you've taken in more than you can chew: you've lost your innocence. You can't unlearn the fact that there's another possibility. A little knowledge can indeed be dangerous because it provokes a re-evaluation of the status quo. The peaceful acceptance of what you've got has been rocked. Maybe eating the apple will restore your inner harmony. Maybe you want to take a nibble, not because you know exactly where that will take you, but because you no longer feel good about where you are. You don't know if you can believe the advertiser's claim, but you do know you can't return to your former ignorance.

If you are holding this book, reading this page, it's already too late. You, as a working woman, already suspect that the place where you could be is better than the place where you are. The return to paradise is stepped along a series of plateaus; you achieve a new harmony, you feel content, and it lasts until the next bit of info comes along. The grass *is* always greener, and the longing for heaven on earth impels us toward it.

This book is meant for the Eve in all of us. It is the serpent *and* the apple: it is meant to discontent, to inform you that the place where you are might be very good but can be even better. The book is meant to take you to your next plateau, which won't be Paradise Regained, no. You will, however, have the practical tools to make your experience of work and others' experience of you more heavenly.

Thank goodness you're not Eve, right? Whether you believe the story of the Garden of Eden is literal or metaphorical, who would want all that responsibility? And yet, the truth is that each of us is responsible for our own physical, emotional, and spiritual wellness. Inherent in who we are is such a deep desire for completion that we never rest content for long. If you believe that everyone else, like you, shares this yearning, think of your journey toward paradise as driving on a crowded road: you can drive self-centeredly, viewing all the other drivers as out to get you or in your way; or you can understand that we're all helping each other get where we're going. There's traffic on the heavenly highway; you have an obligation not only to yourself, but also to others by keeping the flow moving along, exercising courtesy when they signal turns or apply the brakes, avoiding cutting anyone off, moving over when they're passing, and obeying the road signs. But when the road is open, your vehicle is tuned up, your tank is full, and (luck permitting) the weather is clear, you can fly along in the sheer joy of knowing you're on your way. Both serpents and apples are part of the scenery. You will find for yourself that what unsettles you, makes you see your dissatisfaction or discomfort, is your own serpent, operating as a servant to your desire to grow, tantalizing you when you might hesitate, provoking your native curiosity to explore new territory. This book is full of information to help you assess how much of your current situation is Eden-like and how much isn't. You will discover for yourself that what gives you new abilities and new prowess is your own apple, rich with the paradoxical knowledge that everything new is a potential blessing and/or curse, that every ending is also a beginning, and that what you make of an opportunity is up to you.

A word about our own experiences. In the process of birthing this book, we discovered our own apples and serpents. We have tremendous empathy for the difficulties of viewing well-being as the number one route to Paradise. Perhaps that is why we were compelled to write the book in the first place. We respect each other's differences in style and choices: Karen prefers meditation, with a supplement of yoga and aerobics; Kathy prefers working out at the health club with a little weight training thrown in. Karen prefers pleasing herself first and saving work to the last minute; Kathy prefers organizing and pacing herself well in advance of deadlines. Both of us experience entire chunks of time when attention to wellness seems to go right out the window, and it is with effort that we resume activities that perhaps months ago seemed to flow as an effortless part of our daily schedules. We found our heavenly highways to have many detours and roadblocks, but as we strove to practice what we preach here, we were able to find new exits and entries to help guide us. As a result of our journey we feel better equipped to handle life's unexpected turns, blowouts, and times of running out of gas. We also found that the highway is ever-changing. At times we wanted to veer back to the old familiar routes, but we also discovered that the horizon ahead looked pretty inviting.

Make the best of this book by tailoring it to your needs; enjoy meeting the serpents, relish eating the apples. Feel free to say "no" to whatever is useless or conflictive for you; try the things that seem appealing, helpful, sensible, and embrace whatever works. Practice them body, mind, heart and soul, until they lead you to the next step. If, as a result of reading this book, you move to a new plateau, then you will have achieved success!

Welcome to the journey home to yourself, to your well-being at work on every level, to a more heavenly existence during this life. Welcome . . . and *bon voyage!*

PART I
Your Emotional Self At Work

CHAPTER ONE
It's A Jungle In Here

What is it about the word "work" that carries such onerous connotations? The sweat of one's brow, toiling in the fields, bringing home the bacon — earthy images, but burdensome. The agricultural metaphors have necessarily shifted to a more contemporary vocabulary. Now we commute, work nine to five, work overtime; we have white-collar workers, blue-collar workers, and ring-around-the-collar workers; we've gone from plows to professions, horses to horsepower, tilling to technology. We, as a species, work not only to survive; we also work to improve the quality of life for the individual, and we work to make this world better for all. Sometimes we blunder on a planetary scale. Like the unraveling of some Shakespearean tragedy, the very things we do to avoid disaster in fact bring it on — witness the disintegration of the ozone layer and the conflagrations in the rain forests. But sometimes we do things so right! The miracles of medicine and science, comfortable housing, the initiative to feed everyone on the planet, and the development of mechanisms to do this — none of these would be possible without what we call WORK.

So, where's the rub? Why is WORK often a "four-letter word"? Two explanations: the first is that we can never fully foresee the consequences of our choices, creations, actions, plans. Who would have thought that such a technological boon as air-conditioning would contribute to the depletion of atmospheric protection from the sun's ultraviolet rays? And on an individual level, who would have thought that embarking on a career path could jeopardize a marriage? Or that working around asbestos could cause cancer? Even if some sage woman consulted the Delphic oracle or the three witches stirring their brew and was told that her personal and professional priorities would clash disastrously, might she not think, "But I can handle it. If problems arise, I'll deal with them"? We make our best choices believing we will keep disaster at bay as we go along, sometimes ignoring the evidence that damage is accruing.

The second explanation: we distinguish WORK from PLAY as though they are separate entities. For all too many of us, this is sadly true. Work is a job, a chore, a necessity. For others, however, this is not so; they are doing what they love to do, to their own and others' edification, amusement, entertainment — and getting paid for it! O happy day! And sometimes WORK and JOY go hand in hand: we know we're about to welcome a new life when we go into (pun intended?) LABOR — which is to acknowledge that birthing is one of the most physically and emotionally demanding acts of production a woman will ever experience, nearly always culminating in great happiness.

For a moment, consider the ideal: the work of each woman brings her joy and health. Whether she works out of necessity or choice, she deserves personal wellness and happiness as the direct products of her efforts.

Now let's examine the real: for most of us, working involves an ongoing process of maximizing the personal benefits while minimizing the personal costs. This is especially so with respect to emotionality. While many women believe that work is simply a neutral "job," a place to go which occupies a slice of life while services or skills are rendered in return for a paycheck, the majority of the species *Feminina educata* (educated women) attach meaning to and invest their feelings in their career choices. The overlapping of emotions and work can be heavenly or hellish — as working women soon discover.

In her pre-apple days, Eve was neither frightened nor angry. Survival, presumably, was not an issue in Shangri-la. Eve didn't need the knowledge of Good and Evil because, in a world where all is good, judgment skills are not in great demand. No wonder she couldn't evaluate the serpent's invitation! But once Eve took that ill-fated bite she began to experience what we all know only too well — the emotional roller coaster with its attendant ups and downs. Joy. Anger. Sorrow. Fear. Our feelings are primal evaluations of what is and is not good for our survival. They are our most basic knowledge of Good and Evil. In other words, they are value judgments that stimulate us to action. They are called "feelings" because we experience these signals in our bodies, and they are accompanied by distinct physiological changes. If we act, we can resolve them and discharge their physiological aftereffects, as well as their psychological ones. If we fail to act and bottle them up, they will return to haunt us; they become our baggage.

Feelings are the most ancient mechanism for survival which we, as cognizant beings, possess. Climb into your time machine, and head backward about twenty thousand years to observe an ancestress of yours who is out in the forest foraging for food, perhaps humming to herself or preoccupied with the recent torrential rains. Suddenly her senses alert her — a rustling sound, a slight odor, a felt presence. She whirls around and sees a wolf stalking her. What happens in her body? Her heart and breathing rate quicken, her stomach lurches, she begins to sweat, her muscles tense, her body gives her access to stored fuel and extra oxygen, and stricken with terror, she rapidly computes her probability of survival and her options. Her fear — a feeling certainly older than love — is both her assessment and her guide. She must act: will she flee or fight? Her feelings impel her to resolve the situation, and, if she has judged correctly (and luck is on her side), she will live to entertain her band around the firepit with the story that night. Strong feelings can even backfire. The body's mandate to survive can produce panic acute enough to paralyze, to freeze a person — she becomes a tasty snack to whatever is about to devour her.

Come back to the present and take a realistic look at what either threatens or enhances your survival in today's world. Wolves? Rival bands? A rich harvest? A fertility ritual? Not literally, but metaphorically, we are confronted with hundreds of stimuli to which our feelings respond, "Yes! This is good for me," or "No way! I'm out of here!" Or some variation on either of those themes. While our physical survival is no longer on the line daily, our bodies still provide us with signals that other layers of survival are in jeopardy. Sometimes we hear them loud and clear; at other times we ignore subtle messages until sharp emotions motivate us to make changes. At work, we often deny or anesthetize our feelings, unaware of what our bodies are trying to tell us. This chapter will examine three broad emotional arenas: first, the "baggage" each of us brings with us to work, or wherever we go, that determines our emotional outlook; second, the emotional conflicts between work and other priorities; and third, the events and relationships at work that present emotional problems for women. Where these areas overlap, examples will be given of "interface" issues, in which one area can feed into another. Later, Chapter Eight will take a detailed look at the physiology of stress and the profound physical consequences of this . . . and what you can do about it!

What this chapter does NOT do is explore in depth the wonderful positive emotional aspects of work. However, the contributions that working makes to our emotional wellness are worth reviewing, so as you begin to read about the gut problems a job can generate, don't lose sight of the benefits which (one hopes) outweigh the blues. If, however, as a result of reading this chapter, you find that in your own situation you are genuinely miserable — it may be time for major change.

Among the emotional rewards of work, whether yours is a temporary job or a career commitment, are autonomy, self-directedness, and fair financial compensation. If you do your job well, you gain feelings of self-worth, competence, confidence, strength, empowerment, satisfaction. If your job involves creativity, you may experience joy and a sense of maternity or giving birth. If you are in a service profession, you may regularly feel tenderness, nurturing, caring. No matter what kind of work you do, if it is a good use of your abilities and talents, you are likely to have fun and feel playful. When you are absorbed in problem-solving or an interesting task, you may be in the state of flow where you are so involved in what you are doing that you feel timeless, eternal, completely fulfilled. When you belong to a lively, committed team, you will feel love toward and be energized by your co-workers. If you have a good boss, you feel respected and in turn respect her or him. If your work is a challenge, you will grow and learn, and thus retain your vitality and attractiveness.

Furthermore, getting out of the house may gift you with a feeling of freedom. If you have children, sometimes the reminder that comes with a job that you are your own adult person is sweet relief after mopping up spills and reading Richard Scarry's *Best Word Book Ever* for hours on end. For a married/committed woman, having a career rebalances her relationship with her husband/partner. Sometimes in this process there are awkward role redefinitions and challenging control struggles, but if negotiated well the net result can be most rewarding in terms of equality for both members of the relationship.

In our have-it-all society, it would seem that for a woman to do paid work is a logical and secure path to contentment. Ironically, it is the very nature of having it all that has engendered more, rather than less, emotional stress. The expectation that women marry, bear and raise children, hold jobs, be successful, assertive, attractive, and sexual, keep a clean house, volunteer, earn a certain level of income, etc., has created a mighty burden. We need emotional wellness more than ever; for many of us, it remains elusive, though we diligently and *en masse* pursued avenues which have promised that this time we would finally achieve true happiness. We find ourselves overwhelmed, frazzled, stretched thin, depressed, and still grasping at immediate gratification. Even with emotional binoculars, Eden is a mere speck on the horizon of our emotional needs.

To understand where these needs originate, let's begin at the beginning: self-esteem.

MY TRUNK RUNNETH OVER

Each of us brings emotional baggage to the workplace. If you were lucky, both gene-wise and upbringing-wise, you are blessed with an unconditional, unwavering self-knowledge: "I am inherently good and lovable." If Nature's lottery didn't assign you a winning ticket in the first round, but in your adulthood you have grieved over and risen above childhood and adolescent victimizations — abusive or neglectful parenting, poverty, self-abuse, racism, and so on — you may be well clear of the worthlessness and rage that cloud feelings of self-esteem. If the emotional suitcase you carry into your job is filled with positives such as self-respect, serenity, good humor and healthy boundaries, your employer is fortunate to have you, since you are likely to support your own and everyone else's emotional well-being at work!

If, on the other hand, you fall into the estimated 96 percent of us who grew up in dysfunctional families[1], read on. It's scary, but you may identify with a large chunk of this chapter!

Childhood is the time of life when we naturally formulate our sense of ourselves by referencing our experiences against external authority — mostly our parents. The bulk of this process occurs during the first five years of life, a time when our verbal skills are just beginning, our brain cells are devouring learning, and our view of the world is dependent in large measure on how well our needs are met. We also are acutely sensitive to the feelings of those around us, and generally want to please the people we love. Before we are five, we go through a period of what is called "magic thinking" (although some of us never quite outgrow it); we develop unrealistic notions of causality, including the role we play in connection to the events around us.

It makes sense, then, that in girlhood our self-esteem is exquisitely vulnerable and fragile. Generally we may be predisposed to depression and pessimism; our brains develop neural pathways that "lock in" our conclusions about who we are, how the world operates, and how we respond. These are the origins of the unconscious and compulsive emotional reactions which are our automatic survival defenses as we enter adulthood, for better or for worse. To illustrate the range of possibilities, here are a few examples:

> HILDIE'S STORY. I grew up in a very authoritarian, rigid household. My parents, both German, were hardworking and, I think, gloomy by nature. We were taught to be seen and not heard. I remember my mother tucking me in at night, and telling dark fairy tales with forests and monstrous people who ate bad children. I think I felt remotely guilty throughout my childhood, although I can't recall having ever been bad.
>
> For me, work is an essential part of my life, and it's really my universe. I'm conscientious and methodical. I have a good time at office parties, especially the Christmas party, and I bake tons of special

German cookies and breads for it. I try to give my all at work. To be honest, I sometimes think I need my job more than it needs me. It's who I am. I worry that I'll make some horrible mistake and lose my job. I arrange my days so that I have time to review my work and make sure I haven't made mistakes. I dread performance reviews, even though they've always been positive. I would crumple if I were ever criticized, so I work very hard to make sure there's nothing to criticize. I know I'm a nice person and a good worker, but I don't know if it's a facade or if it's the real me. And I never want to find out.

STELLA'S STORY. I love my name! It means "star" and that's how I've always felt — like some lucky star has crossed my path. I knew I was pretty because my parents and my godmother always said so. Somehow, I always knew I would become a model, and I always knew there was more to me than my looks. I don't think I was ever stuck-up or conceited, because I was taught never to brag, that I had been blessed with certain qualities, and other kids were blessed with other things. Somehow, I was always in the "in" crowd without having to work at it, got good grades without much effort — I know it sounds snobbish, and I don't mean it to, but life has always been disgustingly easy for me!

Now, in my modeling, I love my work, the travel, the opportunities to meet interesting people. I see a lot of models who are preoccupied with their weight, their bone structure, their skin — I mean really obsessed, and who complain about the grind. I take good care of myself, but I also enjoy life. It's not important to me to be The Best Model Ever. A lot of people think models are superficial, or willing to use the bed as one rung on the ladder to success. I can honestly say that I refuse to compromise myself, and that I give a lot of thought to what's really important in life. I know I won't model forever, and I've started to think about the logical next step for me as far as a career goes. Maybe P.R. or hotel work, I don't know. For right now, I'm having a great time, saving money, and open to what the future may be.

TERRI'S STORY. Love my work? It's a job, what can I say? It pays the bills. If we weren't so strapped, I guess I'd quit, but I'd have to find another job sooner or later anyway. It's not that the work itself is so horrible. There's a lot to a printing business that's interesting. But my boss is a class-A jerk, great at criticizing, great at the occasional comment about how good I would look in a tight sweater (when he's in a "good" mood), and putting everyone down when he's not. Although I'd have to say that except for the sexist stuff, he's an equal opportunity employer — he gives the men equal opportunity to feel rotten, just like us girls.

I don't know. When I stop and think about it, all my bosses have been jerks. They don't seem bad during the job interview, you know, very businesslike and professional and like they know exactly what they want, then bam! They turn out to be creeps. I used to talk to my husband about it, but he says either stand up for myself or stop complaining. So I don't say anything to him anymore. I just go to work, try to stay out of Mark's way while I'm there, and come home. Once, about five years ago, I quit a job because my boss was coming on to me so strong. About four years before that, before I was married, I lost a job because I was having an affair with my manager and his wife found out — and he told me he wasn't married! What I'd like to know is, how did all these jerks get to be bosses?

Each woman — Hildie, Stella, and Terri — entered the work force with a unique program of expectations, abilities, and feelings of self-worth. There are many reasons why each woman comes to her career or job with her basic emotional position: "I'm good, worthwhile, lovable," or "I'm not as good as everyone else, I'm undeserving." If a woman enters a job feeling less "okay" than her bosses, colleagues, and subordinates, the job will not make her feel essentially better, though it may provide substitute gratification. In fact, she will likely continue to arrange events at work to reinforce her poor self-image.

An extreme form of using work as a "fix" to alleviate or avoid emotional discomfort in other parts of a woman's life is workaholism. What begins in apparently earnest intention and work satisfaction, even passion, gradually creeps over an invisible threshold and becomes a compulsive and unconscious medication for emotional pain. (It is important here to describe what is meant by "emotional pain." In life, everyone experiences times of tragedy which result in intense grief, longing, rage. These are exceptionally hurtful times of trauma and crisis, and not what is meant here. Rather, the chronic, low-grade and dull, often barely felt ache of vague unhappiness that tints the lives of so many women is the starting point for emotional ill-health on the job. This generally shows up as a lack — not being fully happy, alive, joyful, confident, self-loving — rather than as a felt pain. In fact, if chronic emotional pain hurt more, we'd probably act more quickly and wisely to truly dispel it.)

Work, no matter how fabulous the glamour, money, status, tasks, will not cure what ails you, if what ails you is painful baggage and you are in denial about it. Insidiously, your loaded trunk will begin to spill dirty laundry here or there. You can cover it up, but you will be, at some level, aware of its presence. Feelings of insecurity, shame, anxiety, fear — subtle as they may be — will motivate you to perform above or below what is healthy for you. There is a saying: Wherever you go, there you are. So how can you find out what's in your trunk? Time to pull out your pencil and enjoy a spot of self-analysis.

UNPACKING: TREASURES AND TRASH

This section is intended for your own use, to provoke and prod your reflections on your past and present. It won't give you a pat diagnosis; rather, it will offer you a way to examine elements and patterns in your emotional life related to your work. You may want to do this over several sittings; you will find that it takes your brain time to unlock old locks and oil the rusty hinges on the doors to your childhood — but once you get started, don't be surprised if memories begin to pop up at odd times during the day. This is perfectly normal; one memory leads to another.

I. WHAT I LEARNED ABOUT HOW TO FEEL ABOUT WORK

1. What kind of work did my mother do, and why? _____
2. What kind of work did my father do, and why? _____
3. How did my mother feel about her work? _____
4. How did my father feel about his work? _____
5. My mother said that work _____
6. My father said that work _____
7. Other relatives said that work _____
8. My teachers said that work _____
9. My religion taught that work _____
10. In fairy tales or other childhood stories, when it came to work, the women _____ and the men _____
11. One very sad thing that happened to my parents about work was _____
12. Around the house, I was expected to help out by _____ and I felt _____
13. I knew I had accomplished something good when _____
14. As a child, I found that work _____
15. When it came to helping around the house, my siblings _____
16. The best thing about work was _____
17. Any memories, ideas or feelings about work from your childhood_____ _____ .

II. WHAT I LEARNED TO FEEL ABOUT ME

1. My earliest memory of affection toward me is _____
2. My mother said that girls should be _____
3. My father said that girls should be _____
4. I knew I was being bad when I _____
5. I knew I was being good when I _____

IT'S A JUNGLE IN HERE

6. At night alone in bed I felt _____
7. Inside myself I knew my parents were wrong when _____
8. I was afraid of my parents when _____
9. I loved my parents when _____
10. I sometimes caused my parents to feel _____ when I _____
11. I tried my best to _____
12. I felt I couldn't please my parents when _____
13. I was praised when I _____
14. I knew I was lovable when _____
15. Even though I _____ my parents still _____
16. My siblings _____
17. My favorite memory of me is _____
18. A horrible thing that happened to me was _____ and I still _____
19. I was ashamed when _____
20. I was proud when _____
21. The parent with whom I felt closer was _____ because _____

III. HOW I FEEL ABOUT MYSELF/MY WORK

1. On the job I generally
   ___Overachieve   ___Work at my level   ___Underachieve
2. I would say the organization where I work is
   ___Healthy, benevolent   ___Sick, dysfunctional   ___Don't know
3. If I lost my job tomorrow I would _____
4. I respect my work.
   ___Always   ___Usually   ___Sometimes   ___Never
5. I respect my boss.
   ___A   ___U   ___S   ___N
6. I get caught up in office politics.
   ___A   ___U   ___S   ___N
7. At work, other people resent me or are threatened by me.
   ___A   ___U   ___S   ___N
8. When it comes to my work, I am a perfectionist.
   ___A   ___U   ___S   ___N
9. I see myself as an asset to my employer (myself, if self-employed).
   ___A   ___U   ___S   ___N
10. I hate my job.
    ___A   ___U   ___S   ___N
11. If something is poorly done or behind schedule, I will do extra work to compensate for it, even though it wasn't my responsibility to begin with.
    ___A   ___U   ___S   ___N

12. I give a lot of thought to the type of work I want to do, and the place where I want to do it.
 ___A ___U ___S ___N
13. I am recognized and affirmed by others for the work I do.
 ___A ___U ___S ___N
14. I am paid fairly, including benefits and perks, for my work.
 ___A ___U ___S ___N
15. I have a history of working for people whom I like and admire, and parting on good terms.
 ___A ___U ___S ___N
16. At the end of the day, I am satisfied with my work day and able to be fully present at home.
 ___A ___U ___S ___N
17. I take work home with me.
 ___A ___U ___S ___N
18. I work overtime (more than 40 hours a week in a full-time job).
 ___A ___U ___S ___N
19. I would do better at work if it weren't for the people around me.
 ___A ___U ___S ___N

Look at the overall pattern of your answers. What do they tell you about you and your relationship to work, and why or how you came to be this way? Have you come into the workplace, or a certain job, because you were expected to? Was it because you thought it was the best you could do, or you couldn't get anything else? Do you work because it's an outpouring and expression of what you have to offer, or because you need to survive and what else is there to do? Do you like and enjoy work better than anything else in your life? Do you blame others/circumstances for your lack of happiness at work?

Become aware of the little voice in your head, your self-talk. Women with poor self-esteem practice negative self-talk, usually by a critical, parental, irrational spokesperson left over from childhood. We are able to recognize and laugh at this chatter when we see it in movies, as in Woody Allen's *Annie Hall*. But it is much harder to get hold of it in our own lives, because it's so much a part of how we operate that we don't even see it, like blinking. You blink thousands of times a day, yet are rarely aware of it. You do self-talk thousands of times a day, yet hardly ever notice it. Here's an example of inner dialogue that might occur when a woman's boss informs her, at 4:20, that the report for the board has to be redone tonight — probably another two hours worth of work:

Gut: Oh, shoot! Not again.
Little Voice: You know how angry he gets. (Translate: his feelings are more important than yours.)

IT'S A JUNGLE IN HERE

Gut: But this is the third time this month. He doesn't organize his time.

L.V.: I know, I know. But neither do you. (Translate: your mother was right about you. Who are you to judge, little worm?)

Gut: Well, I'm sick of this. I'm tired, and I want to do my laundry and go to bed early.

L.V.: Oh, come on. You can catch up on your sleep another night. (Translate: what are you, some kind of wimp?)

Gut: Carolyn can do it. She hasn't left yet.

L.V.: Oh, that's fine! She already earned brownie points for that great presentation while you asked such a stupid question I couldn't be-

lieve it, and with the recession you know who's going to lose her job, but go ahead, go get a good night's sleep, what do I care? (No translation necessary.)

Gut: Okay, okay, I'll do it. (Translation: But you'll be sorry.)

At times, the little voice is just a soft background tape, sort of like negative elevator music, playing variations on several themes:

I'm no good.
I'm not good enough.
I'm just unlucky.
Why does this always happen to me?
Don't make waves.
What did you expect?
No one likes me.

Getting in touch with your inner tapes, especially if they're negative (and even women with fairly intact self-worth have a few pet self-criticisms) means going through your day in slow motion and listening to everything you think and feel. The little voice is automatic; its origin is the criticisms we experienced and internalized as children, when our worldview was forming. So listen to your thoughts, your inner dialogues. You may even want to carry around a small pad of paper and jot down what you hear, thus tracking it over time. Begin doing this, and it will help you with a technique suggested in the next chapter.

If you're still not clear whether your baggage is positive or negative, you can use your workplace itself as a mirror which reflects your level of self-worth. Companies generally hire people consistent with their own range of autonomy, respect, and integrity. Dysfunctional companies hire dysfunctional members; high-functioning companies hire high-functioning people. There is great wisdom in the concept that we only love or hate in someone what we love or hate in ourselves, and this applies to your job. While there are no perfect companies, and even self-employment can reflect self-abuse, take a look around at what you have chosen — yes, chosen — with regard to work. If you felt better about yourself would you still choose to work where you are now, or would you make a more informed decision? Do you often feel like the green grass is "over there?" This is a hard question, but unless you are honest with yourself, you are not likely to improve what, up to now, may have felt like your lot in life.

EENY, MEENY, MINEY, MOE

The next area of painful gut messages has to do with the tensions and trade-offs which assail professional women when they must choose among various emotional priorities: self-care, social life, love relationships, domestic responsibilities, maternal feelings and duties, and the majority of waking hours — career. If a picture is truly worth a thousand words, this section will result in a clear graph of which options in your life receive the most attention in terms of time spent on each. This in turn will enable you to discern why you may be feeling torn, guilty, or frazzled. Perhaps your actual day is in conflict with your emotional needs, causing you emotional stress. So keep your pen or pencil handy to continue the process of self-analysis.

The primary responsibility for domestic tasks, including cleaning, food preparation, and childcare, as well as managing the social calendar — the "traditional" female roles — still falls to the female head of the household despite the addition of career. Not only management of the feminine tasks but also having an attractive physical appearance is an expectation that women take to heart. This will consume even more of women's time and energy as the Baby Boomers hit menopause, since "matronly" is definitely out (!) but the never-ending battle against gravity and aging wages on. And how about preserving time and energy for intimate relationships and your sexuality? It makes sense that working full-time occupies so much psychic and physical space in a woman's life that it is taken for granted that the disappointments and fights occurring after hours are not connected to that primary dispersal of energy.

The choice to embrace a full-time job can create emotional conflict. It is easier to exist on a career track when there is not yet marriage, or marriage-and-kids, or (harder still) kids-without-marriage. But the single women who have been career-oriented and now hear the booming of the biological clock — it may have been ticking ten years ago, but it's much louder in their mid-thirties — resent the lack of time for a social life because their vice presidencies are all-consuming; or they worry about what will happen to their corporate positions if they do marry and have a child, time permitting.

Emotionally, we are at greatest peace when the structure of our lives is in harmony with our priorities. Sometimes we hit a balance that works for awhile, but the plateau is precarious if, for example, your child begins to have difficulties in school and the school social worker needs to see you (a daytime appointment, of course) and refers you for family therapy (at, let's say, $70 per session every Thursday at 5:30). Suddenly your feelings hand you a package: worry about your child, shame that you're not a better mother, guilt because your mother told you this would happen if you worked, anger at your mother for butting in, anger at your husband for not attending the school conference with you because he was out of town on a sales mission and you hardly ever see him anymore anyway, exhaustion over how to add another appointment to the schedule of lessons, games, and other chauffeuring, frazzled at driving through rush hour to make the appointment, frustrated at getting a fast-food dinner for your starving kids at 6:45, panicked at how to add a $280 monthly expense to the shrinking budget, etc. There goes your weekly workout time on the Stairmaster, which you were lucky enough to squeeze in as it was. Too bad, because at least it helped you physically vent your frustrations.

To carry the scenario a bit further, put yourself in the shoes of the mother just described, and imagine yourself at work. Some days, work will seem like a welcome distraction from all the family problems as you are absorbed in your tasks. But the dreaded phone call will intrude — "We have your son here in the principal's office. When could you come in for a staffing?" — and you'll wonder why your neck and shoulders are in spasm, your mind wanders occasionally, and the worry, guilt, and shame encroach and become a sort of soft-pedalled presence in the pit of your stomach.

Are we having fun yet? To get a picture of how much fun (or non-fun) you are having with your juggling of emotional priorities, do the following:

1. Prioritize by number from 1 to 11 where 1 is most important and 11 is least important, the items on the following list which apply to you.

    — My job (includes commuting time)
    — My marriage/long-term committed relationship (includes time spent directly and indirectly on it) (If applicable)
    — My children (includes direct or indirect time, e.g., making childcare arrangements) (If applicable)
    — Self-care (includes time getting ready for work, exercise, nutrition, beauty, relaxation, shopping for clothes, health and dental care, and solitary play/hobbies)
    — My spiritual life
    — My social life (includes friends, dating, parties not related to work, entertainment)
    — Sleep
    — Meals (does not include meals eaten on the job or on the run)
    — Personal growth (includes school, workshops, self-education)
    — Domestic chores (includes arranging/supervising others' work at home; food shopping and preparation)
    — Other _____

Here are four headings for a worksheet that you may complete. Analyze and break down your day as closely as you can, but don't split hairs;

IT'S A JUNGLE IN HERE

round off your time to units no smaller than ¼ hour. List your categories and the total amount of time in each. (The total number of hours should be 24.)

Schedule	Activity	Category	Amount of time

2. A picture is worth a thousand words. You will next construct a pie chart to get a visual depiction of how your time is allocated during a typical (is there such a thing?) 24-hour period during your work week. As in the following example, you will first list every activity, the category in which it falls, from the list in Question 1, and the amount of time (roughly) allotted to it.

EXAMPLE:

Schedule	Activity	Category	Amount of time
6:30 a.m.	Rise; turn on coffee, shower, dress, fix breakfast for kids, think about supper tonight	Self-care, domestic	½ hr. ¼ hr.
7:15	Get kids up. While they are eating & dressing, do makeup, be available to them	Children	1 hr.
8:15	Drop off kids, drive to work, arrive 8:55; work till 5	Commute Job	¾ hr. 6¾ hr.
	Breaks	Self-care	1 hr.
	Phone call home at 3:30	Children	¼ hr.
5:00 p.m.	Drive home	Commute	¾ hr.
5:45	Change, talk to kids, start supper	Children	¼ hr.
6:00	Meal preparation & eat, clean up, time with kids, husband, start laundry Help with homework; laundry, Kids' bedtime	Domestic Children Marriage	1 hr. 1½ hr. ½ hr.
9:00	Watch TV, finish laundry	Self-care	1 hr.
10:00	Watch news, chat with husband, tidy house	Domestic Marriage	½ hr. ½ hr.
11:00	In bed, hopefully	Sleep	7 ½ hr.

Now list the categories, and the amount of time spent in each. (The total number of hours should be 24.)

EXAMPLE:
    Self-care — 2½ hrs.
    Job & commute — 8¼ hrs.
    Domestic — 1¾ hrs.
    Marriage — 1 hr.
    Children — 3 hrs.
    Sleep — 7½ hrs.

After you have completed the worksheet, transfer your categories onto a pie chart divided into 24 sections, like the one below. You may wish to use different colors, one for each category, or shade each section differently. Label the sections according to the number of hours you spend in each of your own categories. (If you're really ambitious, and want a more detailed picture, make a pie chart for each day of your week, from Sunday to Saturday.)

3. Compare how you rank-ordered the list in Question 1 with your pie chart. Where does the time actually go? What do you find, and how do you feel about it? _____

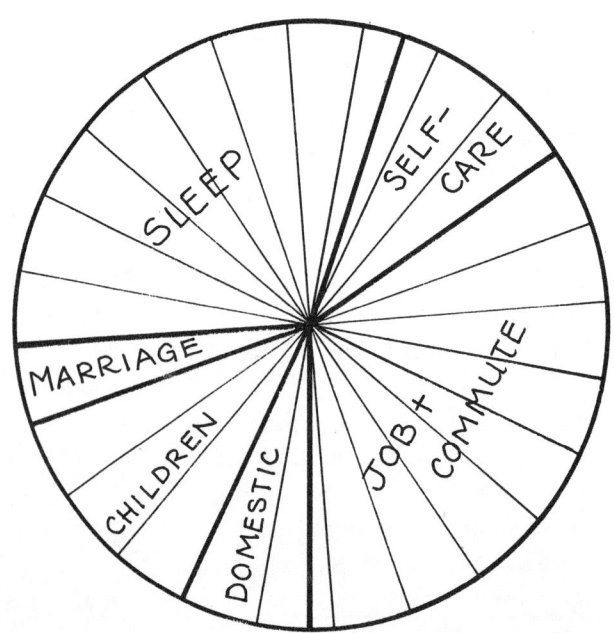

If there are discrepancies between what you believe is important and how you allocate your energy, emotional conflict is inevitable. If your most important relationships are getting short-ended, over time you will experience real unhappiness, as will your loved ones. And if you are already at a low ebb in terms of self-worth, you are headed for trouble. You will begin to cycle through a repetition of frustration and failures that will reinforce your belief that you're somehow falling behind in the human race. Left unattended, emotional conflicts, like toddlers, tend to get into greater and greater mischief. You can't fool your body; your body doesn't lie. First it tries to get your attention with Early Warning Signals, such as frustration, worry, dissatisfaction; these minor discomforts are the message to change or adjust what you're doing because something is interfering with your "survival." Just as fear not only motivates but prepares a threatened person to take action, these feelings can provide you with the incentive and energy to reorganize your decisions. You can, of course, overlook and ignore them, since they often aren't "loud" enough to heed over the clamor of everything else in your life. But the effects of these feelings accumulate until finally they manage to halt you in your tracks: illness, depression, a breakdown, a failure, an accident — whatever it takes, your body will do it.

Working mothers in particular are prone to the overwhelming number of self-debates that occur in balancing work and family, especially when the children are young and relatively dependent. Some days, it almost feels like an Eeny-Meeny-Miney-Moe situation, as if any old choice will just keep the game moving along, and that no choice is any worse or better than any other. The child-care trade-offs tax a working mom in three ways: emotionally, wondering about someone else raising her children; financially, as a large portion of her pay slips through her fingers into someone else's pocket; and structurally, as the child-care provider takes a sick day, or moves, or gets a better job and mom has to take time off from work to scramble for a good replacement. And because conscientious mothers put their dependent children's needs ahead of their own, it becomes easier to ignore distress signals from the body.

Signs of emotional conflict include physical symptoms: headaches; muscle tension, especially in the jaw, neck, shoulders, mid- and lower-back; an ache in the region of the heart; irregular heartbeat; digestion upsets; tightness in the chest or stomach; tightness in the throat; a lump in the throat or welling of tears in the eyes; difficulty eating; a change in one's relationship with food (quantity or quality); lowered desire for sex. Feelings which may occur are: depression, anger, anxiety, confusion, suspicion, jealousy, rage, sadness, grief, frustration, irritability, inadequacy, helplessness, hopelessness, lack of self-control, fear, paranoia, worry.

Behavioral manifestations of emotional conflict are also varied, but be on the lookout for: an attempt to control or influence the behavior of others, especially your loved ones, as a way of managing your own conflicts; becoming manipulative; becoming inappropriately confrontational; blaming (even if only mentally, watch out for holding someone or something else responsible for your situation); withdrawing or isolating; wanting to escape geographically; taking on even more work; becoming increasingly perfectionistic or critical of self and others; arguing more.

All of these traits can be symptoms of emotional distress as a result of conflict, especially if a pattern of symptom/frequency emerges over a two-month period. Everyone experiences crisis, and the short-term appearance of several of these characteristics is generally manageable. What's truly important to be on the alert for is a chronic sequence or presence of indicators that you are adrift on the stormy Sea of Values, and without proper navigation instruments, headed for reefs. Listen to and trust your feelings; when you are in pain, don't ignore it. Let it be your compass to a safer harbor.

THE EMOTIONAL ENVIRONMENT: WHAT YOU DIDN'T BARGAIN FOR

Rarely do women go out on job interviews prepared to screen a prospective employer for emotional and mental health. Since the interview itself provokes anxiety, many interviewees are so relieved at creating a favorable impression that it doesn't occur to them to turn the tables and ask some essential questions. Many unhappy misfits could have been avoided if a) the interviewee had had a basis for discerning how emotionally nurturing and rewarding the workplace might be, and b) the interviewee believed in herself enough to hold out for a more functional situation if this one does not meet her standards. Ask such questions as: How do you respond to employee initiative? What kind of verbal support can I expect if I am hired here? Is there discrimination in your treatment of men, women, and minorities, and if so, what kind? Do you expect me to work overtime, and if so, how much would I be compensated? If you are interested in hiring me, may I interview three employees of my choice to ask them how they find working here? If you promise something to an employee, do you follow through?

The point in asking these questions during the first or second interview is to take a pulse check of the emotional health of the organization. When asked, a prospective employer may or may not be entirely truthful in responding to your questions, and this is hard to detect. There are also telltale signs of gameplaying, authoritarianism, and rigidity which are subtle and therefore easy to overlook when a woman's attention is on how well she's presenting herself, and when she is perhaps worried because she desperately needs a job. Without first asking, the hopeful employee-to-be may be entering a dreadful situation in which she will gradually wither emotionally.

What are the classic "office politics" which take their emotional toll on women, and how do they operate? Three categories of dysfunction (hierarchies, relationships, and communication) will be explored; special consideration will be given to sexual harassment. All jobs have some elements of poor functioning; no perfect position exists. But each working woman has a right to mental and emotional well-being on the job. As you read, read not only for recognition but also for balance: do the emotional assets of your workplace outweigh the liabilities, and by how wide a margin? If the debits cancel out the credits, you are operating in the emotional "red." Prepare yourself to make changes. There is no excuse for abuse!

Throughout the remainder of this chapter, the words "functional" and "dysfunctional" refer to the mental and emotional well-being of the job or company. A functional workplace is one which respects and nurtures growth for the individual and enhances harmonious interrelationships which further the benevolent purposes of the organization. A dysfunctional workplace interferes with the identity, autonomy, creativity, and integrity of the individual and sets up "crazy" or "sick" dynamics among the employees at all levels, from bottom to top. *There is no correlation between the success of a company, as measured in profit, and how functional it is.* In fact, some of the most financially profitable institutions have generated millions of dollars at the expense of their employees' emotional health and that of their loved ones. Interested in how it happens? Read on.

DYSFUNCTIONAL HIERARCHIES

Among other things, a company is a social phenomenon. As such, whether explicitly or not, it has an organizational chart, revealing vertical and horizontal structures of power, roles, and tasks. Generally speaking, the "higher" a position on the corporate ladder, the greater the leadership, decision-making, and other management responsibilities that attend it. Furthermore, being creatures of meaning, we tend to ascribe status to such roles, assign them social boundaries, and award them greater financial compensation. When you first enter a position, you generally do a lot of "down and dirty" learning about who's who in the company, the power of each person, and the likelihood that this power will affect you. Even if you requested and were given a copy of the organizational chart, the paper in your hand might reveal precious little of what *really* goes on. Only showing up for work day after day and observing the dynamics around you will give you the actual picture. In other words, those who are supposed to be at the helm may not be doing their jobs; or they may be doing their jobs but also making everyone else nuts in the process.

The structure of a company is dysfunctional when its members abuse their power. "Pyramid" models, in which a few people at the top make decisions affecting many below them, are more likely to permit misuse of power than "collegial" models, in which dialogue and consensus form the basis for decision-making — albeit less efficiently. There is nothing inherently wrong with the pyramid model; in large institutions, it works, especially when there is a vertical flow of communication and feedback between levels. When the ideas, needs, and morale of the members at one level receive an open hearing at higher levels and management is appropriately responsive, power is used as a service, rather than as clout. Members of the organization are likely to thrive emotionally in such a situation. However, when a pyramid houses top members who are domineering and rigidly authoritarian, insensitive to morale issues, or conversely, leaders who are ineffectual, helpless, and chaotic — those beneath are inevitably going to pay an emotional price. In the former instance, members' creativity, spontaneity, self-esteem, and freedom suffer; in the latter instance, members must "cover" for incompetent leadership by glossing over mistakes, scrambling to meet deadlines, and informally deciding how to manage a crisis. In effect, they take on responsibility without recognition, rank, and financial rewards. Both hierarchical flaws abuse the earnest goodwill and talent of the lower echelons. The resulting emotions include: bitterness, anger, confusion, depression, disgust, disrespect, suspicion, paranoia, fear, anxiety, panic. Or, in the case of members shouldering management burdens which are not properly theirs, they may temporarily experience good feelings, even euphoria, about themselves as they overfunction on the adrenalin high, but this is doomed to burnout from exhaustion, since the goodness is the illusory result of the hyperadapted stage of stress. Eventually, these cooperators in the dysfunctional hierarchy will experience some form of emotional, and perhaps physical, collapse. The problem is that everyone within the context "buys" that it's okay to keep these people because the hierarchy itself does not have adequate built-in methods for self-evaluation and is therefore in denial. Members who rock the boat by confronting the problem do not last; the company finds some way to silence, scapegoat, or banish such employees, while everyone else quietly suffers low-grade dehumanization.

A second form of dysfunction in hierarchies is disparity of expectations — too high or too low. An incoming employee generally has no way to evaluate whether or not the expectations are abusive until she is in emotional pain, either stressed-out or bored beyond belief. In fact, companies with unreasonable expectations (such as working 130 percent, inordinate travel, taking work home) are asking their membership to embrace the corporation as a priority greater than any other relationship; marrying a company is not what most of us wanted to do when we grew up! These companies have clever ways to camouflage their request: the privilege of joining a Fortune 500 corporation, the generous use of a company car, making a bonus, being on the "partner track"; perpetuating the how-great-we-are fable through internal propaganda and keeping the adrenalin cranking through a crisis can keep employees overfunctioning and numb to their own needs and feelings. To participate in unreasonable expectations, we have to buy elaborate illusions and myths. These hierarchies damage their members emotionally in two ways: delusion and drain.

A third form of hierarchical abuse is the use of guilt and shame to control members' behavior. This can be very subtle and diffuse throughout the organization — a vague sense that mistakes are unacceptable, that there's something "wrong" with you if you use your personal/sick leave, that telling the truth is not okay, that meeting your own needs is selfish and bad, etc. Or the abuse can be situational and quite blatant: the supervisor who berates you as a person when your project is overdue, the performance review in which a disapproving voice tone is used — even when the words are positive, the "I thought you were better than that" attitude or comments by management — these are just a few of the thousands of ways that "shame on you" can creatively be imparted. No one enjoys making mistakes; mature women acknowledge, correct, resolve, and move on from them without having to be told, and if need be, they will bring problems to the attention of a supervisor and solve them together. But when a hierarchy implicitly sees its underlings as naughty or ignorant children, this erodes the self-worth of its members. Ask yourself: am I currently working in a situation where I feel as though I can't afford to make a mistake and I dread what will happen if I do? If the answer is yes, examine both your own baggage (are you carrying around a load of shame?) and the structural practices of your workplace. This is one of those "interface" areas between personal and professional arenas which are all too common, especially for women.

A fourth hierarchical abuse is institutionalized discrimination. The word "discrimination" is used here to mean irrational and disparate standards of treatment for different groups. Chauvinism, racism, elitism, ageism — these obvious forms of prejudice have gone underground since the EEOC (Equal Employment Opportunity Commission), the courts, and vocal minority groups have confronted cases of unfair bias. Nonetheless, in many companies there still exists a double standard which quietly manifests itself in the unwritten policies toward persons of color, women, gays, older people, and the handicapped. Behaviors indicative of these prejudices include limited advancement in spite of equivalent qualifications, status issues, repeated promises which somehow never come to pass, the telling of stereotypical and denigrating jokes, disproportionate assignment of unpleasant tasks, exclusion from informal socializing, and so on. Be on the alert for signs that your business operates in a prejudicial manner; also be on the lookout for how much of it you may be ignoring, tolerating, or even practicing. Cooperating with the system hinders your own emotional development, as you ultimately must lie to yourself that this stuff doesn't bother you.

DYSFUNCTIONAL RELATIONSHIPS

For a relationship with a superior, colleague, or subordinate to be unhealthy, both parties must collaborate in maintaining it that way. The purpose of this section is to identify both the markers of dysfunction in any relationship and the ways in which you may unwittingly be participating in dysfunction. Throughout this section, be aware again of "interface" issues between the context of your job and what you bring to it.

What Boundaries?

Relationships, *any* relationship, involves the establishment of boundaries, or emotional limits. A useful simile is the personal, physical space around each of us. When people with whom we are not intimate move within eighteen inches or so, especially face-to-face, we experience a physiological reaction sometimes verging on panic. Automatically we feel violated and need to draw back. Past the perimeter of eighteen inches to about three feet there is a social zone for friends, acquaintances, and business associates, and beyond that, a zone for strangers and enemies. These are literally physical boundaries, practically universal in our society, and generally honored by healthy individuals.

Likewise, each of us needs emotional zones: intimacy, friendship, acquaintances, business, strangers, and enemies. Because relationships change, and the possibility of becoming closer always exists (even with enemies!) these emotional boundaries must be flexible or permeable. However, when they are too adaptable, they become diffuse, and we get caught up in the emotional needs and reactions of other people and they with us. On the other hand, if they are rigid, intimacy is impossible, and even empathy can be difficult. In our culture, women more than men are expected to be sensitive to the feelings of others. However, *anyone* who grew up in a dysfunctional family, we now know, almost has radar for the feelings of others, whether conscious of it or not. By simple virtue of being mammals, we pick up many cues which inform us that someone else is emotional: facial expressions, choice of words, voice tone, and posture, certainly. Less obvious indications of emotionality, but which we nonetheless sense, include pupil dilation, breathing rate, muscular tension, involuntary eye movement, change in body temperature, change in skin tone, perspiration, and even certain smells; all these alert our own brains and nervous systems. Therefore, if you are in good health and your senses are operating, you will be aware that another person is feeling something. You almost cannot NOT know when someone is feeling something. This may account for what is sometimes referred to as tuning in to someone's "vibes" or "vibrations." You may not correctly know the feeling (for example, you may read impatience as anger), nor why the person feels that way. But you *will* know that an emotional response is occurring. Thus, emotional boundaries are always permeable to some degree (unless you are dealing with a zombie, a sociopath, or Mr. Spock of "Star Trek"). This is important, and bears repeating: whether we know it consciously or not, we are virtually always tuned in to emotionality in other people, which usually results in arousal of our own feelings. Herein lies the potential for dysfunction.

Inappropriate Intimacy at Work

By definition, the workplace is precisely what its name says: a place to work. Workers are contracted for their contributions to a goal (usually helping the company make money). This is what distinguishes "professional" from amateur, hobby, avocation: you are paid for what you do. If what you do is dependent on becoming intimate, you are probably working in a profession such as psychiatry, psychology, social work, the ministry. Ethically, such service providers are expected to stay personally and sexually uninvolved with their clients, so there are certain boundaries which safeguard the trust necessary for intimate revelations by the client. Other than the human services and medicine, intimacy is not a part of anyone's job description. However, in today's "future shock" society, where families are "blended," single parents abound, where corporations liberally relocate workers, and many adults have shied away from the religious affiliations of their youth, many people find the workplace to be their primary source of socializing and community. Hence, many women look to the job to meet their needs for closeness. It is thus hard to recognize and accept that becoming so close with someone on a job that it interferes with one's performance, judgment, and other work relationships is inappropriate. This applies to friendships as well as love relationships. It is further complicated when such intimacy occurs across hierarchical lines, when secrecy is involved, or when two people who work closely together are married to each other. This is not to say it can't be done. Many people have successfully negotiated intimacy and work. The criterion of dysfunction is efficacy: is work still receiving the same quality and quantity of energy, attention, and talent as the contract requires? If not, trouble is smoldering, and at least one person is going to get burned. If you've ever gotten "involved" and "broken up" with someone at work, you know what a bad taste that can leave, and how complicated going to work can be, especially if you have to encounter this person. This is emotionally abusive to you, even if to no one else.

Another form of intimacy gone awry at the job is being too open and vulnerable with co-workers who have not earned such trust, or lending a perpetually available ear to someone who needs to spill her guts. Sometimes women feel as if they somehow owe baring their souls to a manager or colleague, or as if they shouldn't refuse someone who desperately wants to talk. These types of encounters gradually deteriorate, even though they may begin by feeling good and helpful. Initially they are hard to recognize as potentially dysfunctional until the listener begins to feel used, as if the speaker is some type of parasite, and then pull back; the speaker then feels hurt, angry, rejected, abandoned. Here again, what may be operating is a powerful interface between a personal pattern of getting close and a convenient work situation.

Another variation on inappropriate intimacy is gossip, or the rumor mill. Dysfunctional companies keep their members energized and titillated by tolerating the spread of intimate details about someone's personality, work habits or personal life — true or not! This is very sad and represents both a statement about human nature and the failure of a company to channel curiosity and extroversion in a healthy way. Gossip is hurtful and demoralizing; ultimately the company itself becomes the victim of gossip, as workers go home and complain to others what a "sick place" it is! Gossip also becomes something of a competitive race; participants must keep ahead of each other so as not to become the brunt of a rumor. This pattern perpetuates itself out of fear and is stressful.

Even if you personally believe that you have healthy emotional boundaries, you will eventually feel drained if you work in a situation where others' boundaries are diffuse when it comes to intimacy. How healthy is your job situation with regard to intimacy? Not very, if there are affairs, rumors, exclusionary friendships, workers who are "a mess" because they're breaking up with someone else at work, etc. Take a good look at your own intimacy behavior on the job as well as that of the people around you. Ask yourself if you're satisfied with the way things are. If you're not, look for suggestions in the next chapter on improving your situation.

Inappropriate Defenses

Each of us, at one time or another, is subject to emotional assault. It would be wonderful if everyone we met had the intention and know-how to meet all of our emotional needs. In fact, it would be wonderful if we even fully knew and understood our emotional needs, so we could ask to get them met! Life is not perfect (oh, sigh) and so each day presents opportunities to be emotionally abused or neglected, or to dish it out to someone else.

Inappropriate defenses on the job include both too few defenses, which have to do with diffuse boundaries, or too many defenses, which comprise rigid boundaries. When a woman disintegrates over an unfavorable critique of her work, when she takes things personally and is preoccupied with them, when her heart goes so far out to a fellow employee whose performance is slipping that she covers for this person on top of her own work, when she feels ignored or neglected — these are all signs that her boundaries and defenses are inadequate for the situation at hand. Personalizing and emotionally overreacting to the actions and feelings of others drains precious energy, stimulates a stress response in the body, and ultimately lowers one's self-esteem.

Too many defenses can also gum up the works. Our primal resources for dealing with invasion or threat are "flight" and "fight." The forms of these seen most often at work include withdrawal, isolation, outright denial, minimizing, distorting, placating, avoiding, excusing, rationalizing, distancing (forms of flight); and anger, hostility, sarcasm, blaming, scapegoating, arguing, demanding, and pulling rank (forms of fight). A form of defensiveness which combines elements of flight and fight is passive aggression, which means arranging to make life miserable for others in such a way that it is difficult to be held accountable. This also avoids the real issue. For example, a woman who is given a last-minute research assignment by a boss who habitually does not organize well for deadlines may be furious because this is the third time in a month she's been taken advantage of. Rather than refuse the work or confront her boss' ineptitude, she silently takes the assignment and finishes it, but in anger decides not to finish a proposal due at the same time and says nothing about her decision until asked for the proposal. Then she accusingly retorts, "Well, what did you expect? You told me to get the research data, and you knew I was working on the proposal. Did you think I could do both?!" as if her boss is at fault. If she's really good at this, her boss will feel angry yet helpless.

All of these defenses interfere with teamwork and problem-solving by establishing impenetrable boundaries. They keep alive the illusory and extreme form of "I am an island," and often inadvertently place people on the defensive.

Finally, a defense which wreaks havoc with relationship boundaries has to do with alliances, or triangles. How often we turn to a third party to vent our feelings, only to have that person catch the contagious emotional energy, perhaps becoming an ally or a rescuer, only to be seen as a persecutor later on. These cycles, once begun, are extremely difficult to halt.

Each of us needs emotional autonomy, and each of us needs community. Life is an almost daily juggling of these two; our defenses are the tools with which we are equipped to keep the emotional scale in balance. Our defenses are operating in a healthy manner when they keep out intruders we have not invited in — including those who turn to us for help when we don't have it to give as well as those who would berate or rescue us — and when they are not so much in control of us that we can quiet them and reach out to others to meet our needs for sociability, assistance, and affirmation on the job.

Methods for moderating your own defensiveness and for effectively responding to the defenses of others will be discussed in the next chapter.

Inappropriate Responsibility

Responsibility. Ah, such a loaded word. Don't you just remember those childhood voices?

> If you lost it, it's your responsibility.
> You can't have a dog because you're not responsible enough.
> You're the oldest, so you're responsible.
> Who's responsible for this?
> When will you ever learn responsibility?

And then there were indirect messages:

> NOW look what you've done!
> Make sure your room is clean by the time I'm back.
> How could you do this?
> You make me so mad . . .

Well, you must have done something to upset your brother.
You're old enough to dress yourself now.

The issue of personal responsibility incorporates concepts of accountability, as in getting your work done; culpability, as in guilt for making a bad choice; self-control, and free will. As we grew up, we learned about responsibility from our parents, teachers, and religious figures. Then the media, in publicizing court cases, communicated to our developing awareness that insane people, even temporarily, were not as responsible for their actions as sane people, and that some ends justify the means. We may have learned in our early work experience that individuals with power and money hold a greater obligation to help society. What we have probably all gone through ourselves is an evolution through different understandings of responsibility at different points in our lives.

In the workplace, as in every other area of our lives, we must determine what "belongs" to us, what is our part in work and interpersonal relationships, and what is someone else's. We need healthy boundaries when it comes to responsibility, so we achieve a comfortable moderation on the spectrum between laziness and martyrdom. If you consistently do as little as possible, never check for mistakes, plead ignorance, wait for others to take the initiative, daydream, use work time, supplies, or the telephone for personal purposes, then you are falling short in your responsibility to your employer — even if your employer is yourself. At the opposite end of the spectrum, if you believe no one can do a job as well as you, if you continually try to fix or solve problems when you haven't been asked or it's not in your job description, if you constantly need to take care of everyone else's needs, if you are chronically "overseeing" and judging the performance of others, you may have stepped across the border into over-responsibility, which is a form of (dare we say it?) grandiosity, even narcissism. Of course, certain personality types and an alarming number of oldest daughters enter maturity and the work force with an Olympian ability to know how everyone else should run his or her life, and a most generous willingness to help them with this. You know who you are, you Wonder Women of the World out there! And if you work for this type of person, you know how frustrating it can be to have your mind read, your needs wrongly anticipated, and your work critiqued or, worse yet, interfered with. And even though such driven types run the risk of burn-out, their stamina can sustain them for years!

The complimentarity between the lazy and the omnipotent never works indefinitely. Both doing too little and doing too much are breaches of professional etiquette when they persist. And organizations that tolerate either extreme only suffer in the long run, as the quality of work suffers from injustice, inconsistency, and the resulting emotional strains on their members.

SEXUAL HARASSMENT (OR DO YOU SAY HARASSMENT?)

In the fall of 1991, public attention was focused on the confirmation hearings of Clarence Thomas, nominee for a seat on the U.S. Supreme Court, and on the charges of sexual harassment brought against him by Anita Hill. These hearings again stirred the pot of public awareness and opinion over exactly what constitutes sexual offenses against women. There was mixed agreement on what they are, or who bears responsibility for them.

The most telling symptom of this societal ambivalence to which we, as women, fall prey was the disagreement among ourselves over whether Anita Hill was telling the truth. Try to recall conversations you took part in or overheard at the time. Weren't they lively, if not actually heated? Did you yourself believe she was truthful, or lying?

If you have ever experienced firsthand the bind of feeling "on the spot" because some man at work was treating you with sexual disrespect — from telling obscene jokes in the presence of others, to propositioning you, to threatening you outright — you are not alone. In a *Chicago Tribune* article (October 10, 1991) it was reported that ". . . more than 45 percent of women experience sexual harassment at work, according to Melissa Josephs, a policy associate for the group (Women Employed), in Chicago."[2] You may genuinely not have known how to assert your rights, or even what they were. Those hours of TV exposure on the hearings were the Great Projection Test for the sexual ethics and traumatic experience of millions, male and female alike. It was nearly impossible to get down to the core issue of how inadequately we, the women, still deal with being sexually harassed on the job. This form of dysfunction in the workplace encompasses all the types of emotional dysfunction previously described: hierarchical abuses, lack of boundaries, inappropriate intimacy, poor defenses, unhealthy responsibility, dysfunctional communication. Yet sexual harassment is a unique form of "unhealth" precisely because it IS sexual, and don't we still have some double standards floating around our society about male and female sexuality!

While there have been tremendous improvements in female equality politically and economically, women, more than men, are still viewed as sexual objects, and it is from this attitude that sexual harassment originates. And we can neither look to nor wait for legislators and courts to end the problem. Laws have been made and cases won, but the vast majority of victims do not initiate effective or formal complaint procedures.

In the workplace itself, women must decide what is and is not acceptable behavior, and reinforce it.

Many men and women still harbor the vestigial belief that women are somehow responsible for stimulating men erotically. Many men and women still expect women to be pure of thought yet able to be "one of the boys" when the conversation at the water cooler turns off-color. Many men and women still hold the archaic view that women who dress "provocatively" are "asking for it." Et cetera.

Sexual harassment is illegal in the U.S. according to a 1980 interpretation of Section VII of the Civil Rights Act of 1964. That means it is a Federal offense to sexually harass a person. According to the law, "Unwelcome sexual advances, requests for sexual favors and other verbal or physical conduct of a sexual nature constitute sexual harassment . . ." when employment or employment decisions are conditional to submission to it (which is extortion), and/or work performance and environment adversely suffer as result of it.[3] In other words, any verbal or nonverbal message (including pictures or objects) which implicitly or explicitly convey, "My mind is on sex right now, not on work, and won't you join me?" constitutes harassment, even if there is no threat attached. This can take the form of jokes, flirtation, gestures, touch, body position; it can range from direct messages to innuendo. The word "harass" means to be consistently bothersome, as if occurring over time. But even an isolated incident that makes you uncomfortable, and which you in conscience did not initiate or invite, can affect you personally and professionally.

The majority of sexual harassment occurs between men and women, the men usually being the offenders. However, all gender combinations are possible: male-to-female, male-to-male, female-to-male, and female-to-female. The essential components of sexual harassment on the job are:

1) the uninvited sexual objectification by one person toward another,
2) which interferes with the receiver's work ability, time, and/or energy,
3) and which creates emotional/physical/mental discomfort for the receiver.

Realistically, no workplace is devoid of sexual energy. We are sexual beings. Generally, we enjoy adorning ourselves, presenting a pleasing image to the world. We unconsciously evaluate others' attractiveness, just as they do ours, and this is a naturally occurring phenomenon. Some social analysts and psychologists have hypothesized that in our urban, media-oriented culture, we are bombarded with more sexual stimuli (rush hour on the sidewalks, crowded elevators, ads, movies and TV shows) than our biology has evolved to handle. In a broad sense, all of us are "sexually harassed"; just take a gander (but not a leer) at the magazine covers, particularly some women's magazines, at the grocery checkout line. This in no way, however, excuses lewd or exploitative behavior at work — or anywhere else.

Here are the damaging effects of harassment on the individual: hurt, confusion, anger, self-doubt or guilt, pressure, physiological stress, fear, withdrawing, the burden of secrecy, shame, betrayal, disgust — any, some, or all of these may be present in an individual. It is no surprise that such feelings would distract a woman from the ability to do her job. Often the victim of it falls into further difficulty. First, many women do not clearly identify, right at the moment, that they are feeling violated. Sometimes it may take days, weeks, months, even years, to comprehend and name what was happening. One woman related that she did not understand how bothered she was by her boss's leering remarks about her husband being such a "lucky" guy until she had worked for a new boss for eighteen months who never once made a remark about her husband!

Second, once identified, it may be difficult to confront the offending party. Women are all too often raised to be gentle, polite, respectful, sensitive — in other words, what are we supposed to do with our justifiable anger?

Third, if the situation is severe enough to warrant intervention or legal action (that is, if direct confrontation does not put an end to the situation and the grievance procedures at work have failed) where should the injured party turn? In a dysfunctional organization, going over the offender's head may be logical, and may be the procedure dictated by policy, but in practice this may not be safe. Involving a lawyer can be quite costly in money and time, not to mention the emotional drain. Some women fear winning the battle but losing the war: their jobs, reputation, whatever. Although the law against harassment is drafted to prevent such reprisals, they can happen anyway. If a person is being sexually harassed, there is a chance that she is not the harasser's first victim, but how can one find this out? If there were other complaints, these cases should have been handled confidentially. Then too, women who have gotten out of an unpleasant situation do not readily renew memories, feelings, and pragmatic risks by revealing what happened. So the helplessness and isolation of the victims of sexual harassment further detract from their professional and personal well-being.

Those who have experienced sexual harassment know how intimidating, frustrating, and humiliating it is. Those who sought help through the established channels (through their company or the legal system) may have encountered skepticism, disbelief, and disrespect — possibly ending up feeling as though there were something wrong with *them* or that they were crazy.

Each woman has the right to work in a healthy environment, free of sexual innuendo, pressure, and impropriety — not as an object but as a human being deserving of respect. Chapter Four, in examining roads to emotional wellness at work, will offer options for personal and corporate efficacy in dealing with the problem of sexual harassment.

Sexual harassment, dysfunctional hierarchies and relationships, power abuses — these are worms in the apple of your self-esteem. Worms can be gotten rid of, but the apple itself has to be a healthy and whole product of a tree that's deeply rooted and nourished, grows in ample air and light, opens its blossoms to the necessary bees — yet still receives protection from the storms that can traumatize it. The knowledge of who you are, and what you can and can't do is a critical component of emotional well-being in a less-than-perfect world. The next chapter offers advice on developing a more celestial work life by valuing yourself.

CHAPTER TWO

Turning Wounds Into Wonders

A highly qualified MBA, Victoria Victim, has just landed a vice-presidency with Megamonolithasaki, having negotiated a six-digit salary/benefits package. Secretly, however, she battles depression (she's on medication and sees her shrink twice a week); she has compulsively and competitively overachieved since first grade and fears that unless everyone knows how responsible she is, they will see her as a shameful failure.

In one sense, adulthood is the time of life during which we cleverly disguise ourselves as well-adjusted individuals but in fact often act out of childhood feelings of shame and worthlessness. It's as if the authority figures from our growing-up years still tower over us, looming there, waiting to victimize us with their I-told-you-so's. Many women spend their entire day motivated by cringing. Of course, even the most emotionally traumatic girlhood is no excuse for abrogating accountability for one's actions; we must continue to grow in moral responsibility. On the other hand, to deny one's baggage, if it's there, perpetuates compulsivity, anxiety, and therefore unsatisfying participation in our professional tasks, the work community, and the effective political and ecological generosity needed to intervene in our troubled world.

It's not fair to blame Eve for all our rotten apples. You could spend a lifetime looking for a better orchard, a shinier apple. Learning to cultivate, prune, fertilize, and harvest the orchard you've got is the subject matter for this chapter.

If you, in your own estimation, have a solid core of belief in your precious worth, and are not easily shaken by the opinion of others, you may wish to skip this section. Otherwise, the resources this chapter offers for reinforcing self-worth are: autogenic messages; affirmations from outside yourself, and inner dialogues for handling "shame attacks." To deepen the experience of these techniques, use them in conjunction with the breathwork in Chapter Seven.

Please note that your self-worth is not all in your head. Mind over matter is naturally crucial — you have to decide to use the techniques in this book and plan to structure them into your life. This takes a certain amount of intellect, will, social support, and physical and emotional wellness.

AUTOGENIC MESSAGES — A MORE HEAVENLY YOU

Positive self-talk is the process of internal affirmation. It's very difficult to just stop playing old mental tapes; it's much easier to begin deliberately playing new ones, and they will gradually supplant the old. This is so because willful suppression of an idea or behavior puts it in the spotlight. Try the following: Whatever you do, don't think about sex. . . . Almost immediately, what happens? The harder you try to NOT to think about it, the harder it is to think about something else. Now try this: Think about your favorite place to play when you were little. . . . What happens? Bet you didn't think about sex! In order to avoid the inevitable preoccupation that occurs when we try to forcibly end a pattern, it works much better to simply begin a new one.

To help you believe in and feel good about yourself, we offer the following menu item. It may be done sitting or lying down, at home or at work. Try it first at home, in a time and place where you won't be distracted. Once you are adept at it, it can be done anywhere. It takes about three weeks of daily practice to be able to use it in most situations.

(Read the directions over until you are familiar with them, or make a tape for yourself, reading slowly with five-second pauses between each positive statement.)

Close your eyes. Take a slow complete breath, relaxing as you exhale. Take another complete breath, deepening your relaxation. Then breathe at a normal pace.

Take a few moments to allow your mind to gently consider and then release your cares and worries. When you have surrendered them away, you are ready to begin.

Mentally repeat each statement three times, pausing about five seconds between each repetition or statement.

1. Right now, I am good .... (3x)
2. I am becoming better each day .... (3x)
3. I am capable of change .... (3x)
4. I am precious and good .... (3x)
5. I desire to be my best self .... (3x)
6. My desire is my goodness .... (3x)
7. I am becoming the best I can be .... (3x)

Lie still, and feel the goodness within you at your heart center. Let it slowly expand until you are filled with it. Rest there for a few minutes. Then take one or two deep breaths, and when you are ready, open your eyes. Allow your attention to return gradually to your day.

Begin using this technique, or any portion of it, as frequently as you can at work. Not only does this make *you* feel good, it will also become contagious, affecting the peace of mind of those around you. Just as a negative person can grate on everyone, a positive person can uplift others. You will also begin to work even more productively and with better limits as you embark on the journey of sanity-through-self-esteem.

FRIENDS AND WONDER BREAD

The makers of Wonder Bread used to have an advertising slogan that told consumers their product would ". . . build strong bodies 12 ways." We all need to find the things in life which build us up, and this is even more important with regard to self-worth. Some of you are going to recoil at the following technique. You will mentally say things like, "But that's embarrassing," or "That's so conceited," or "I couldn't do THAT," or "My self-esteem isn't in such bad shape that I should bother someone else," or (worst of all), "I don't deserve it." Just listen to that inner voice when you read this suggestion: Contact your close friends, female and male, and ask them each to write a letter to you about all the good things they see in you. (Hear those objections in your brain?) Do it! Wouldn't you do it for one of your friends who asked you? Would you think, "Oh, she's not worth it!" or "What a jerk! Who does she think she is?" You have no idea how moved you will feel, how appreciated, when you read the letters. A sign of whether your self-worth tank is running on empty or not is the degree of squirming you do as you read them. The more you writhe, the more you need it!

Keep them in a file at work. Add to it. When a customer, supervisor or colleague pays you a compliment acknowledging a specific job well done, ask that person if she or he would put it in writing. Most people rarely think to do that, but are glad to. If they say yes but don't follow through, it usually means they, like you, got caught up in their own daily hustle and bustle. But if even 20 percent write those notes, your self-worth file will thicken. Read it often, read it in times of crisis, read it whenever. Lift out sentences and phrases that you can use as autogenic messages. If one of your friends writes, "You are such a good listener," use "I am a good listener" to add to the tape library in your mind. Let yourself take it in and be nurtured. Friends build strong self-esteem in lots more ways than Wonder Bread's 12.

INNER DIALOGUES

In the previous chapter, there was a conversation between Gut and Little Voice (alias L.V.). By now, you know that your Gut is the primal evaluation system otherwise known as feelings. But who (or what) is L.V.? It is all the authority figures you internalized in your much younger days, most often your own parents and probably especially (gasp!) your mother. We don't know why mothers get such a bum rap in particular, but Mumsy's (and whoever else's) opinions of you are alive and well in your Little Voice. For many women, the Little Voice hits them where they are most vulnerable, in their shame. But this makes perfect sense; a crash course in Self-Help 101 will help you understand that Mumsy's (or whoever's) opinion of you as a child sprang from her own fear that if her children were flawed it meant she failed as a mother, thus causing *her* shame. So we kids had to be good so Mumsy wouldn't have to deal with her baggage, and a Mumsy who is trying to avoid feeling ashamed uses shame to control the kids. Voila! Baggage and a Little Voice for you! You follow? (Of course, we all had to learn to behave and follow rules so that we could grow up and live and work together without harming ourselves and others. It's HOW we were made to follow these rules that sets up our baggage, not the rules themselves.)

From time to time, the L.V. gets the upper hand, but if the Gut voice is capitulating unwillingly, there's always a price to pay. It may be some form of self-sabotage, such as not getting a report done on time, or once again arguing with that co-worker you were determined to avoid. L.V. often uses criticism, guilt, and shame to "win" in discussions with Gut, although she can be the voice of parental wisdom and reason. However, Gut can also be the voice of childhood wisdom and reason, and between the two (and with the gift of experience/education) you can be true to yourself in a mature way. The trick is learning how to respond to L.V. when she's in her critical mode.

Let's return to the inner dialogue from Chapter One and see how it might play differently if we imagine that Gut now also has had a booster shot of self-esteem. Enter the boss, who informs Loyal Woman at 4:20 p.m. that she must stay and redo the packet for the board meeting tonight. Lights. Cameras. Action. Roll tape:

> Gut: Oh, shoot! Not again. This is not my problem. I gave him the draft two days ago.
> L.V.: Say yes. You know how angry he gets. (Translation: His feelings are more important than yours.)
> Gut: I get angry, too, and my life is as important to me as his is to him. This is the third time this month. He doesn't organize his time.
> L.V.: I know, I know. But neither do you. (Translation: Your mother was right about you. Who are you to judge, you little worm?)
> Gut: Hmmm. Interesting thought. I hear you saying that because I was disorganized as a kid, which most kids are, I do not have adult skills, and you are wrong about that. Please apologize for defamation of character.
> L.V.: Oops! (Aside, to audience: She's on to me. I'll have to try a new approach.) Sorry, Gut.
> Gut: I'm tired, and I want to do my laundry and go to bed early.
> L.V.: Oh, come on. You can catch up on your sleep another night. (Translation: What are you, some kind of wimp?)
> Gut: You are right that I have the option to make up my sleep some other time, but I choose not to use it. I need my rest in order to function well at work, and you know that. Carolyn can do it. She hasn't left yet.
> L.V.: Oh, that's fine! She already earned brownie points for that great presentation while you asked such a stupid question I couldn't believe it. I was actually embarrassed to be in your body. And with the recession, you-know-who's going to lose her job first, but go ahead, get a good night's sleep, what do I care? (No translation necessary.)
> Gut: Whoa! How many judgments can you throw in at one time? First, I resent your bringing up the question issue. We'll discuss that later. Second, I refuse to compare myself with Carolyn. We have different strengths. Third, the boss may have poor time organization, but he recognizes my contributions and values my skills. I don't believe I'm in danger of losing my job. There's been no talk of cutbacks, and while it's true there's a recession, I refuse to violate my physical limits over your fantasy of what might or might not happen. It's more important to me to take

> care of myself in the short run so I make the best use of my skills in the long run. I'm tired, I have plans for tonight. I'm leaving at 5:00. I'm going to tell him so politely, and I would appreciate your help with choosing the right words. Agreed?
> L.V.: Oh, I guess so. But don't be surprised if something bad happens. Don't say I didn't warn you.
> Gut: Look, it's just a choice right now. I'm scared to go in there, okay? Are you coming in a spirit of good will, or not?
> L.V.: Oh, all right. Now, here's what you need to say . . .

In order to use your inner dialogue, you must first know when and how it's occurring. You may have begun tracking it already. If not, carry a small pad of paper around with you for a week, jotting down each dialogue of which you become aware. This is the first step. Continue to use your autogenic messages during this period.

Next, each time your inner conversation begins, try some slow, deep breathing to help you gain a calm center. (Part III contains detailed breathing techniques.) This will give you time and oxygen to think more clearly. When you've got a good start on the slow breathing, move on to the third place of change. Insert the words from the autogenic messages into the "script" which your Gut uses to respond to L.V. When L.V. says, "Why are you wearing that skirt to work? It makes you look fat," let your Gut calmly reply, "I feel bad when you tell me I look fat. I am a good person, deserving of praise. Don't tell me what I do wrong; tell me what I do right. I desire to be the best I can be." Nondefensive internal honesty can hush L.V.'s anxious critique. Often L.V. is simply repeating what Mumsy (or whoever) said *ad nauseam*. When L.V. is confronted with Gut's clarity that "Someone else's shame is not MY shame," often L.V. will apologize and back down.

Be prepared, however. It took a lot of years and mountains of influence to form L.V. She will not easily leave. Persist in your efforts to integrate the autogenic messages into your inner dialogue. Eventually L.V. will believe you and begin to settle down. In times of acute stress, however, when you've neglected your program of wellness, L.V. will be right there, jumping in to reassert her authority and control.

If you practice slow, deep breathing, as part of your physical well-being, you will gain the added assurance that it works for your emotional health on the job. Your inner dialogues arise from your own anxiety that you are about to become ashamed of yourself in this situation or that. You will discover how well you can manage your inner conversation by integrating breathwork and autogenic messages.

WHO? ME?

No one is responsible for your emotional health and healing besides you. While it helps to understand that your baggage — whether light or heavy — originated in the interrelationship between the organism (you) and your environment, it is useless to blame Mumsy (or whoever) and hold on to your past as an excuse for poor behavior or performance at work (or anywhere, for that matter). Since the majority of your waking hours and your prime energy go into a full-time (plus) job, use it as a golden opportunity to experiment with awareness and choices. Then you will not only be cooperating with your own desire/need for emotional sanity, but you will also position yourself to fully develop and implement your social conscience. Healthy self-esteem and regard for social needs go hand-in-hand, and can even grow simultaneously. That's why this book addresses emotional AND spiritual wellness at work. More on that to come.

Meanwhile, back to personal responsibility. Random events occur. We experience them as helping or hindering our life's journey; you can eat the healthiest organic food and still contract cancer, perhaps due to your genetic heritage; you can be a raging alcoholic and never get into an accident or get caught weaving in traffic. The data from life itself does not give us accurate, clear feedback on personal responsibility.

The measure of personal responsibility is simply, really, how you choose to see it. This changes over time, as it does for society at large. In terms of emotional health, if you're interested in increasing it, your best bet is to gently hold yourself as accountable as you can, and know your limits. It can be just as responsible to say "I can't" as "Here, let me." It is possible to be dysfunctional in terms of responsibility. It is grandiose to be responsible for everything; it is a cop-out to be responsible for nothing.

If all the world is a stage and your script reads, "Why does this garbage always happen to me? HE did it! SHE did it! THEY did it!" it will be hard for you to move into emotional health unless you are willing to stop blaming. This means not blaming yourself, either, since blamers tend to think (dysfunctionally), "Well, if they're not to blame, then it must be me!" The blame game is a dead end, because it's simply a covert way to avoid resolving hurt and anger. Accepting responsibility nondefensively for the legitimate consequences of your actions can occur only when you are honest with yourself. In fact, the emotional consequences of accurate accountability are wonderful: relief, autonomy, self-confidence, and self-worth. At work, you have a job description; that is the responsibility delegated to you and to which you agreed. If it's too much or too little, get it handled with your manager. Any other responsibility which you voluntarily take on or accept must be judged, situation by situation, to be appropriate to your abilities and contracted with concerned parties. In other words, get verbal agreement before you: give advice (is that what the person is asking for?), fix what's broken (do you know the whole situation and do you have what's needed to fix it?), change how something is done (have you informed the appropriate people?), or make decisions (are you the appropriate decision-maker?). Simple agreement protects responsibility boundaries for both parties. The section on Active Listening (see Chapter Five) will help you establish a foundation for this agreement. For the receivers (sometimes the victim) of another person's well-intentioned taking of responsibility, this behavior may come across as controlling, demeaning, manipulating, intruding, creating confusion, anger, mistrust (as an adult, did you ever experience your mother's taking responsibility for you when you didn't want it?). For the doers (sometimes unconsciously acting out their baggage) taking responsibility may overextend and ultimately exhaust the person, creating resentment, irritability, a feeling of being taken for granted and unappreciated, and a greater need to control. Either way, the emotional milieu of a job deteriorates.

To discern appropriate on-the-job responsibility, honestly answer these questions for each instance in which you are tempted to step in and take charge:

1. Is this in my job description?
2. If not, have I been formally asked or required to do it?
3. Do I clearly know the consequences of doing this?
4. Am I willing to fully accept the consequences, positive or negative?
5. Am I able to do it?
6. Am I willing to do it?
7. If not, am I willing to suggest and negotiate an alternative?
8. Will I harbor negative feelings if I choose to do it, even though I'd rather not?

Never punish someone else for your choices. Nothing creates an uglier emotional atmosphere at work than scapegoating. And never allow yourself to be scapegoated if you genuinely were not the problem. Use appropriate channels to air grievances if you feel you are being unjustly accused of something that was NOT your responsibility! Place accountability squarely and realistically with Number One. Honor it, and you will be happier for it. See Chapter Four for tips on how to recalibrate responsibility.

NEEDS AND LIMITS

In conjunction with responsibility comes knowing what you are and are not able to do as a human being. The surest source of such knowledge is your own body. An unfortunate by-product of the development of Western theology and philosophy has been the dualism between body and soul. The implication of such a split was that the soul was a "higher" being which could enjoy eternal happiness as long as the flesh did not interfere by indulging in pleasures. This assumption, or variations of it, filtered into homes, schools, and churches over the ages, suggesting to millions of people that the body could not be trusted. (The psychological paradox is that the harder people try NOT to pay attention to something, the more obsessed they can become; another psychological irony is that the more worried people are about the body being "bad," the more energy and attention will be devoted to disciplining it. So without anyone realizing it, the very structures that were attempting to focus their members' attention on the soul were inadvertently putting spotlights on the body!)

Hopefully, you weren't raised to believe that your body was bad — a potential source of temptation and evil. If you were, you will have a difficult time learning that you, as a whole being, ARE a body that is good, trustworthy, and communicative. Even if you did not receive negative "flesh" messages, it would be no surprise if you learned very little about how to listen to, correctly interpret, trust and honor the many signals your body flashes at any given moment.

Here is an exercise in listening to and trusting your body in order to get a clear fix on your needs and limits. It involves fine-tuning your awareness as you search for bodily sensations that are the result of pushing yourself daily to go beyond your limits, of saying "YES" with your mouth when your gut is yelling "NO." Of course, there are many times when it is necessary to override a felt need or limit in favor of someone else's; compromises are a part of life and work. But there are also countless times when women violate themselves needlessly because of perfectionism, workaholic-rooted beliefs, being overly and inappropriately sensitive to the needs of others, or attempting to control and manipulate others. Whether you have misused your body out of genuine necessity or misleading beliefs, the results are the same: physical symptoms of emotional abuse, which are easy to ignore in their early stages but can become debilitating if not attended to.

So take a pen or pencil, and prepare to let your body "talk" to you.

Directions: You will be focusing your attention on various parts of your body, one at a time. With each part, take a few moments to *feel* any sensations (tightness, numbness, tingling, a dull ache, throbbing, pain, etc.) or to *recall* any sensations (headache, stomach ache, sinus problems, etc.) which you have experienced within the past three months. Jot down any sensations of which you are aware. Also, take note of any work-related images/memories which may pop into your mind as you do this. For example, you may feel tension in your jaw recalling the incident yesterday when a customer was rude while you clenched your teeth and held your temper. Or, as you feel how tight your shoulders are, you may realize how tense you become when loading mindless data into the computer. You may even get a lump in your throat or tears in your eyes over your unfulfilled desire to play with the art program on the Macintosh instead. Let your body speak, and be open to any information or responses it gives you.

1. Begin with your head. Think of your scalp, your face, your eyes, your jaw, the muscles around your mouth, your sinuses, any headaches. Record on paper whatever sensations and images come to mind.
   Sensations: _____
   Images: _____
2. Focus on your neck and throat. Pay attention to the muscles on the sides and back of your neck.
   Sensations: _____
   Images: _____
3. Focus on your shoulders, arms, and hands.
   Sensations: _____
   Images: _____
4. Focus on your back.
   Sensations: _____
   Images: _____
5. Focus on your chest, lungs, heart.
   Sensations: _____
   Images: _____
6. Focus on your abdomen and internal organs.
   Sensations: _____
   Images: _____
7. Focus on your hips, pelvic area, groin, and buttocks.
   Sensations: _____
   Images: _____
8. Focus on your thighs, knees, calves, ankles, and feet.
   Sensations: _____
   Images: _____

If you have been patient, thoughtful, and thorough, you will have a range of sensations/images written down. You may not have something written in each category, and perhaps one or two are quite full. Not all sensations correlate with events, relationships, or the environment at work. Some are more personal but spill over into your work day. However, the information you just recorded is your body's way of communicating with you about your unmet needs. Continue with the following reflective questions:

1. Which situations at work energize you, make your body feel good? _____

2. Which situations at work trouble you, cause physical tension or discomfort, or other physical symptoms? _____ _____.

3. What do you need? (List everything that comes to mind. Do not censor or critique anything.) _____ _____.

Now reread what you have written. At this point, any discomfort from your body (tension, headaches, stomach upsets, etc.) is feedback about your needs and limits. Or you can think of these as messages from the serpent, telling you that paradise is not all it's supposed to be. Naturally, not every need can be met, not every limit honored. But your HQ (Happiness Quotient) will increase when you meet the majority of your needs, respect the majority of your limits, and are making conscious, balanced choices about where you are willing to sacrifice, overextend, and take the consequences.

Continue with these questions:

4. Are you feeling resentful, depressed, or hopeless because you have important needs at work that are not being met? If so, what are they? _____

5. Are you feeling violated in some way because you have gone beyond some of your limits at work? If so, what are they? _____ _____.

Now go back to the needs listed in item number 3. Next to each one, assign it a letter value, as follows:
    A — Could be easily handled with a minimum of changes and some, creativity.
    B — Could be handled, but logistically difficult, requiring great creativity.
    C — Too difficult to handle at this time.

Next to the letter, assign a number as follows for each item:
1 — Very urgent — I'm really hurting!
2 — Painful, but I can cope.
3 — No big deal.

This will create a range of categories. While the letters and numbers you have assigned are arbitrary, they can help you discern where to put your energy:

1A: Here are needs which are urgent, yet solvable. Examine what has been preventing you from addressing them — perhaps intimidation (fear of rocking the boat), low self-worth (don't deserve it), over-responsibility (I can handle it). Listen to your body. Take care of these needs now!

1B: Needs which are urgent and manageable with some effort require discernment of your available resources/energy. Think carefully about the trade-offs. Try addressing these needs. If you make two attempts and the situation is not resolved, get help.

1C: Needs which are very urgent but too difficult to handle create a sense of despair and being overwhelmed. Get outside help (your manager, human resources department, industrial psychologist, or private therapy) as soon as possible!

2A: These needs are creating discomfort, but you're coping. Ask yourself: how long are you willing to cope? Sooner or later, you will violate your own limits and hate yourself for it. If your needs are easy to meet, go ahead so you free up energy to use elsewhere. Take care of it now.

2B and 2C: Needs and resources may tip the scales pretty evenly. Assess how long you can maintain the balance. Ask yourself: how will I know when the scales are tipping too far to one side or the other? Will I be willing/able to act if my needs begin to outweigh my ability to cope? Don't let this situation run on too long. You are under stress and depleting your body's resources.

3A: Minor needs or those easily managed should either be met immediately or ignored in favor of more pressing needs. Choose your battles. You can afford to neglect these for awhile if your investment of energy/creativity is better used elsewhere.

3B and 3C: No big deal. Forget about doing anything about these for now, but continue the body check-in every other week for signs that they need your attention.

This way of prioritizing needs and limits puts the focus for change on those you assigned 1A and 3A. Handling the 1A needs will give you the experience of success and reinforce your self-esteem ("I'm worth it!"). Those needs designated 3A will either gradually erode your ability to perform on the job or create a breakdown/crisis of some sort. Use outside help to clear them up as soon as possible. For all other needs, take some time and thought to determine how and when to move on them.

One reason it is important to know your needs and limits is that the only one who can meet them, or arrange/negotiate to get them met, is you. And it should come as no revelation that unmet needs and overextended limits become emotional problems if left unattended. The other reason for knowing what you can and can't do is that this understanding is the foundation for healthy emotional boundaries. When you begin to feel anxious, hurt, resentful, neglected, ignored, angry, upset, etc., in a relationship, take a look at whose needs are not being met. Chances are they're yours! You have a problem; and you can either smother your feelings of resentment and let them fester, or find a way to set better limits. To sum up, when you are not meeting your own needs, you will drain yourself and hate others (especially if you believe their needs are being met at the price of yours).

Of course, there are many times when you will be in a position to help others with their needs. Refer to "Restructuring the Relationships," #2, in Chapter Four, for a suggestion about this. Do not take on someone else's needs to the detriment of your own . . . UNLESS you understand the consequences to yourself and are absolutely willing to accept them without holding it against the other person. This will ensure your emotional well-being; and your maturity, sensitivity and honesty in assessing your ability to help others will also facilitate their well-being.

Many events and pressures at work can disrupt your sense of well-being and continue for what may seem an interminable period. Keep two things in mind:

1. Sometimes you may feel so negative that it creates the illusion that you're worse off than you are. In fact, negative feelings don't necessarily signal that you're not happy or healthy. They may, in fact, merely be red flags of warning urging you to act preventively. As one woman said, "Just because you feel like garbage doesn't mean you're not coping."
2. Knowing when to run a white flag of truce up your emotional pole is just as important for well-being as knowing when to fight for your needs. If something irksome cannot be altered by you, let go of it. When you are powerless, surrender. Use the tools in Chapter Six to help you with this.

PMS OR PMA?

Every human being has ups and downs; every family, every system, even global weather patterns, have rhythms and shifts. Because of hormonal cycles, women of menstrual age have a built-in mechanism (more intense and longer in some than others) for viewing their lives through a particular lens. For many women, this means having less tolerance for minor irritations, feeling blue over things that would not usually bother them or retaliating with an anger that seems to have awakened with the suddenness of summer lightning — out of nowhere. And, of course, many women rarely have noticeable mood fluctuations but are nonetheless aware of a kind of emotional opportunism that helps them scrutinize and review their work situation from a special angle.

PMA, or Positive Mental Attitude, is a prime ingredient of sanity. This does not mean pasting on a phony smile, oozing a saccharin enthusiasm over everything others say to you, or telling yourself you're not really in pain when you are. It means being willing and open to look for the up side in any situation, even while acknowledging the legitimate difficulties of it. *Life isn't fair, but it isn't unfair, either.* The events of life, nature, systems, are neutral; fairness, or justice, is a human, and only human, capacity. So if life is neutral, then philosophically and psychologically it makes sense to interpret it in the way most favorable to emotional well-being, regardless of your mood at the moment. Moods change, so when you catch yourself having a negative emotional reaction to something or someone, use your mental abilities to frame it in a more positive way. Here are some examples:

DON'T SAY	INSTEAD, SAY
This is a problem.	This is a challenge.
I'm stuck.	I have an opportunity to experience creative license.
She's trying to manipulate me.	I know what I want. How can I negotiate that with her?
I'm having an awful day.	My body's telling me to slow down and listen to it better.
I work in such a sick place!	My well-being does not depend on what's around me. What do I need?
I hate my boss.	I can use this to learn about my own issues.

The key is to be able to view everything as an opportunity for growth. You don't have to choose to grow; there will be many times when you simply won't have the energy to do anything more than say to yourself, "Well, I know what I could do to handle this differently, but I just don't have what it takes." Pat yourself on the back for viewing the situation as a potential positive lesson, and don't berate yourself for not having the resources to do what you "should" have done differently. Part of emotional well-being is knowing when to take it easy.

Whether you're a CPA or a CEO, a VP or an MP; whether you clean someone else's house or someone else's teeth, your emotional wellness determines how heavenly your service will be to the recipient. Reflect on your experience of being a client or customer for something that was important to you. What if you, let's say, need elective surgery and have a chance to interview two surgeons; let's say both are equally qualified and competent as far as you can tell; and let's say they charge roughly the same fee and involve the same amount of travel time, etc. If all else is equal, the one with whom you feel the safest and most connected, the one who seems to understand you and respect your needs, the one with the positive outlook, will most likely be the one you pick. Why? Because when the chips are down in the human condition, when we feel farther than ever from paradise, we gravitate to those who will make us feel safe, warm, appreciated. Conversely, when you are emotionally sound, you are more likely to attract business. We all desire to get back into the Garden of Eden. Become emotionally healthy, and you provide a little paradise for everyone else.

CHAPTER THREE
Resolving Inner Conflicts

You may be wishing that Eve had left that apple alone and told the serpent, "What?! Do I look like I have the IQ of a zucchini? Eat that stupid apple — and lose all this? I know a good thing when I've got it. Shove off, Snake!" Apparently, Eve did not foresee the consequences of what must have seemed like a relatively small action. And this happens all the time. In large and small ways, each of us discovers that seemingly positive choices sometimes result in unexpectedly negative fallout. Something else Eve could not possibly have foreseen: we, her "daughters," have an array of choices in a world that would have astonished her. We want to believe that we can, indeed, have it all. Yet our own experiences living out this desire reveal that the road to Eden is full of trade-offs: this road is shorter, but beware of falling rocks! That road is faster, but the tolls are expensive. And the third road has spectacular scenery . . . but no gas stations for the next 300 miles.

Most of us would greet with envy, not skepticism, any woman who would calmly claim that she has no problem juggling a full-time job, attending her children's plays and school conferences, hiring good household help, preparing gourmet meals, and maintaining a fabulous sex life with her husband. What, did she come equipped with some owner's manual for managing chaos when she was born? Does she have some Magic Holographic Road Map To Life invisible to the rest of us?

Let's consider one example. Karen looks back nostalgically on two remarkably different periods of her life during which her days were the most simple and free they've ever been. When she was 18, she entered a convent. There, for the first three years, every day was absolutely and precisely structured for her: meditation, chores, classes, meals, recreation, worship; there was no money to earn, no bills to pay; her responsibilities were clearly mapped out for her and her main decision-making had to do not with whether she participated in the structure, but to what degree. This was life lived as closely to a road map as one could get! The second period of her life, out of the convent for years and married with two kids, was a ten-month nomadic existence, living off savings, hauling a travel trailer around the U.S. The only "structure" was determined by night and day, heat and cold, when the baby needed to nurse, and when everyone else was hungry. No two days were exactly alike; the decision to stay or move on was generally made the night before. Life happened one day at a time, full of wonder, surprises, and occasional unforeseen difficulties, like when the Wagoneer engine caught fire on the interstate. The only road maps were the ones you could fold — or try to fold!

For Karen, these two experiences are opposite metaphors for ways to resolve life conflicts. There are two basic approaches to handling the array of emotional priorities confronting working women. Some women prefer to develop a predictable structure, adhering to it as faithfully as possible, organizing, scheduling well in advance and fine-tuning it as necessary, keeping change to a minimum unless it's well thought-out and planned for. Other women prefer the gypsy approach to life, taking one value at a time, waiting to see what will seem important next.

Each approach has its blessings and its curses. The structured approach minimizes frequent decision-making by using advance strategy. It helps the practitioner juggle chaos by timing which ball to hold when, though she may not have enough hands if a number of balls come down at once (as happens in life from time to time). The flexible approach helps the practitioner stay sane by being adaptable and able to go with the flow, as if she had seven or eight arms. She doesn't feel the need to keep track of every ball, so sometimes she loses sight of her governing values as she becomes Octopus Woman, trying to hold as many balls as she can, tangled up and paralyzed by embracing too many priorities.

No matter what your approach, your emotional health will stay sound if you 1) know what your primary values are, 2) organize your time accordingly, 3) leave ample room for flexibility, and 4) re-evaluate periodically.

PIE CHART, PIE CHART ON THE WALL, WHAT'S THE CLEAREST THING OF ALL?

Before reviewing the Pie Chart from Chapter One, make a list of the ten most important things in your life right now. This could include yourself,

RESOLVING INNER CONFLICTS 51

JUGGLING PRIORITIES

THE STRUCTURED, ORGANIZED APPROACH

THE FLEXIBLE APPROACH

WHICH STYLE DO YOU PREFER?

loved ones, activities, money, world peace . . . whatever. Don't worry about any particular order. Next do the same for your work/job/career. Write down the ten things that are most important to you.

          My Life   **My Work**

1. _____   _____
2. _____   _____
3. _____   _____
4. _____   _____
5. _____   _____
6. _____   _____
7. _____   _____
8. _____   _____
9. _____   _____
10. _____   _____

Now take what you consider to be the top three from each list, and write them in order of importance, with 1 being the most important. Use the headings "My Life" and "My Work" for your two lists.

        My Life   **My Work**

1. _____ 1. _____
2. _____ 2. _____
3. _____ 3. _____

Compare the two lists and your pie chart from Chapter One, and answer the following questions:

1. What do both lists and the chart say about me as a person?
2. Are there any elements in common on all three? (For example, relationships with people are more important to me than accomplishing tasks.)
3. Each of us develops priorities by weighing what we are taught is important against our experience. How did I learn that these things are important to me?
4. Do I ever take any of these things for granted?

You may have had to struggle to get three items off each list; rank ordering them might have been even more difficult. Whether you realize it or not, you have powerful emotional attachments to the things that are meaningful to you. You can intellectualize, debate, philosophize all you want about what *should* matter in life. But the truth is, when you have to make tough choices, your heart always knows clearly what you want, rational or not. There are many times in life when you will have to sacrifice your heart's immediate desire for a greater good, but this too will ring true to your heart if your choice is in the best interest of someone who matters as much to you as you do. Otherwise, when you ignore what is important to your heart for some flimsy rationale, you will eventually pay a price for it. This is not to suggest that you throw intellect to the winds. You will need all of your rational powers to assist your heart in balancing its desires.

Here are two life experiences that illustrate this theory:

Felicia was always career-minded. She became a buyer for a sophisticated New York women's store, and gradually worked her way to higher echelons in the fashion world. At 34, she met and a year later married a stockbrocker. Neither had a strong desire at first to start a family. But guess what Felicia heard ticking when she was 37? The alarm on her biological clock rang loudly on her 38th birthday. After a lot of deliberation, anxiety, a brief spell with a therapist, and a long talk with her personnel director, Felicia (and her husband, of course) decided she would try to get pregnant. The speed with which she conceived was astonishing. Felicia felt as though she never had much of a chance to digest her decision — let alone her dinners from the previous nights, as she had terrible morning sickness during the first trimester. All this time, Felicia waited for some happy pregnant glow to hit; she waited for the nesting instinct; she waited to feel maternal. These never happened. She worked right up until the birth, and when her son was born, she took a three-month maternity leave.

Felicia really *tried* to do "the mother thing." She loved the baby, all right, but something was missing. She read books, talked to her husband, talked to friends. She felt guilty that she wasn't content, that she somehow felt deprived. She had expected, and feared, that the baby would eclipse her feelings about work. She knew that children are supposed to be uppermost in a mother's life. And Felicia knew that she loved this little boy in a way she had never experienced love before — but she missed her job terribly. She thought that if she didn't get back to work soon, she would go crazy. She spent the third month of her leave interviewing nannies and au pair services until she found a live-in (which she could well afford) whom she trusted. Once she was back at work, she was scrupulous about being home on time, enjoyed mothering tremendously, felt that she mastered the "quality time" concept with regard to her son, and was the happiest she'd ever been. Her life felt complete, and she finally had the space she needed to adjust to motherhood. In fact, she was open to the possibility that sometime she might, in fact, want to try being a full-time mother, but not at this juncture of her life.

Aleesha, on the other hand, took the opposite path. She considered herself a feminist, and very liberated. She worked as a ticket agent for a major airline and thoroughly relished taking advantage of the travel benefits for herself and her husband. When they decided to have a baby (the initiative came from him) she made it very clear that she intended to work until she went into labor, that she would take the six-week leave she was entitled to and then go back to work. If her husband wanted this baby, he had better do his share of childcare, lining up sitters, etc. He more than enthusiastically agreed! Much to Aleesha's surprise, however, she bonded so intensely to her son that she was wracked over the thought of going back to work. As each day of her leave passed, she dreaded the separation, even though her husband's schedule was staggered with hers so that they would not be leaving the baby with hired help all that much — which they couldn't really afford. They depended on her income, so with a heavy heart she returned to work.

As the months went by, Aleesha tried to tell herself that her son was lucky to have his dad around so much, that children are resilient, that she loved those travel perks, that she was glad she was so independent. But she grew increasingly depressed. Finally she realized that her paycheck, and all that it meant, was not as important to her as her relationship with her son. Her job did not permit part-time arrangements. What to do? She had a long talk with her husband, who did not want to work harder to pick up the financial slack if she quit, and who also enjoyed his time with their son. So, for the time being, Aleesha continued to work, but by the baby's first birthday, she was confused and resentful. She never dreamed, in her pre-pregnancy days, that she would feel this way. That, too, added to her emotional stress.

The stories of these two women illustrate that the heart will not take "no" for an answer without a good reason. What about your own heart? Review your top three priority lists once again. Are these choices really your heart's desire? If not, refer back to your ten-item lists, and see if anything else is. If need be, change your top-three lists so that they represent what matters most deeply to you. Right now, are you aware of whether or not you are actually putting your time and energy into your fundamental values? Can you tell, just by the way you feel about your life, if you are in synch with your heart? Let's take a closer look.

Turn back to your pie chart from Chapter One. Look at how much time you devote to your topmost priorities, to auxiliary activities, and to unrelated activities. Of course, everything you do has SOME value to you, or you wouldn't be doing it. The problem of conflicting values which working women encounter is one of fundamental priorities and jammed schedules! Compare your three top life values with where your time actually goes. Compare your top three work values with how you really spend your time at work. And compare your three top life values with your three top work values. Just take a few minutes to let your brain absorb all the data from the pie chart and priority lists.

One final step: What is your body feeling, what emotions trickle/flood into you when you consider the whole picture? If there's tightening in your stomach/abdomen; if your shoulders or lower back twinge; if your heart rate speeds up, your breathing becomes shallow, you feel an imminent throbbing in your head; if a lump in your throat or tears in your eyes make their presence known . . . the serpent is speaking to you. It could be better, it could be less frenzied, less doubt-provoking.

STAR LIGHT, STAR BRIGHT

You probably know the old nursery rhyme that prefaced many a child's wish. If your work- and life-styles are not in harmony with what you say you believe is important, you are either fooling yourself or your wishes are bruised. You have three basic options for restoring balance.

First you can change what you've been telling yourself is important. One woman in a career support group made a remark during a discussion of goals, a remark which bespeaks a healthy attitude toward priorities. She said, "In life, I take careful aim. Then, whatever I hit, THAT becomes the goal."

Celeste was brought up to believe that she should always give more of herself than what was asked. "Don't wait for others to do 100 percent," her mother instructed her. "Give 150 percent yourself and you'll never be disappointed." Once Celeste was ensconced in her sales career, however, she had little time for a social life because of her travel schedule. When she finally fell in love, she nearly went crazy trying to give 150 percent in both her work and her relationship with her boyfriend. She grew frazzled and depressed, and both involvements began to suffer. "I kept waiting and hoping that some miraculous revelation would emerge and show me how to manage everything. I was starting to burn out. I was crispy around the edges," Celeste confessed. She had a long talk with her best friend, who pointed out that for as long as she'd known Celeste, Celeste was overly conscientious about everything and could afford to cut back, relax, give less. Instead of trying to cram everything in, she pointed out, just do less. Celeste was thunderstruck. But a bit of reflection helped her become more honest with herself: Did it really matter in the universe whether she gave 75, 100, or 150 percent? Because of how stressed she was, she wasn't giving 150 percent anyway; in fact, some days she actually got in the way of her own and others' performance. Why not just change her values and cut the percentage? Naturally, it was easier said than done, but she kept reminding herself that her body didn't lie, that her body could not and would not give 150 percent to both work AND potential marriage. In Celeste's case, the priority in her mind and the priorities in her body were on a collision course; it's not that one was good and another bad, it's just that she had to reorganize her thinking and her values. So sometimes it makes more sense to jettison a particular value than to tie your life in knots trying to honor it. This is the Zen riddle of life: aim carefully, then appreciate what you actually hit.

TIME MANAGEMENT

Your second option for greater congruity between what you say and what you do is to realign your time to fit more closely with your values. Have you ever been amazed at how some people can fit so much activity into one day and yet rarely tire of filling their lives to the brim? Besides making the choice to be active, they also carry it off successfully and without emotional friction. These people obviously have developed the skill of effective time management.

To help you get a clear idea of how you spend your time, keep a time diary for two work days of all aspects of your life. Carry a small notebook with you on these two days. Be honest. (This is exactly what people do in preparation for changing their relationship with spending or eating, only in this case you're tracking your relationship with time.) Mark in the amount of time you spend on each event from the moment you awaken until you retire to bed. Even indicate how long you lie in bed before arising. This assignment may be challenging for you, especially if it's difficult for you to keep track of your minutes and hours in the first place. But there's no better *time* than the present to change. See this time diary as an opportunity to make some good adjustments in your life, not an unpleasant discipline.

Upon reviewing how you spent your two days, you might be surprised at ways you used or wasted your time. You are the only judge. In your time analysis, are there changes you'd like to make? For instance, would you like to spend more time on one aspect of your workday and less on another? If so, make goals for yourself. Setting goals is similar to reading directions to a new game. Just as the instructions tell you how to play to win, your goals lead you successfully through your life. Think about both immediate goals and future goals because they are equally important and feed off each other. Make a chart, using the heads below. Once you write your goals, make notes on how you can actually reach each one. Some of your goals will be easy to obtain, and that's good because realizing them will provide you with a sense of accomplishment. Others may be outrageous. It's okay to stretch your goals to the MAX. That's often how dreams come true, but also be aware of the need to avoid shaming yourself or berating your efforts if your goals don't materialize or seem to move slowly.

GOALS FOR THE DAY	GOALS FOR THE WEEK	GOALS FOR THE MONTH	GOALS FOR THE YEAR

Unlearning old habits can take a while. Give yourself several weeks or months to integrate your new style of operating at a new level of efficiency into your work life. As with learning any new skill, you may slip and slide at first. Celebrate when you see progress. And learn from your slips to make firmer your stride forward.

If you need help with this, consider using a time-management system. On the job, for instance, if you value direct customer contact but find that bureaucratic paperwork and record-keeping keep you at your desk for hours, you may intellectually recognize that you could a) delegate the paperwork; b) condense it; c) restructure your job description; d) get another job altogether — but somehow not be able to implement any of these. If you *know* what you should be doing but find yourself stuck, there are excellent time-management products on the market, such as the Franklin Day Planner or the Ultimate Organizer, which come with a complete training program to teach you to integrate the use of the planner with your governing values (see Appendix IV for more information on these systems). While the up-front dollar cost may seem daunting, the consistent emotional rewards of using such products are priceless. Be honest with yourself: if you invest upwards of one hundred dollars in a problem-solving tool such as one of these, would you follow through by listening to the tapes or attending a short seminar to learn how to use it effectively? Would you be willing to carry your planner with you wherever you go? If the answer is yes, such a tool could be a life-saver if disjointed use of time is driving you crazy and you are tied up in emotional knots trying to address all you believe is important in your work and life. Faithful use of such a system will give you more time for what's most important to you if you use it as designed.

YOUR HEART'S DESIRE

Your third option, if you experience chronic disjunction between your values and your daily chores, is to accept the possibility that you are out-of-touch or intimidated by what you REALLY want. Many women fear their own power and the power of their dreams. There is good reason for this. Depending on the historical context, women's ambitions have been met with incredulity and scorn; they have been ignored, even punished. During the Renaissance, there were women artists whose brilliance rivaled that of da Vinci, Raphael, Michelangelo — yet have you ever heard of Artemisia Gentileschi (1593-1652) or Properzia Rossi (c. 1490-1530)? Even getting into art classes has been a hard-won struggle, let alone getting recognition! Some women were actually severely punished for simply pursuing the development of their talents. We often face so many negative messages about our dreams. One woman poignantly relates how even her mother scoffed at her desire to change careers from sales to food service, something she'd always thought she would love: "Oh, no one will even look twice at you! You'll need to go back to school, and besides, you don't know the first thing about the industry." (Not that her mother did, either.) As a result, she and thousands of other women might find it easier to bury a dream rather than live with the discomfort of believing they can't have it, or the threat of reprisal if they achieve it.

Try this simple exercise — but only if you're willing to take a chance. Trust that a little knowledge — self-knowledge, that is — isn't too dangerous, that you really do know exactly how you'd like your professional life to be. Directions: (You can do this with eyes open; write your answers on a sheet of paper as you go along.)

RESOLVING INNER CONFLICTS

A. Picture yourself standing in the middle of your workplace, and everyone is gone. The building is empty, with the hush of expectancy. Imagine yourself in a beautiful, shimmering, magical robe, alive with great power. Take a deep breath, feeling your energy. In your vision, feel your entire being tingle with the ability to have whatever you want. Look around your work site. Take in as many details as you can . . . Now feel your heart beating. Is it beating with pain because you are unhappy, or with the excitement and possibility of what is to come? (Either way, it's all right. Just feel your heart, feel the center of your being, and cherish it.)

B. Now ask yourself, as you look around your workplace: What do I really want? Do I want to continue in this job, or would I like another? (Be honest) _____

C. If I want to stay, how would I like things to be? (Don't limit your thinking. Imagine everything you'd really like.) _____
_____.

D. If I want to leave, what would I love to do? Where? How much would I like to earn for doing it? (Go for it — tell all — unburden your heart!) _____
_____.

E. Now come back to the present moment, and reread what you've written. Answer this: What would be one small, concrete step you could do before the week is up to believe in your vision? (e.g., talk it out with a friend, think about it every day, tell yourself it's about time, etc.) _____

F. Next, what would be one small, concrete step you could take within the next two weeks to move closer to your vision? (e.g., talk to personnel or your boss, call career counselors from the Yellow Pages, put the word out to your network of friends that you want a change, etc.)_____

G. Are you willing to do this? ___Yes ___No ___Not at this time. If yes, make a commitment. What will you do, and by when? _____.

H. If no, or not at this time, do not shame yourself for not pursuing your dream. There are many good reasons, also flowing from your governing values, why you say no to your heart's desire — and besides, believe in your future! Why are you not willing or able to pursue your wish at this time?_____
_____.

Be tender and merciful toward your wishes. It is the childlike heart that glances longingly out the window when it is claustrophobic, suffocating.

It is the power of the dream that reveals our wishes, and therefore, the values that we sometimes keep secret even from ourselves. When we are afraid of our dreams, we project negative images onto them, seeing them as temptations rather than as servants. Try to accept the possibility, if you are stuck and unhappy, that you have nothing to lose by uncovering your desire. Trust that all of your other values of love, morality, and responsibility will modulate any hidden desire, no matter how wild, forbidden, or crazy it may seem at first. Listen to your heart — it always wants to be happy and healthy.

TUGS ON THE HEARTSTRINGS

The greatest area of emotional and values conflict for a woman is the pull of home vs. career, especially if she has developmentally dependent children and/or is in a committed relationship. This situation is amplified by the plethora of how-to books on raising children successfully and "having it all" in relationships, which increase pressures by raising expectations to the level of perfection — thus generating stress. Women who can't seem to manage this conflict of interest feel guilty as well as out-of-control. In spite of literature to the contrary, most conscientious working moms at one time or another fear they are doing their children a disservice. If you factor in bonding hormones at birth, the desire to protect children, and the behavior of the children themselves at times of separation, you have a formula designed to produce genuine anguish for many women as they walk out the front door or drive away from the day care home, leaving a wailing child behind.

Besides children, a marriage/committed relationship can also fall prey to the ravages of work: time apart, especially if a woman works overtime or weekends; competition, depending on each partner's need for salary, status, or just plain dominance; lack of psychic energy if the job is emotionally consuming; and conflict over one's share of domestic responsibility since both parties work full time! These conflicts of interest tax any woman's ability — and agility — to please herself and others. What sweet fruit is available to curb the appetite of women whose inner emotional battles leave them starving for a simpler existence? If you are looking for guidelines on minimizing the conflicts between work and family issues, read on. Otherwise, skip to the next chapter, "Savvy Systemic Solutions."

REDUCING DOMESTIC DISCORD

Eve was presumably a full-time mother, trying to keep a clean cave and food on the fire, and even at that couldn't keep Cain from bashing Abel.

How much greater the anxiety when someone else, usually a stranger, has responsibility for your precious children?

Virtually every working mother has had to deal with the sitter who cancels, the laissez-faire attitude of some overwhelmed day care providers, the shock of learning what a qualified nanny gets paid and expects. Employers should be concerned about the impact of inadequate child care, since their employees' productivity demonstrably decreases and absenteeism/tardiness increase as working mothers (and fathers) must field phone emergencies, cover for absent sitters, and struggle with their own preoccupations about home while trying to attend to the tasks at work. The phenomenon of employers seeing women of child-rearing age as suspect, somehow inferior workers, is part of a larger and vicious circle of inadequate day care and inflexible hours. Companies which provide on-site day care and flex-time keep their female employees, their productivity and their loyalty. Those that can't or won't inadvertently reinforce their own myth that women are not suitable for promotion because they can't be counted on to place work over a family, a form of sexism/reproductive discrimination, and misplaced values. While women must continue to lobby for company involvement in the issue of child care, not just for mothers but for fathers as well, here are some tips on minimizing the structural and emotional problems surrounding the practical details of being a working mother:

1. If your company has on-site daycare, interview the care providers before placing your child there to assure your peace of mind. If there is no on-site child care, but your company is large enough to potentially provide it, team up with other working moms in the company to advocate the establishment of such a facility. The closer you are to your pre-school child, the greater your security and the more you can monitor the quality of care.
2. Find out if your company has a referral service for child-care providers they've screened. Some corporations offer this, and it reduces your search time.
3. The advent of computers makes it possible for employees in some type of jobs to get a computer link-up at home, so their home becomes an extension of work. While this may become complicated and boundary-less in the long run, in the short term it may solve child-care dilemmas for many women.
4. All states currently have licensing requirements for day-care centers, although this is not the case for employment services which provide child-care workers. While licensing does not guarantee a stimulating learning environment for your child, it usually means that the provider has had to establish safety and does not exceed the maximum number of children allowed. Interview several.

5. If you desire in-home child care, professional nanny services are the best alternative to a trusted relative — although much more expensive. Nannies are specifically trained and experienced to care for children, and expect to be treated as professionals. You should interview several to find a good personality match. Be prepared to pay wages, deduct taxes, and provide vacations or other benefits. Nannies are neither housekeepers (light housework) nor babysitters. They are generally more reliable, and less transient, than providers from other sources; they are definitely more expensive, and what you pay them may significantly cut into your own earnings, making it not worth it to work (even though you'll miss the other benefits of working).
6. Other sources for sitters include: employment/domestic help services; classified ads; networking and word of mouth. While you can pay less than you would for a nanny, you must decide: if you want an English-speaking person (or the language spoken at home); if you want to become involved with tax evasion (yours or theirs); how many prospective employees you are willing/able to interview and how many references you are going to check. Think all this through before you begin your interview process. (Always ask for and check three references per candidate.)
7. Remember that hiring from these sources increases the likelihood of transiency, which is as hard on your kids as it is on you. Get agreement on how much notice you expect if the person decides to quit so you aren't left in the lurch.
8. Ask questions, including hypothetical ones: If my child said a swear word, how would you handle it? If my child burned herself, what would you do? Asking these types of questions during an interview gives you an indication of the maturity and responsibility of the candidate.
9. Remember that you are the employer. Pay fair wages, be upfront about the duties and expectations, review/evaluate performance, offer raises.
10. If you are married/partnered, involve your mate in the process.
11. Know signs to watch for that indicate your child is in distress. While these might not have to do with poor child care, there's always the possibility that the person you hire is verbally, emotionally, physically, or sexually abusive. Young children exhibit stress by somatic troubles (such as stomachaches, headaches, difficulty eating or sleeping, nightmares, bedwetting) and emotional/social problems (fear of strangers, aggression, withdrawal, excessive daydreaming, sexualized affection, sexual precociousness, persistent sad facial expression, unusual and persistent mood shift); and of course, any suspicious or poorly explained bruises,

burns, sprains or other injuries are also potential warning signals. Children cannot articulate problems in the same way as an adult. If your child seems genuinely and chronically uncomfortable or fearful about your child-care person, don't hesitate to communicate your concerns to the care provider, and don't be afraid to take a strong protective stand. It's your job to shield your child; if you err, better it should be in the direction of too much defense rather than too little!

There are no quick fixes to the childcare dilemmas confronting working moms. The more groundwork you can do, the greater the likelihood of a good, nurturing, and stable childcare worker. A word to parents of older children and teens, especially single parents: the increasing independence of pre-teens and adolescents brings a new set of challenges. Know your own children. While they require less supervision and protection, they face great pressures to be sexual, experiment with drugs, etc. They probably have more physical stamina than you do, and can certainly outlast you in an argument. It is easy to get caught up in control struggles with them, especially if you feel like your parenting has been running in the red and you're trying to make up the deficit. A terrific resource for working parents of teens is a support group — particularly for single parents. Groups like Toughlove or parent support groups offered by your local high school or mental health agency give barraged parents ideas, resources, confidence, clarity, people to call in stressful times, humor, companionship . . . the list goes on and on. And you don't need to wait until your teen is "troubled." Use these groups as prevention. If you suspect a drug problem, get your child immediately evaluated at a chemical dependency/alcoholism facility. These evaluations are free, will steer you to appropriate help, and early intervention has been shown to prevent worse problems. Someone once said that the two worst times of life are being a teenager and being the parent of a teenager! This ain't necessarily so, but if it's hard for you to work and know how to be an effective parent of a teen, the bottom line is — get help. Don't do it alone.

Just as crucial to the well-being of your children is the health of your marriage or primary relationship. Your priority for your family should be the maintenance of a strong commitment and intimacy. But the stresses and strains of a job certainly can take the edge off that romantic glow — not to mention your ability to fight fairly and sustain clear, intimate communication. To preserve your marriage/primary relationship, follow these guidelines:

1. Be aware of your fairy-tale expectations . . . you know, the knight in shining armor who will provide for you, romance you, rescue

you. Your "knight" is probably just as needy as you are after a long day. Be realistic.
2. Maintain good health. Preserve your storehouse of energy and immunity. Ask your mate to be involved in this also.
3. Review your romance by making a date to tell each other the story of how you met, courted, committed. Review the dreams, desires, visions that you had in the beginning, and re-evaluate where each of you is now with respect to them.
4. Schedule lovemaking for a time when you are both likely to be available and awake. Don't rule out spontaneity, but don't count on it either.
5. If you have children, keep conversations about them to a minimum. Set a timer for ten or fifteen minutes, and end the topic when it buzzes. Too many marriages gradually erode into child-centered, role-oriented arrangements. Deliberately use time together to talk about each other, your relationship, your deepest feelings.
6. Make appointments to settle disagreements. Pick a time close to the actual conflict or provocation, when you won't be distracted or exhausted. Call a time-out if the fight becomes too heated; make an appointment to return to it. Be courteous when you fight.
7. Keep "in touch" with each other — literally! If weeks go by with no hugging, stroking, shoulder rubs, etc., but you expect yourself to be responsive in bed . . . good luck. Busy work schedules distract couples from frequent tender physical contact, whether it's sexual or not.
8. Create rituals: a candlelight dinner once a month; a weekly love note; a surprise "Thinking of You" card sent to his office on his half-birthday (six months). Work is highly ritualized; reflections of caring need to be as well.
9. Give each other space to adjust upon arriving home from work. Ten or fifteen minutes of solitude to change clothes, breathe deeply, get centered and present are vital before the barrage of "Wait till I tell you about my day," or "Could you talk to that daughter of yours?" or "Thank God you're home. I can't get the lid off this damn jar!"

The Adam-and-Eve-in-Eden model of marriage vanishes before your eyes when the specter of juggling work-marriage-kids rears its head. The irony of a necessary and valuable job becoming a detriment to healthy relationships is no joke. No woman ever takes a job with the intent of harming her loved ones. It hurts to cause hurt. And an even greater tragedy can occur if the vicious circle of dysfunction begins: Work can seem happier and more rewarding than tension at home, so you work long hours, which creates MORE tension at home, so you work LONGER hours to escape . . . off to the races! If your career seems happier than your domestic life, it's time to listen to the serpent: It could be better . . . Listen to your heart. No job is worth sacrificing a family for. No amount of money can buy the love and respect of children or win back an alienated spouse. Do what you need to make your home as heavenly as you can.

CHAPTER FOUR
Savvy Systemic Solutions

Up to this point, your emotional well-being at work has been considered primarily from the perspective of you as an individual: examining the baggage you bring with you, bolstering your self-esteem, clarifying the priorities of your heart to minimize internal conflicts. You are not an island, however. If you begin to alter your behavior, it will certainly affect the people with whom you relate; more indirectly, any change affects the broader emotional system of which you are part. If all you are cognizant of is the impact of one person's frustration or impatience on you, you may be missing a large emotional ripple passing through your office.

An obvious instance of this is a company with an expansionistic executive who is an excellent manager in bullish economic times, but whose skills fall short during recessionary phases. Early during the lean times, employees begin to feel the difference in subtle ways, questioning his decisions and practices. Very small ripples, indeed. Then, 18 months later, he regretfully announces that 20 percent of the workforce will have to be laid off — although the company has a contract with a career specialist who has been hired to help these people get jobs. Major ripples: the anxiety, resentment, anger, muttering, competition, self-protection, etc., are like waves ebbing and flowing through the company.

On a much smaller scale, each person's feelings and actions also create effects around you, though not nearly as dramatic. It is vital that you, as one individual, acquire an understanding of and respect for the system you are part of. It is equally important that you develop tools for 1) protecting yourself against the system's ravages if it is not a benevolent system; 2) participating healthily whether the system is or is not benevolent; and 3) monitoring and changing your participation in the system to influence its functioning in a healthy way.

Whether literal or mythical, we attribute to the loss of Eden the "human condition": power struggles, emotional conflicts, territorialism, ups and downs . . . in short, the stuff of emotional systems. The notion of living in utter harmony and bliss is an enticing Utopian ideal, motivating humans to communicate and to negotiate individual self-interest into communal contentment. At least on a microcosmic level, women seem to be more adept at this than men, as research into matriarchal tribal societies evidences. We don't know what a macrocosmic society governed with the addition of feminine principles would be like because none exists. We do know what patriarchy hath wrought: tacit expectations, sexual maneuvering, jockeying for power and status, compulsive ambition, ulcers and heart attacks. Women who buy into the assumptions behind such behaviors fall into the same patterns and diseases.

This chapter offers techniques for dealing with the emotional environment of an office, studio, restaurant, store, factory . . . the scenes change, but the processes remain constant. Therefore, the following sections offer suggestions for acquiring systemic skills in coping with dysfunctional hierarchies, improving communication, creating healthy power, dealing with sexual harassment, influencing a healthier environment. Getting as close to emotional Eden as possible is a longing in each of us. You have as much right to develop that at work as anywhere else in your life. This chapter addresses the interconnections between your behavior and feelings and those of the people around you.

HAPPIER HIERARCHIES

The sphere of your influence is determined by your position at work, how you manage your personal effectiveness, and your personality. Obviously, a high-energy, extroverted, well-organized compassionate executive will have significantly more direct control over the environment than will a low-key, introverted research librarian or postal clerk. In other words, whales create bigger waves than do goldfish. Being realistic about how effectively you can produce positive change is important; so is having faith that every positive alternative you select is a thread in a tapestry. Never doubt your ability to affect a system for the better! The model for this faith comes from the emerging study of the science of chaos, based on mathematics and physics:

Tiny differences in input could quickly become overwhelming differences in output — a phenomenon given the name "sensitive dependence on the initial conditions." In weather, for example, this translates into what is only half-jokingly known as the Butterfly Effect — the notion that a butterfly stirring the air today in Peking can transform storm systems next month in New York.[1]

Loving the Leadership

Dysfunctional abuse of authority occurs as a matter of degree: tyranny and ineptitude are extreme forms of behaviors which otherwise make for balanced leadership when they are present in appropriate proportions — 1) the giving of direction and 2) the practice of laissez-faire, or hands off.

For those readers who are in management or leadership positions, the appropriate use of authority facilitates a healthy emotional milieu by creating trust, allowing for competent independence and creativity, motivating satisfying levels of performance commensurate with a worker's abilities, and encouraging an open flow of communication. The following list of behaviors is intended as a gentle reminder of those management styles which reinforce emotional wellness for workers:

1. Give clear directions. Avoid confusion in your instructions.
2. Promulgate decisions which will affect workers. Meetings (both one-on-one and group), memos, the bulletin boards, the in-house newsletter all serve the function of informing employees of change. Proper use of each one helps minimize rumors, which siphon off employees' energy and morale. This also prevents confusion and ill will, and provides a foundation for problem-solving. Trust is built by letting people know what's coming, however unpleasant.
3. Review performance regularly. Always focus on the positive before bringing up something that needs correction. Raise issues by explaining the context for what you are about to say so that the employee is less likely to take your feedback as personal criticism.
4. Don't wait for a performance review to correct a problem that suddenly begins to appear. Sweeping something minor under the carpet will only lead to greater aggravation later for both parties.
5. Check in with employees frequently to see how they're doing.
6. When appropriate, solicit input and suggestions from employees prior to making decisions that will affect them. This gives employees a sense of ownership.

7. Be frequently seen and not frequently heard. Smile a lot, encourage, reinforce whatever is going right. Your nonthreatening presence gives the message that you're available. It is better to let employees seek you out when they need help rather than have you rush in to fix, correct, problem-solve — which may be perceived as controlling behavior and therefore arouse resentment.
8. Listen carefully to insure that you understand an employee before you respond.
9. Make your expectations clear. Provide written job descriptions for all employees.
10. If you promise something, follow through.
11. If you say there will be a negative consequence if an employee does not do what is expected, follow through if the employee fails to come up to par. If employees perceive "empty threats," they will continue to behave poorly, which will lower morale and anger you.
12. Respond swiftly to grievances.
13. Do your "personal" homework. Know your own baggage so you do not overreact or project your own issues onto employees.
14. Be human. Don't put on a mask of authority to fit some intellectual idea you have of how you think you should be. You will be perceived as phony and this will create suspicion and resentment.
15. Perform your own job.
16. Delegate appropriately.
17. If it's not broken, don't fix it.
18. Treat everyone equally and fairly. Develop personal contact with each employee you supervise. This will help minimize alliances that can form when employees have only second-hand experience of you and rumors or gossip about something you've said or done.
19. Have a sense of humor.

These guidelines will help you use your authority to give your employees the message that they deserve and have respect.

For those readers who are "below" someone else (and most workers are), the following principles apply to all situations. Those especially germane to dealing with dysfunctional authority are asterisked:

1. Know your job description and do it as well as you are able. If there is a chronic mismatch between your ability or interest and the tasks assigned to you, don't wait for a performance review; bring it up before the pain is too great.
2. When you need help, ask for it. Many requests can be handled informally, with a quick question to a colleague or your supervisor. For more detailed requests, get your thoughts organized and

written; make an appointment and keep a dated copy for your records of your request.

*3. If you do not receive the help you need after a reasonable period of time, repeat the request, and say what you will do if there is no response within a week. Generally, you can legitimately name one of two consequences. Either 1) without the help, you cannot do the job, or 2) you will go up another hierarchical level in asking for help. Again, keep a written copy for your records.

*4. Do not personalize someone else's abuse of power. If management is inept, it's not your job to cover it up or compensate for it. This is misplaced loyalty. If management somehow blames you and you know you have been doing your job well, it's not your fault. Defend yourself by documenting, in writing, how well you have been fulfilling your job description. Keep a copy for your records.

5. Support your boss/supervisor/manager by acknowledging what she/he is doing right, well, etc. Let her/him know you appreciate the work, effort, support, listening, etc. Leadership needs to know what's working. Behavior that's ignored or taken for granted tends to make itself extinct. If your boss provides a healthy emotional milieu, reinforce it!

6. As a general rule, do not become sexually involved with anyone at work. Every woman who does believes she is the exception and can handle it, but the history of working women is littered with lost jobs, betrayed hopes, broken hearts, and shattered self-esteem. This rule especially applies to relationships with those who are hierarchically above you. If you value your emotional health, honor this limit. If you are currently in such a relationship, end it. Seek professional counseling if necessary.

*7. If your management/supervisor/boss is verbally abusive or disrespectful of you, take a clear stand. Do not buy into this emotionally; this is how dysfunctional leadership manipulates with guilt and shame. Point out the words/voice/tone which are degrading and make it clear that you are open to a critique of your performance but not of you as a person.

*8. Make sure you understand your boss before you act or respond. Listen carefully, especially with regard to directions or changes which may affect your performance; accurate hearing saves time and effort. Remember the computer adage: garbage in, garbage out.

*9. Do not respond to controlling behavior with equally controlling behavior on your part. Get some distance from the incident; think about what happened, where it might be stemming from elsewhere in the system, and about what you need. Talk things

out with a trusted friend away from work to vent some of your feelings. Decide what you can and can't do, and carry out your plan as a way of empowering yourself. If you get into a power struggle with your management, probably it's you who will lose.
10. Stay in touch with your feelings. Check in with yourself. If you are not happy, take responsibility to do something about it. Do not hold your boss accountable for your unhappiness. This is a victim's position and will only hurt you. In the system, victims wear a "Please Take Advantage Of Me" sign — an open invitation for others to behave in ways that reinforce the victim's view of the world.
*11. If you believe you are being discriminated against in some way, do the following:
 a) Document incidents, and keep your records in a safe place. Include the names of witnesses.
 b) If you don't already have one, get a copy of the personnel policy. This should contain both the principle of equal treatment and the grievance procedure. Follow the grievance procedure as stated.
 c) If there is no personnel policy and no grievance procedure, contact the U.S. Equal Employment Opportunity Commission (1-800-USA-EEOC) for counsel.
12. Do not gossip about authority figures (or anyone else, for that matter). If you decide to begin to relate differently in the hierarchy, keep your decision to yourself or perhaps tell a trusted friend outside the company. You will avoid emotional complications and triangles this way.

Both foregoing lists of guidelines are things which can be done by you as an individual. What about the system as the whole?

Dysfunctional hierarchies are hard to identify from within. New employees are not likely to rock the boat by pointing out power abuses. Instead, they quickly become absorbed into the system and cooperate with the tacit power politics. They may even put a good face on the matter by telling themselves that certain things have to be done to get ahead, or congratulating themselves at how well they are learning to play the game without losing their integrity. Alas! The phrase itself, "playing the game," makes light of a dehumanizing, defeminizing reality. When a company values competition, advancement, ambition, status, and performance over the human needs of its workers for satisfaction, affiliation, creativity, and recognition, it is sadly entrapped in a cycle which will eventually sweep itself and its members into stress and burnout at best, collapse at worst.

Be aware of what's happening around you and the part you play. If you suspect or know for certain that your workplace permits abuse of power, then understand that you must map out the likely ramifications of your decision to stop "playing the game." Will there be reprisals from above? From below? If so, what will they be? Could you lose your job for confronting the use of shame tactics? Will others join in? If so, will this result in the formation of alliances, factions, polarized groups? If there are unpleasant results of your choices, how long are they likely to last? Will concerned parties be open to talking about them as they arise? Your decisions are bound to affect more people than just yourself. Take time to think through any change in how you relate to the use of power. Act in your own best interest, but always take into account such systemic shifts as you can foresee and then prepare for them.

Restructuring the Relationships

In Chapter Two, unhealthy emotional boundaries regarding intimacy, defenses and responsibility were explained. Each woman's boundaries are shaped by her personality (for example, extroverts and people who value taking each others' feelings into account have more diffuse boundaries by nature than do introverts and those who value taking rational, demonstrable, factual data into account). Other factors affecting boundaries are a woman's ethnic background, her previous experiences and baggage, and her current circumstances and maturity.

This section contains suggestions and tools for rebalancing your relationship boundaries if they are overly rigid or diffuse. Because each person is unique, a range of techniques is offered. If something sounds useful, try it; adapt it to your own situation. Having healthy boundaries and understanding the impact which readjusting them may have on others is a step toward claiming your personal power and peace, and therefore your happiness.

If you habitually keep your emotional distance and never let your guard down at work; if you wear an "I'm an island unto myself" mask, even though you feel lonely and isolated; if you've been hurt, and you're NEVER going to be vulnerable again — your boundaries may be impermeable and rigid. If you want to experiment, try one of the following exercises:

1. Increase the amount of time you maintain eye contact while conversing with someone at work. Keep your face relaxed and open, breathing slowly and consciously as you do so. While maintaining eye contact, especially while listening, silently say to yourself,

"This is a precious person, just like me. I am able to take this person in without judging or criticizing." Simply be aware of your feelings as you do this.
2. Take one small risk per day. Pick relatively safe people at work — those you generally perceive as gentle and open — and say hello, asking how they are. When asked back, try being just a tiny bit more honest about yourself than you would usually be.
3. A safe way to a more permeable boundary is offering people the gift of listening. Keep your face relaxed and expressive; maintain gentle, empathic eye contact, and paraphrase what you hear the speaking saying. (See "Active Listening" in the next chapter.)
4. Sometimes people have difficulty disclosing who they are because they simply aren't sure. Spend more time becoming intimate with yourself; keep a journal; meditate; do something nice for yourself, minimizing your distractions (TV, romance novels, compulsive housework, etc.). Often, just becoming more companionable with and toward oneself automatically begins to flow into diminished interpersonal barriers.
5. For three minutes at the start of your workday, in a quiet place free from intrusion, picture yourself initiating or participating in a conversation in which you say something meaningful about yourself. Picture a favorable response, whatever you'd like, from the other person. Try this for three weeks and then begin to implement it. You may be amazed at the difference.

When you begin to open your closed boundaries, you pave the way for enhancing your participation in the teamwork implicit or explicit in most jobs. Others begin to identify you as a member of the emotional team, even if your job is a solitary one. This is a contribution to general wellness at work.

If you are the type of person, on the other hand, who wears her heart on her sleeve, who is everyone's shoulder to cry on, who is righteously indignant over other people's pain and ready to do battle on their behalf, who is always open about her personal life, even to relative strangers at work . . . perhaps your emotional boundaries are loose and diffuse, and need a little tightening up. A few pointers:

1. When other people have strong feelings, positive or negative, and you literally begin to *feel with* them, take a deep breath, acknowledge yourself for being sensitive and caring, and remind yourself to let go and let them have their own feelings. It is an act of respect to assume that people can have and handle their own feelings. You can be empathically happy or sad, or extend understanding, but it is a waste of your primal energy to jump on the emotional bandwagon of others.

2. When you learn that someone else at work has a problem or difficulty, and you just KNOW you have several perfect solutions to offer, do yourself (and the other party) a favor. Before you open your mouth, do the following three simple things:
   a) Repeat the problem, as you understand it, to the person. Wait to hear if you are correct.
   b) Offer your availability. Wait to see if it's needed.
   c) If it is, ask what you can do that would be most helpful. The bottom line is to be courteous about offering help. While you may have the best ideas in the world, if they're not truly wanted or appreciated, you may seem obnoxious, controlling, or intrusive. Check it out first.
3. Give others a chance to shine. Hold back a little in group situations and meetings. An operating principle of systems is: when a role is vacated, someone else will eventually step in to fulfill that function. If you are the "party person," the office socialite, work on developing your interiority, your reflective side. Give it about a month before you despair and rush right back in. Shifting roles keeps the emotional system flexible and healthy. In the meantime, you may discover some long-neglected aspects of yourself gathering mold in the corners of your heart and mind.
4. Ask the people at work you are closest to for feedback. Sample questions: How do I come across to you? How do you think I come across to others? Do I sometimes seem pushy, too open? It is scary to request information about yourself, but it will help you assess to what extent your "guts" are hanging out.
5. Avoid rumor mills and the gossip circuit. These will only get you stirred up and sucked in.
6. Have a healthy emotional and social life outside of work. Do not use work as your sole source of community and communion.

Emotional openness and honesty are refreshing when the person is congruent, that is, credible because the inside and outside match. In many companies, however, these qualities are not valued. Before you rock the boat, know how well you can swim. Employees can be scapegoated and isolated for expressing emotional honesty, even more so if it's perceived as criticism of the company. On the other side of the coin, if you *are* disgruntled, confused, frustrated, you stand a better chance of producing change on your and others' behalf if you clearly state your feelings as well as produce a logical, written report of the problems you may be encountering.

For example: Juanita is shy and unassuming. She has worked the night shift as a radio ambulance dispatcher for three and a half years. Twice she has requested a transfer to the daytime shift but has been ignored or passed over. After all, she's nice and polite and isn't likely to be very assertive. However, she kept a record of each request, both delivered in writing and in person at the time, to her supervisor. Now she takes the time to write up her performance and attendance records, mentioning the time she was featured in a news program for saving a child's life by her quick response, and she pulls the copies of her earlier requests from her file at home. She wants to make a case for her loyalty and dedication, as well as her uncomplaining patience over the previous rejections. She arranges a meeting with her supervisor, coming in an hour earlier than usual for the meeting. During the conference, she matter-of-factly presents her track record and the turn-downs. Then she says, "Frankly, Bill, I'm hurt and confused. I think I've done a conscientious and dedicated job, and I don't feel appreciated. I've seen other people's needs accommodated (she does not mention names, and she is not whining). For personal reasons, a daytime job makes a lot more sense for me at this time (she does not owe an elaborate explanation of her situation), and I would hate to look elsewhere for a daytime job. Can you help me with this?"

Juanita maintains a boundary around the details of her life; she presents a rational case in writing, and reveals enough of her pain to convey how serious she is. If her supervisor is a person who makes decisions using logic rather than regard for her feelings, her rational arguments speak his language. But the power of straightforward emotionality is a universal language. Because our species is generally altruistic when we recognize need, her plea would strike a responsive chord in most people. If Juanita can look him in the eye, keep her voice in calm control, and maintain a centered, erect physical posture, she begins to change the system without having to be offensive or manipulative. She retains her dignity and implies that her supervisor is equally dignified.

Defending Defenses

Every person needs emotional defenses. The work world is generally benign but can be experienced as hostile, threatening, uncaring. At work, a woman's pride and self-esteem are often on the line, especially in male-dominated businesses and fields.

Emotional defenses are Nature's way of buying time. They are protective mechanisms in that they enable us to distance ourselves from an event, digest it, and develop an appropriate strategy. Sometimes defenses can work against us. Repression can interfere with memory, even blocking out a painful occurrence altogether. Rationalization and excuses can seem feeble, creating the impression of a whining victim. And snapping back with sarcasm may give a clear, "Back down, bud," message, but at the risk of alienating office-mates, bosses, and subordinates.

Having too few defenses, being emotionally thin-skinned can set you up for an invitation to a low rung in the pecking order. In a sense, it's like being the proverbial ninety-pound weakling, bullied and laughed at by the big guys. If you crumple when criticized, easily feel ignored or rejected, take teasing personally, believe that you are the favorite subject of gossip — chances are you could use a little more emotional padding. Look over these hints, and see if any seem like attractive possibilities:

1. When others seem invasive, or you sense someone's anger about to intrude into your world, or the dreaded performance review is at 3:00, use deep breathing, close your eyes and conjure up a meaningful protective image. For example, picture yourself in a suit of lightweight (and stylish!) armor; or envision a protective shield of white light or a clear bullet-proof dome descending all around that will keep you from emotional harm. Some women use more aggressive pictures, imagining the "assailant" as a creature they can intimidate and banish at will, something like St. Georgette and the Dragon. If you are short on images, think back over the childhood stories, fairy tales, and myths you were told or read. Choose a heroic character and let that person work on your behalf in your mind's eye.
2. Take a course in the martial arts. Knowing that you can defend yourself physically is a great confidence booster and creates a living metaphor for handling the knocks of unthinking, unfeeling colleagues.
3. Learn to draw attention to someone's hostile behavior, intended or not, in a straightforward but non-attacking way. An expression of surprise on your face often alerts the offending party that she/he has stepped over the line; adding a quiet question with direct eye contact can break the pattern: "What are you doing?" may have the effect of communicating, "Don't mess with me."

If, on the other hand, you are *too* well defended, you may yourself be clobbering people's feelings with anger, sarcasm, isolation, excuses, scapegoating, arguing, demanding, pulling rank, etc. Ultimately, you are shooting yourself in the foot and interfering with the serenity of those around you. This is a tough nut to crack, because if you're reactive, you probably have had good reason to be so in the past, and you may not be aware of how fully defended you are. You may want to consider some form of therapy to get beyond whatever traumas haunt you. In the meantime, here are suggested resources.

1. Rely heavily on deep breathing/relaxation when you feel attacked so you don't lash out in response or "disappear" and withdraw (see Chapter Seven).
2. If your primary mode of defense is some form of toughness and you rarely cry, give yourself permission to cry more often — in private, of course. Let the energy out as sadness and grief rather than generalized hostility — which is how toughness comes across. You probably have a lot to be sad about or you wouldn't be so well defended, so go ahead and cry.
3. Get three good nights of sleep before you respond to an incident. Your feelings, and those of the other person, will keep. Restore your mind and body and gain perspective by resting for a few days. Then, before approaching the other person, write out what you see as having happened, taking responsibility for your part in it. Sometimes this is in itself enough action. If not, make an appointment and calmly discuss it with the other person.
4. Take a good hard look at your baggage. Take ownership for it. Never blame someone else for what you may have set up, even unconsciously!
5. If you go too far, and wittingly or unwittingly attack another person, catch yourself, if possible, stop it, and apologize. If you're really hot-tempered, you'll recall and regret your outburst later. Go back to the person and apologize; offer to make amends. Do not leave a trail of wounded hearts and bitterness in your wake.
6. Avoid creating a triangle. Conflict can only be resolved between two people. Generally, even the most well-intended third party will inevitably be perceived as an ally of one person or the other. This will only increase hard feelings, so don't bring anyone in to your emotional rescue. Exception: Asking your manager to appoint a mediator not known to either party may be a reasonable solution to the problem between you and someone else if you have tried to resolve it one-on-one and it didn't work. The reason not to use your manager as an arbiter is that he or she may not be entirely objective.

(Note: Women can be very tricky, very clever, when it comes to enlisting emotional help. Letting your feelings of hurt or anger at someone leak out when you walk into a room is a sure way to invite someone to ask, "What's wrong? You look awful." Now the stage is set. Here it is: your golden opportunity to enlist this person on your side. You might say, "Oh, that Sharon! She gets to me with her know-it-all attitude," or "Oh, it's really nothing. I just found out someone is dating someone else, and it caught me off guard." If your office/company has a robust rumor mill, the person to whom you are speaking knows (or thinks she knows) *exactly* who "someone" and "someone else" are, and if "someone" has a bit of a reputation for being love-'em-and-leave-'em, you can gloat over having added a hot coal to a pile of ashes on his head. As for Sharon, you may have diminished her in the opinion of your listener by your sneering remark. So keep your feelings about other people to yourself, or deal with them without the concerned party. This is a matter of healthy personal boundaries.)

7. If your defense is to isolate yourself, withdraw, give the silent treatment, storm out of a room, etc., you are eroding the possibility of teamwork. Use slow breathing and relaxation to work on staying present just a little longer. Know that you can leave or withdraw any time you want, but try staying put, hanging in, for perhaps three more minutes than you usually would. If this works, aim for five minutes next time, then ten, and gradually progress to a point where you don't need to disappear at all. Never push yourself to the verge of excruciating discomfort.

8. What if you are passive-aggressive, that is, your way of defending yourself is to take revenge by *not* doing what's expected of you, but being very sweet about it and having a perfectly logical explanation? Work on these things:
    a) When you don't like what's happening, say something as soon as you are aware of it. Sweeping incidents and your feelings about them under the carpet means you'll only trip on the lump sooner or later and revert to your old ways.
    b) Be honest about the behavior you don't like and your feelings.
    c) Ask for what you need to rectify the situation, or explain your limits. People who are passive-aggressive behave that way because they perceive it to be the only way to achieve justice when they are being put upon or not getting their needs met. Directness helps to avoid the pitfall of being passive-aggressive, which only generates mistrust and anger in the long run.

How could you respond when others are defensive? In a lifetime of working, you will encounter many, many people with hair-trigger responses to the way you consciously or unconsciously come across. Sometimes their defenses are appropriate; other times they are reading into a situation or projecting their own baggage onto you. In either case, your first order of business is always to reduce the other person's defensiveness by modifying your own behavior. Make a conscious effort to present an open, listening, non-threatening posture, both physically and verbally. *As much as possible, drop your mental agenda for where or how the situation should go.* Ask gentle questions about the other person's experience of the situation, and listen carefully. Validate the person's experience and feelings. *Be open to the part you may have played in creating the situation.* You may not see things the same way; you may have entirely different feelings. Until the other person feels accepted, however, there can be little movement in his or her perception of the situation. This is how defenses operate. Human beings can be so busy expending their psychic energy on protection that there are few scraps left for changing their conclusions. Can you recall becoming more open-minded once you felt entirely heard by at least one other person? For a healthy, happy team environment to exist at work, defensiveness has to be kept to a minimum. It is in your interest to help other people protect their own self-interest. If you try to force change, something breaks.

Recalibrating Responsibility

Here comes the fun stuff! Has the big red "S" (for Superwoman) on your blue leotard been burning a hole in your chest? Is your middle name "Atlas" because you shoulder the world's extra burdens? Have you gone that "extra mile" so often that you feel as if you've circumnavigated the globe? Does responsibility loom in your life like a mythic giant, but you keep climbing to the clouds anyway hoping for some promised reward . . . and all you get is a chopped-down beanstalk? Do you need to feel (dramatic pause, please) . . . INDISPENSABLE? Then this is the section for you!

Boundaries around responsibility are difficult for conscientious people — of whom you are one, right? And women enter this arena through their own unique passageways. Women at birth experience a surge of hormones designed to help them bond with their dependent, often exhausting children. This is Nature's insurance that we won't drop the ball when the demands of childrearing become overwhelming. Women historically have bonded with each other in coffee klatches, quilting bees, consciousness-raising groups, etc. Certainly many have bonded so powerfully to their mates that they are unwilling to separate even when being battered. Similarly, women can become bonded to responsibility . . . even when it's abusive! This can begin as early as girlhood, when girls are taught to help mom around the house and with younger siblings, in taking on babysitting jobs as a way to earn money, in being expected to be "more mature than boys." Figuratively speaking, women generally say "I do" to an invisible partner, Responsibility, long before they don a gown and march up an aisle to wed a man. (This is not to imply that men are less responsible than women but to approach the experience of deciding to be responsible through the general feminine experience in our culture.)

In the section on priorities in Chapter One, you analyzed and rank-ordered what's most important to you. Take a moment to go back over that section and review what you wrote. It is true that the pragmatics of life dictate that we cannot always devote the time we'd like to what we desire most fervently. Responsibility and preference do not always align as perfectly as we might hope. On the other hand, we sometimes become caught in a responsibility trap leading to depression, disillusionment, burnout. Dysfunctional boundaries around responsibility operate as both cause and effect: they create disharmonious, lopsided systems in which some people are overadequate while others are underadequate, and they are an end result of dysfunctional use of power when expectations are unclear and unrealistic. Thus, being over- or under-responsible keeps an unhealthy system sick by perpetuating elements of a cycle that feed on each other:

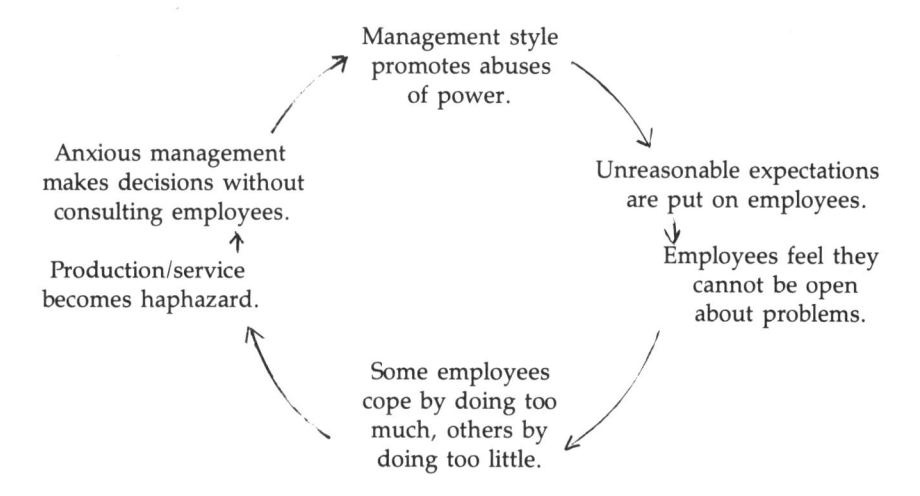

```
                    Management style
                →   promotes abuses   ╲
               ╱      of power.        ╲
                                        ↘
Anxious management                   Unreasonable expectations
makes decisions without              are put on employees.
consulting employees.                     ↓
       ↑                             Employees feel they
Production/service                   cannot be open
becomes haphazard.                   about problems.
       ↖        Some employees       ╱
         ╲      cope by doing too   ╱
           ╲    much, others by   ↙
                doing too little.
```

If you work in such a system, what options do you have for greater individual/systemic well-being? Before you proceed, be honest with yourself: are you an under-responsible person or an over-responsible person, or do you feel you've struck a healthy balance?

The under-responsible person is usually feeling demoralized, discouraged, hopeless, pessimistic. Working in a dysfunctional power system for years can undermine even the most stalwart employee's determination to do her best. Under-responsibility, not to be confused with laziness or sloth, is characterized by chronically incomplete or late work; quality below the competence level of the worker; shifting tasks to other workers, either through helplessness, request, or default; and abuse of work time to conduct personal business, distract oneself and others, daydream, or other activities irrelevant to the job. Under-responsible workers may elevate the ability to look busy while idle to an art; however, over time, their poor output tells the tale of an unmotivated, uncommitted worker.

If likeable, or favored by the boss, such a person can exist in a job for a long time, tolerated for personal reasons though resented professionally. If unlikeable, such a person cannot last long and floats from job to job, taking a toll on the good will and morale of an organization.

For you readers (hopefully few) who fall into this category because you have long since lost the will to work, you may wish to consider the following:

1. Perhaps you are not working up to par because you're in the wrong position or field, and therefore miserable. Get out! You are doing yourself, your employer, and your co-workers a disservice. See the Resources section in Appendix IV for career guidance.
2. If you are under-working because management is dysfunctional, you like the content of your work, but are discouraged or intimidated because your contributions don't seem to count, try voicing your problem to your immediate supervisor. Keep a record of this conversation — what you requested, what the response was. If, after a month, nothing has changed, go over your supervisor's head to one person whom you feel you can trust. Bring your documentation of the previous conversation and your work since then. (This is to convey that you have followed protocol and that you are willing to be an active contributor to the company's success.) As before, wait a month, during which you work at top level. If, after this period, there has occurred either a) no change, or b) negative consequences, why stay? Leave on a gracious note, having two months of solid performance under your belt. Those two months will give you the energy and confidence to seek new employment, legitimately being able to declare during interviews what you have to offer. Those who leave an unpleasant job cynical and depressed experience relief but don't come across credibly in a job interview because their recent history is one of underperforming, and that's what shows. No matter how unhappy you are, you can manage two months of effort, knowing you're trying to use the system to your advantage. Muster what it takes; if nothing happens, scoot!
3. If you are underworking because you perceive that high-powered co-workers are hogging all the work and glory, take a look at the role you are filling in the system. You are making everyone else look good, meeting their emotional need to succeed, at your own expense! They owe you a debt of gratitude . . . but you'll never get it. The only way someone can be over-responsible is if someone else is under-responsible. Systemically, this is difficult to change, because people in the glory roles do not want to give them up . . . and why should they? They're basking in the limelight. You have two basic options. You can ask directly for them to share their work

load with you (not as farfetched as it sounds if you approach a person who's both sensitive and overbooked). Or you can yourself work harder and faster, completing your own tasks so efficiently that you can begin to badger your boss for more work. This will take about three weeks of consistent and true labor and effort on your part. It will feel like a slow, unrewarding uphill trial. Remember — you're not just changing yourself, you're dealing with the context of pressure in a system that, until now, has needed your role in it. Persist. If you leave a vacancy, either someone else will step into your shoes, or the system will eventually shift into an abundance mode — there are enough goodies for everyone and no one needs to be short-changed.

In contrast to the under-functioning women, the over-functioning women show up much differently. Emotionally, their self-worth is tied up with performance; secretly they may fear failure and have a compulsive need to outwork others. They are their own worst critics, generally expecting more of themselves than anyone else expects of them. They fulfill a heroic role in the system. Sometimes the system rewards them with recognition and money, but often they are unsung heroines, martyrs to their own and the corporation's twist on the Protestant work ethic. If they are organized and likeable, they may appear to others as competent, highly professional, perfect, inspiring, motivating. If, however, they are driven but disorganized and abrasive, they can still be an asset in terms of productivity but will be detrimental to the emotional wellness of those around them. These people come across as obsessed, perfectionistic, self-righteous, judgmental, defensive, harried. They are difficult as managers, co-workers, and subordinates, yet may be doing an inordinate amount of work.

Over-responsible workers generally contribute well to the production/service end of a business. The toll they exact, however, includes damage to their own well-being (they are actually generating stress in their own bodies, remaining in a hyperadapted state in which their bodies seem to have ample energy — an "adrenalin high" which will eventually erode their immunity). There may also be a toll on the morale of those who are not as driven to succeed but who are performing at a reasonable level. Are you an overachiever? Are you taking on more than your tasks legitimately require of you? Is your job description unreasonably demanding but you carry it out without questioning it? Are you chronically competitive and driven to meet your own standards? Here are some tips:

1. Have you forgotten how to play? Hopefully, it's not too late to rekindle your spontaneity. Take a daily play break without fail!

Spend five minutes of your work day doing something childish: spin a yo-yo, doodle, listen to/tell jokes, go outside to catch a bug in a bug jar, look for figures in the clouds, etc. Not only are you de-stressing your body, you are also enhancing your creativity.
2. Ease up on yourself. Ask yourself where your high expectations come from. Are you becoming a workaholic? Many overly responsible adults were the childhood family heroes, the one the family could be proud of, in families where some type of addiction or dysfunction existed. While this was a loving thing to do as a child, it was completely unwitting and compulsively masked underlying pain. If this sounds familiar to you, treat yourself to psychotherapy, or join a support group such as Adult Children of Alcoholics or Codependents Anonymous (see Resources in Appendix IV).
3. If you are regularly working more than 40 hours a week to the detriment of other relationships/commitments/priorities, and physical self-care, try diminishing your work week by one percent each week until you are down to 40 hours. Does your job description explicitly stipulate more than 40 hours a week? If so, why did you agree to it to begin with? Go back and reread #2.
4. If you consistently take work home, acquire better time-management and delegation skills. Learn to shut the door on work at the end of your workday. Let the door itself become the physical boundary on your responsibility level.
5. Learn to meditate daily using a book like Anne Wilson Schaef's *Meditation for Women Who Do Too Much* or Ellen Sue Stern's *Running on Empty: Meditations for Indispensable Women*, usually available at your local bookstore or easy to order.
6. Go back to your priority list from Chapter One and put "My Needs" at the top of each list. If you don't have a clue about what your needs are or have difficulty developing the means to meet them, consider either therapy or a workshop on codependence.
7. If one of your traits is feeling responsible for the emotional well-being of everyone around you, reread the section "Restructuring the Relationships" earlier in this chapter. Develop clearer, stronger emotional boundaries. The more you meet your own needs while offering empathetic courtesy rather than compulsive problem-solving, the healthier everyone can become.
8. If you're usually among the first to volunteer to help out in a crisis, strap that hand to your side when it gets the itch to raise up like a banner of rescue! Give someone else a chance. ("Oh, no," you protest. "I tried that, and no one else volunteered. Somebody had to do it!" Well, you didn't wait long enough. After months or years of everyone else learning that Superwoman — you! —

SAVVY SYSTEMIC SOLUTIONS

would fly right in, why would they jump up and enlist?) Sweat out your discomfort. Eventually someone else will rise to the occasion. That's a promise.

9. Experiment with judicious helplessness. The two best sentences for over-responsible women who want to get off the hook are "I don't know" and "I can't." And you can really have fun with them. One woman, who describes herself as a recovering perfectionist, said, "I feel like giggling a lot. I realized one day that I thought I had to know all the answers to people's questions at work, but I don't know it all. It's amazing how resourceful everyone else became when I suddenly became ignorant. I used to waste so much time finding the answers to questions I didn't know. Now I just do my job. I feel so liberated!"

10. (This is usually the hardest change for over-responsible women to make.) Begin asking for help. Once a day, make yourself ask someone for directions (even if you know how), ask someone to do a small task for you (even if you have the time yourself), ask someone to listen to your idea and critique it (even if you already know it's fabulous). Practice, practice, practice. Then, when the chips are down and you legitimately need help, you'll be able to ask. Often, overachievers simply cannot ask for help when they need it because they never learned how. We all need each other. It is as much a gift to be the receiver as it is to be a helper. Give the gift of letting go and letting others do it for you.

Healthy work systems have a harmonious and flexible rhythm of reasonable responsibility, with various people rising to the crises which spring up from time to time. Healthy, mature people develop a conscience which includes generosity and altruism. If you read this book and think, "From now on I'm only going to meet my own needs," you've missed the point. Wellness is a matter of balance. Relationships, leadership, defenses, and responsibility must all be used flexibly. Being a healthy team member requires the give-and-take of responsibility, empathy without fusion, protecting yourself without walling people out, decision-making without dominance. Where will you hear the whispering serpent? In the imbalance in your own body each workday. Having too few or too many boundaries requires a little knowledge of what's good and what isn't. When you feel out of sorts, grab an "apple" — take a bite out of one of the suggestions which applies to your situation and give it a try; this will help you expand your knowledge of what's good and what isn't. Trust that the system will shift to accommodate you — perhaps in a way that you could not have accurately predicted. If it's really important to you to work toward your own health, believe that in some way the consequences of your change will ultimately produce an opportunity for your health elsewhere in the system — even by becoming someone else's "serpent."

One final thought about boundaries and dysfunctional work systems: workers who do more than their share may be inadvertently protecting an unhealthy system. Naturally, each woman has a vital interest in protecting her own job. But when her job is in the context of an abusive, unethical company which keeps her miserable, is it worth it? Each person must weigh this for herself. But consider this thought. What if all those who were overworked in a dysfunctional corporation suddenly kept to ONLY the limits of their work within ONLY forty hours per week? Perhaps some customers wouldn't be served and would move to a different provider. Perhaps some reports wouldn't be made, fewer good ones would be produced, etc., until the CEO's worst nightmare occurred, and he or she was replaced — with luck by somebody wiser. Pain becomes the only teacher left when organizations fail to heed every other message to change. And sometimes this is the moment of truth: Can a system hear its own pain and make constructive changes? Many have and do. Many have contracted with outside consultants who came in and put bandaids on everyone's psychological wound but left the members as powerless as they found them — so nothing really changed afterward. But when individuals listen to their own emotional pain and draw the line, this occasionally creates ripples and groans and spreading burdens until finally the message of illness reaches the upper echelons — the ones who should have been feeling the pain and making better decisions all along!

To put it simply: If you work in a healthy system, your limits will be honored, your wants heard, you needs responded to. Healthy companies meet their employees' needs not because it will help raise profits (although in most cases it will), but because leadership knows that meeting needs is a necessary human and just behavior. Period. If you work in a sick system, you can always try the straightforward approach, pointing out what isn't working for you and suggesting change — even something simple like yogurt-and-juice vending machines instead of (or as well as) candy-and-pop machines. But if all is tried and fails, then the greatest favor to yourself is to shore up your boundaries and be willing to batten down your hatches through the systemic storms which may follow. If you happen to feel better yourself but the pain begins to be experienced elsewhere, believe that the entire system will be better off for it. If not, abandon ship. Your moves toward wellness will have become your own private flotation vest and life raft, fully equipped to see you to another shore.

POWER WITHOUT POLITICS

Male models of power have traditionally fostered dominance, competition, status, and acquisition of material symbols of might and glory, including wealth. Is there such a thing as a female model of power, or a non-gender model of power? Or is it somewhat of an oxymoron to talk about female power? Think of women you know whom you consider powerful. What do they have in common? Do you consider them feminine? Nasty? Rational? Sexy? Or are these categories irrelevant? Who has been the most powerful: Margaret Thatcher, Nancy Reagan, Jane Fonda, Mother Teresa? Each in her own way, has represented a different type of power, force, or influence.

There is a difference between "power over," which involves an implicit or explicit contract between two people, allowing one to make decisions which the other will follow, and personal power, which involves integrity and congruence, and for which the exercise of "power over" is not necessary for it to be recognized. In other words, these two types of power do not always overlap. History is full of charismatic figures who lacked integrity and congruence, but whom people followed anyway. Women who radiate personal power may or may not occupy positions of designated leadership. In your own life, you can probably think of relatives, teachers, friends whom you experience as powerful women. This has to do with their wholeness as human beings, their ethics, and their spirit. This is equally true of quiet women and high-energy, outgoing women.

In the workplace, power politics are prevalent. Status, rank, and competition are artifacts of the power game. Games can be fun, but sometimes the profit motive skews the use of power so that the whole person — body, mind, heart, spirit — and the wholistic needs of human beings become flotsam and jetsam in its wake. An alternative to being the victim of abuses of rank and conquest is personal empowerment. Many women, sad to say, are unfamiliar with, even afraid of, their own strength and power. This may be because we, as a species, still confuse power with dominance. In the business world, we have to be tough, live in the fast lane, get the jump on the next guy, stay on the cutting edge; ideas get shot down, unless they're razor sharp (but sometimes they still bomb). Words of violence, images of weapons are vestiges of conquest in the name of power. Because the female experience, the business world aside, involves so much affiliation and bonding, it is the antithesis of dominance, violence, conquest. Dominance relegates people to mere objects — things used to further the goals of power. Bonding acknowledges people as free, whole, good, able to participate in adult relationships as equal, autonomous partners. The bonding mode is cooperation; the contributions of each member of the partnership or team are considered as valuable as someone else's. Every contribution is a precious gift to the functions of the whole unit, be it a dyad or a group. Currently, many corporations are integrating such modalities as quality circles, consensus models of decision-making and collegiality as ways of circumventing the human pitfalls of traditional power pyramids. There is, of course, no perfect way to include everyone's needs — but consensus clearly works better than competition, if the criterion for a good model is affirmation of every worker as valuable.

You can claim or reclaim your power: I accept myself as strong, precious, valuable; I will not let anyone take advantage of me; I am a gift, and will follow the goodness in me to find ways to make life better for all; I am free to choose what is right for me; my love is my power; etc. In a sense, each woman who takes a stand for herself pushes the work system a notch toward consensus, away from competition. This is markedly so if she consciously promotes finding other approaches to influence and decision-making through education, workshops, experiments. Each woman must decide for herself where she can afford to make compromises: when to "play the game" or act like "one of the boys" because it makes good business sense. There are also times when she will be utterly confounded, when none of her alternatives seem fruitful, as in dealing with an executive who is an alcoholic, workaholic, or other kind of addict. Nevertheless, striving toward consensus as an alternative to competition is the direction of hope for workplaces desirous of wellness.

Consensus is based on the dual assumptions of abundance and empowerment. There is enough to go around: enough resources, enough power, enough room — everyone gets to share the goodies. A functional work environment, much like a healthy family system, is characterized by open and honest communication, flexibility, respect for individual growth and limits, provision for employee needs, and employees' sense of ownership and participation in the success of the company. Smart companies enlist everyone in creating such an atmosphere simply because it's the right thing to do, not just because it might raise the peak on next year's profits graph. The role of the individual in moving the company along is crucial. Besides following the beacon of your own wellness, you can also begin a network within your company of like-minded women (and men, too!).

Listen carefully to lunch conversations, the chatter during the breaks. Look carefully at the practices of each person. You know who's out to manipulate and cheat, you know who's ambitious to the exclusion of courtesy, you know who's a chauvinist — male or female. You know who's ethical. Begin to structure your social contacts at work away from those who abuse their bodies and their power (negative peer pressure) and start selecting acquaintances who are attentive to their own wellness. Listen for talk about exercise and nutrition, concern about how to promote so-and-so's idea, disgust with obscene and stereotypical jokes. Find the people whose ideals and pain are similar to yours. You are more likely to bring about positive change when several of you are operating to consciously infiltrate well-being into the office. You can reverse the flow of peer pressure in your favor — but you have to find your peers first. Don't hesitate to toss out conversational topics and questions as bait, and see who bites. Leave a copy of this book, or others, on your desk. If you commit to your own wellness, you will be amazed at who picks up on your signals, as well as how many others appear whom you never guessed shared this desire. At the same time that you are actively seeking to team up, remember your boundaries. Since society is so fragmented, and the former structures of community and social support (clubs, churches, extended families, neighborhoods) have gone through cycles of disintegration, many women look to work to meet their needs for community; this is where they spend the majority of their waking hours and see the same people from day to day. Start your team off on the right foot — each of you can do only just so much and meet just so many needs for bonding. This is, after all, a place of work. Don't make the same mistakes with your allies that you're trying to address regarding the way the company deals with its employees. Start off healthily with clear relationship and responsibility boundaries. Avoid the seduction of falling back on Parliamentary procedure, electing officers, etc. Get a few books on consensus, and begin at the beginning to operate with each other as you would do for yourself, and as you want the company to do for you.

Settling Sexual Harassment

The most insidious abuse of power is sexual harassment, because it violates such an intimate aspect of a person's identity. It is both an issue of sex and power. The range of behaviors which constitute sexual harassment is wide. Offering favors in return for sex, or threats (implicit or explicit) if sex is refused constitute gross misconduct. Less obvious, but still establishing a hostile environment, are such things as obscene jokes or remarks, touching, and posting lewd photographs. The Equal Employment Opportunity Commission is responsible for enforcing discrimination laws, and this includes sexual harassment.

What can you do if you have been harassed or are concerned about this issue? The emotional stress of having been victimized, and the potential added trauma of initiating procedural action, being stigmatized, and incurring further reprisals keep the majority of victims from seeking justice. There is no way of knowing how many women have experienced this violation, since so much goes unreported. However, for those who do report, the fight pays off. Taking into account both internal company settlements and formal outside grievance procedures, including legal battles, up to 90 percent of women who raise charges of sexual harassment win their cases — which means a monetary settlement, the return of a lost job, the gaining of a withheld promotion or a guarantee of no further harassment.[2] It is worth it to file a complaint and pursue it, even though the well-publicized Clarence Thomas confirmation hearings discouraged many women.

All companies should have a policy statement regarding sexual harassment in their employee handbook or personnel manual. It is in a company's best interest to draft and promulgate such a policy, since the courts have set a precedent for holding employers accountable for the actions of managers, employees, and even customers! Companies then get hit where it hurts — in the wallet! Legal bills and just compensation can take quite a bite out of profits.

The profit motive aside, companies need to spell out what constitutes unacceptable behavior and what can be done about it out of a moral obligation to the human beings who work there. You, as the worker, should possess a copy of the employee handbook or personnel policy. If you don't, obtain one and read it. If it does not contain a specific section on sexual harassment and resulting grievance procedures, bring this to the attention of the personnel office and ask that they draft one and distribute it. Even a small office should do so.

Sexual harassment is an abuse of both power and sex. You personally can put a halt to unwanted overtures of a sexual nature by assertively and calmly using "I-Statements" such as this one: "When you tell off-color jokes, I feel uncomfortable. Please stop." This is your own empowerment. NEVER ignore unwanted sexual behavior; don't try to be one of the boys or laugh about it with the guys, as that only encourages it. If the behavior continues, document each incident: the date, time, place, person responsible, any witnesses, and the content — as well as how you felt. After two or three incidents, launch a confidential complaint with the personnel office. Most corporations make provision for a victim to approach any manager, if the victim feels that the personnel office or her/his boss is not trustworthy. Follow the procedures laid out in the policy manual. If there is not a procedure, or if you do not get satisfaction, the next step is to file a complaint with the local office of the U.S. Equal Employment Opportunity Commission (see Resources at the end of this book). The office can direct you in the proper action for your case. It is so important for your own self-esteem, the health of the company, and the protection of possible future victims that you act. Perpetrators of sexual harassment do not usually have only one victim — this is a lifetime pattern. Do whatever you need to muster personal support for yourself in terms of sharing what happened with your spouse, friends, a close relative. You may wish to protect your confidentiality at work as much as possible to minimize the stress of the incident itself. On the other hand, if you are not the only victim at work, you may wish to ask the personnel office if anyone else has filed a complaint against the offender, just so you know you're not alone (they cannot, of course, release names). You may also wish to ask discreet questions of your fellow employees. Each situation is unique. Follow your instinct and needs.

Do take action. Defend yourself. There is no excuse for sexual harassment. Listen to your own discomfort, and let it guide you. While harassment should never occur in the first place and can range from damaging to devastating in its aftereffects, seeking justice is both healing for the individual and an investment in the wellness of future generations of men and women.

Finding Another Garden

A 53-year old executive secretary, Indecisive Inez, had stayed with her company for 17 years, waiting for things to get better. Nothing was horribly wrong, but neither was anything amazingly right. Inez had a private dream of opening a small restaurant (she was a great cook, and loved to make big dinners). She didn't think she was miserable, but she knew she wasn't happy. Day after day she came to work, did her job, got flowers on Secretary's Day from her boss, went home at night, and cooked dinner, imagining herself in the bustling, steamy kitchen of the Friendly Cafe. During the past five years, she learned she had a mild heart condition (there was a history of heart disease on her mother's side); she developed occasional tension headaches and her lower back began to bother her. Her daydreams became more compelling, but she knew she would be foolish to leave the security of her job, and what bank would ever lend her the money when her only restaurant experience was waitressing to put herself through secretarial school? Inez came to feel imprisoned and depressed, but she kept telling herself how lucky she was and how happy she should feel.

Inez is in trouble. If she stays where she is, her heart trouble, literally and metaphorically, is likely to worsen. If she tries to make a move, her lack of energy and her malaise are going to come through to bankers and restauranteurs. And she's not getting any younger. She's getting into a deeper hole every day.

How do you know when it's time to leave a job — especially if it's one that you really wanted years ago and felt lucky to get but now you think you might want to do something different? Or if you're truly unhappy because your boss is a sick-o, but the economy is horrible and the unemployment rate is terrifying and your best friend was just laid off?

There isn't a pat answer to any of these questions. However, here are some guidelines, and some resources.

1. If you love your job and your company is benevolent and you are being fairly paid, stay where you are and continue to deepen your wellness. If, in the future, you want to change jobs or careers, your well-being and stress-management skills will have been a worthwhile investment to see you through the transitions, as well as make you an appealing candidate to a prospective employer.
2. If you love your job but hate your company, see what you can do from within to improve your working conditions: a lateral transfer, your own wellness program, developing a team. Set a reasonable limit on how long you will wait to see what happens in response to your own efforts, with three measurable objectives. (e.g., Within eight months, I want one idea of mine implemented; a cost-of-living wage increase; and a manager who tells me, at least monthly, one thing I've done well without being asked.) If, by the end of the designated time period, you have not achieved two of your three objectives, prepare to move on.
3. If you hate your job but love your company, do your best work for three months, then go talk to your manager. If you are a valued employee (and you probably are, or you wouldn't have that much affection for the company) and if you are clear about what you want to do, it may take some time but a position can be restructured to accommodate you.
4. If you are fantasizing about doing something different, e.g., becoming a travel agent, begin to explore this new direction on your own time. Talk to travel agents, take a workshop, read books, go on a cruise. If your idea is an accurate reflection of your heart's desire, you will have already begun a network; if not, you will soon run out of energy for your exploration without being any worse off — except maybe a little poorer because you went on the cruise (but you had a great vacation, anyway).
5. Hate your job and your company? You've read every page of this book so far and you're still thinking, "This will NEVER work because of how awful my office is!"? Take a look in the mirror. What are you doing to yourself? No job justifies throwing your

life away. If you're that unhappy, get out and get some help, so your misery doesn't sabotage you in your attempt to find a better position!

In terms of resources, there are hundreds out there, and while anyone (practically) can find employment, not everyone can create a position of their dreams without guidance. The resources in the back of this book (see Appendix IV) list materials and books on the market which can help you. In addition, there are several types of services available to you. These are arranged in order from the most discriminating (that is, the perfect person for the perfect position) to the least discriminating (basically a crap shoot). If you are looking to change jobs or careers, here is a simplified guide to employment services:

RETAINED SEARCH FIRMS ("Headhunters")

For those earning six figures and up, these firms cover 50 percent of the total job market. The company pays the fee, and the search firm locates the ideal candidate and makes it worthwhile to take the position. Because they know exactly what they're looking for, search firms are not interested in people who want employment coming to them.

CONTINGENCY SEARCH FIRMS (Also a type of headhunter)

For those in the $30,000 to $100,000 salary range, these types of firms offer about 25 percent of the jobs available. They are paid by the company upon locating a person for the position, so two or three companies might be working on filling the same position; the first one to produce a candidate gets paid. Again, they are usually not interested in candidates coming to them.

EMPLOYMENT AGENCIES

These services offer mostly general office and clerical positions, with a salary up to about $30,000. They offer 8–10 percent of the available jobs for a given candidate. The company pays the fee; they are interested in you if you are a good fit with the companies they work for. The advantage of using this type of service is that they put some effort into matching openings with candidates.

CAREER MARKETING FIRMS

The client pays the fee, and these services do two things: they help the candidate clarify exactly what kind of job is sought, and they help the candidate interview in the published and unpublished job markets. Collateral services include resume writing, interviewing skills, one-on-one counseling, group support. Generally, they serve people making $30,000 and up.

INDEPENDENT CAREER CONSULTANTS

The client pays the fee; they offer a range of services similar to but not necessarily as comprehensive as career marketing firms. Usually listed in the Yellow Pages. Call several and do a phone interview to find out what they offer/charge.

MAIL MARKETING FIRMS

The client pays. They assist the client in clarifying what is wanted and conducting a mail campaign of letters/resumes. They may not provide much coaching in getting the interviews or how to conduct them.

VOCATIONAL GUIDANCE

The client pays. They provide testing and counseling to determine what the client desires/is suited for, but do not help market the client.

RESUME AND SECRETARIAL SERVICES

The client pays. They help with the administrative end of marketing yourself — writing and producing resumes and letters.

CLASSIFIED ADS

Only a small percentage of the actual job market. Basically a lottery. Inefficient way to find a good match.

If the serpent is hissing in your ear that it's time for a change, and you don't have a clear and specific idea of what you want (the type of work, the size company, how much money you want to make, the structure of your hours, the location, etc.) your best bet is a career marketing firm or an independent career consultant. These services both clarify your goals/talents and aid in marketing you to the hidden job market. Ask around to see if anyone you know has used such a service; if not, check the Yellow Pages under "Career." Interview several firms and individuals. Since you will be paying the fee, be an informed consumer. Is the counseling one-on-one, group, or both? Do they use standardized vocational tests? Will they help you with your resume? Will they help you with networking interviews in the unadvertised job market? Is there a guarantee? Will they help you negotiate salary? Refine your interview skills? Some career marketing firms, such as Bernard Haldane Associates, are well-established, reputable, and located in most major cities across the U.S. Other independent career consultants come and go, so ask how long they've been in business and ask for references from previous or current clients. Career marketing firms and career consultants help you create the ideal position and should walk you through every step of the process. This is, for your initial investment, your best value in your search for the employment Eden of your dreams. Most people who use such a service report tremendous satisfaction with it and the position they ultimately end up with; they generally recover their fee with their first year's salary, thanks to help with the salary-negotiation process.

You deserve the job of your dreams. Who wouldn't like to do what she loves, and get paid for it? When work, play, and bliss coincide — and money, too — this is truly a taste of Paradise. The timeless ecstasy that occurs in moments of being who you are while doing what you love is a priceless phenomenon, given to those who take the time to know themselves, listen to their heart, balance their needs, and fulfill their missions. This is the road back to heaven; at times it is Eden itself.

CHAPTER FIVE

A Word on Communication

DYSFUNCTIONAL COMMUNICATION

You must have played the party game "Telephone," in which one person whispers a complicated sentence or tongue twister to another, who then whispers it to the next person, and so on. After seven or eight people, the final statement is often such a garbled rendition of the original as to be sidesplitting. The participants also laugh because, as in most humor, there is recognition of the truth: human miscommunication often results in sheer buffoonery. Many great comedies, from Shakespeare's to Woody Allen's, are based on misinformation and misinterpretation.

At work, however, the results of poor communications are not so funny. Dysfunctional communication refers to inaccurate and incomplete information loops including emotional information. While there are vast numbers of articles and books on managing effective corporate communication, this section deals only with interpersonal miscommunication and how it can create emotional problems on the job.

"Say what you mean, mean what you say." We often believe we are doing that, and that if communication goes awry the fault lies with the other person. Let's break down human communication into simple components so we can take a closer look at where mishaps can occur.

STAGE I

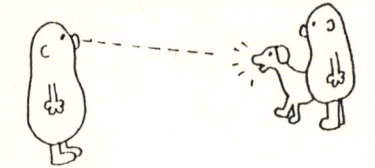

A stimulus (in this case, an unleashed barking dog) occurs, and is sensed by Person A.

STAGE II

Person A has a feeling about the barking dog, and is aware of it.

STAGE III

Person A must correctly identify and name the feeling.

STAGE IV

Person A must decide to tell Person B.

A WORD ON COMMUNICATION   99

STAGE V

[Person A speaking to Person B with dog: "DOES HE BITE? I WAS BITTEN ONCE, SO I'M A BIT NERVOUS."]

Person A must tell Person B.

NOTE: HAS COMPLETE COMMUNICATION OCCURRED YET? NO!

STAGE VI

[Person B responds: "SOUNDS LIKE YOU'RE SCARED. HE'S REALLY FRIENDLY."]

Person B has to let Person A know what he or she heard. THIS IS CALLED FEEDBACK.

We will be using this word a lot, because it is very important to healthy communication.

STAGE VII

[Person A: "I AM AFRAID OF DOGS. COULD YOU HOLD HIM AS I PASS BY?" Person B: "NO PROBLEM. WALK ON BY!"]

Person A knows if she has been accurately heard, and can affirm or correct the message. In this case, she was correctly heard and the situation resolved in a mutually satisfying way.

Now let's see the possible breakdowns at each stage:

Stage I

If person A does not sense or perceive correctly a given stimulus, even an internal one, no complete communication can occur. If you are angry at someone, and the target of your anger seems to be oblivious, you know how frustrating and enraging that can be. Aside from physical handicaps, there are hundreds of reasons why someone would simply not sense an incoming signal. These range from emotional defenses to personality type to attention focused elsewhere. Remember: we can take in and process just so much information at any given time, and each person is unique in terms of sensitivity.

Stage II

This stage has to do with self-consciousness. If Person A is unaware of a feeling, idea, or other reaction/response to the stimulus, then, for all practical purposes, there *is* no feeling. How a person is raised and sensitized, and one's personality will determine whether or not there is conscious knowledge that a feeling response is occurring.

Stage III

As we develop and mature, hopefully we become more adept and truthful at correctly identifying our own feelings. Since we often experience more than one emotion at a time, this can be a complex and confusing process. The more accurately we can self-analyze and name what we experience, the more accurate communication will be. Both recognition and honesty are essential. When was the last time you told someone, "It's okay, I'm not mad," when in fact you were seething — or at least ticked off? Much communication breaks down because of inaccurate or incomplete self-identification.

Stage IV

Let's say Person A has feelings and honestly knows what's going on inside and why. How does she know when to verbalize it to Person B? Not everything in life is meant to be disclosed because some information may genuinely inflict greater hardship than the lack of it. It is up to Person A to judge the level of risk involved and how vulnerable she is willing to be. Whether consciously or not, we are always deciding whether or not to reveal ourselves to another. Person B does not have a degree in mind-reading. Unless Person A decides to share what's going on with her, effective communication is not possible.

Stage V

The decision is made, and Person A is about to speak. She has three fundamental options: a "You-Statement," or an "I-statement," or an indirect statement. The first type of message generally puts the receiver on the defensive, even if only slightly. These are ways of informing the receiver that she/he is the cause of the speaker's feelings, and therefore is the problem. In contrast, I-statements reveal the feeling of the speaker directly, honestly, and with accountability for explaining them and proposing a solution. REMEMBER: NO MATTER HOW CLEAR AND HONEST THE I-STATEMENT, COMPLETE COMMUNICATION HAS NOT YET OCCURRED. And, when Person A makes an indirect statement, this increases the possibility that Person B may not get the correct message. Only feedback can clarify the situation.

Stage VI

The process of giving feedback, or describing to the speaker what you believe you've heard closes the communication loop, thus completing it and setting the stage for the ensuing loop. Person B repeats, or paraphrases, what she has heard from Person A, who then can affirm or correct the message. If the message needs correcting, feedback must also be given to the correcting message. Remember, there are four previous stages (not counting Stage I) during which communication might have broken down, so feedback is essential!

The emotional impact of poor interpersonal communication is usually low-grade and pervasive in organizations, so an employee does not really feel such acute pain that she needs to remedy the situation. In other words, we all put up with a lot of slipshod verbiage and use our defenses to make tolerable having to work with each other. We often do not convey to each other the emotional ups which would support, inspire, and motivate. We fail to confront each other constructively and in a non-blaming way with the minor emotional bumps and bruises inadvertently dealt out, thus "stuffing" or suppressing our own feelings, adding them to our baggage, and later dumping them out unpleasantly or even explosively.

The next sections will demonstrate how essential I-Statements and feedback loops are in ensuring emotional well-being on the job. Clear and complete communication can be tedious and arduous to practice in the beginning, but if you've ever done it or seen it done, you know how heavenly it can be.

COMMUNICATION SKILLS

Books and workshops on communication skills abound, and serious pursuit of this subject will lead to a wealth of resources. Therefore, this section is intended to be a down-and-dirty *a la carte* menu rather than an elaborate seven-course banquet. Three topics are covered briefly: Active Listening, I-Statements, and Assertion Skills.

Learning to Listen

The first topic, Active Listening, is such a simple skill that many women take for granted that they use it and practice it correctly. Even if you've been trained in it, or have read books such as *Leader Effectiveness Training* by Thomas Gordon, chances are you've become a bit lax in using it as often and completely as you might. So this section can be a handy pick-me-up to get you back into the groove. If you've had no previous acquaintance with this essential component of accurate and complete human communication, welcome aboard!

A quick review of the steps of communication early in this chapter shows, in Stage 6, what is called feedback, or repeating/paraphrasing what the listener has heard the speaker say. This is Active Listening. It is like a mirror reflecting the speaker back to her/himself. It is crucial because feedback makes it possible to close this communication loop, giving an accurate understanding from which to begin the next loop. It is active because it demands work on the part of the listener: shutting down her own thoughts and agenda, suspending judgment and defenses, keeping communication in manageable units, therefore interrupting every few sentences so her brain doesn't have to track piles of content, and using her imagination and previous experience to make educated guesses about the feelings of the speaker, all the while checking those out as well as the content. Sound complicated? Let's break it down.

In almost everything you hear from another person, there are two components: content, and feeling (or emotional process). Content is generally the words themselves, describing an idea, fact, incident, etc. It's the news. Process, on the other hand, is usually conveyed in other ways besides the words, though the verbiage itself may name feelings: voice tone, pace of the words, facial expressions, posture, breath rate, energy level, etc. Process can alter, even contradict, the meaning of the words themselves. Take, for instance, someone who comes up to you and says enthusiastically, "Great suit!" What do you hear? A lovely compliment. On the other hand, your worst enemy walks up to you, casts a sneering glance at your new outfit, and sarcastically drawls, "Gre-e-a-at suit . . ." What do you hear? A vicious put-down. And you can do the same thing back. In the first case, you might beam and bubble, "Thanks a lot, Ellen!" In the second, your eyes narrow to slits, and with your voice honed to a surgical sharpness, which you hope will excise her heart, you hurl your most hateful barb, with special emphasis on her name as if it's a pin in a voodoo doll, "THANKS A LOT . . . *DIANNE.*"

Another case: You direct an art gallery, and one of your sales staff, Jim, seems to close a lower percentage of sales each month. It's Saturday, and you decide to schedule a meeting with him for the next week, before the situation gets any worse. In Scenario One, you've had a good, productive day; you just received some pieces which you're confident will move well and are a sound investment; you've been busy but not overly so. It's about a half-hour before closing, and you notice he's not with a customer. You approach him, smile, and in a friendly way you say, "Jim, please step into my office. I want to set up a meeting with you about your recent sales. I think you could use a little help." You wait till he's by your side, and the two of you begin to walk toward your office. Well, Jim's been dreading this moment, but he perceives that you are not going to toss him out. In Scenario Two, you've had The Day That Wouldn't Die — a shipment of sculptures seems to be lost somewhere west of Des Moines, a wealthy but irate client claims the provenance of an eighteenth-century painting is fake, you spilled salad dressing on your silk blouse at lunch, the gallery has been bustling all afternoon and you feel a migraine coming on. But you promised yourself you'd get moving on the problem with Jim. A half-hour before closing, you notice he's not with a customer. You excuse yourself from chatting with a very interested browser, stride quickly over to Jim, and scowling from your headache, pressured to get back to the customer, you blurt out, "Jim, please step into my office. I want to set up a meeting with you about your recent sales. I think you could use a little help," then abruptly turn and head quickly for your office, heels tapping rapidly on the floor. Well, Jim's been dreading this moment, and now he's sure he knows why! Same words, two different processes. A little Active Listening on Jim's part in Scenario Two might save him a lot of anguish over the weekend.

Active Listening requires conscious effort on the part of the listener. The first task is NOT to jump to a conclusion, prepare a defense, judge the speaker. In the case of Jim, because he's already anxious (he knows he's been selling poorly) it will take calmness and maturity on his part to keep an open mind about the state you're in; his impression is that you're furious with him and probably about to fire him, so he's going to have to ride herd on his belief about that. You can certainly think of times in which you were sure you knew what the other person meant and why, or in which you heard what you wanted to hear, only to discover later that you were in error.

Another task for the listener is to "chunk" the communication into manageable units. If, when you were a child, you were ever lectured at, you probably tuned out the angry adult after the opening sentences. When emotional communication is coming our way, one of our defenses is to tune out what is unpleasant, which generally infuriates the speaker. It therefore behooves the listener to do the work of getting the speaker to halt every three to five sentences, even at the risk of seeming rude, to recap the ideas and feelings. Ultimately, most speakers appreciate this because it lets them know you're still with them, attending, following, understanding. This is one of the hardest parts of Active Listening, because 1) we are taught not to interrupt, 2) it means putting our own responses/defenses on hold; and 3) we may find inertia, tuning out, just plain easier.

A third component of Active Listening is paraphrasing the process as well as the content. "I hear you saying that this is the third time this quarter that I was rude to a client, and that you're angry, worried about losing the client, and concerned that I'm going through a hard time," would be a very comprehensive reply to a manager who might have said, "Shawna, that's the third time since January that you've snapped at Mr. LeGree, who's always been a loyal client. We've talked about this before, but you haven't seemed to have gotten a handle on this. What's going on?" Think of all the ways Shawna could have responded that might have escalated or complicated the content/process further between herself and her manager. Instead, she has calmly bought herself (and her supervisor) some time, and she has tried to openly digest what she's hearing. If she has listened correctly, she will respond more effectively.

The benefits of Active Listening include: calming the speaker down if he/she is upset (the speaker feels validated, heard); slowing the communication down (buying time); clarifying in your own mind what you think is being said; giving the speaker an opportunity to hear how she/he is coming across (feedback); allowing the speaker to correct/modify his/her communication so it is more congruent with intent; helping the listener moderate her tendency to compulsively "fix" the situation before it's clear that she is being asked to do so; and shaping the ability of the listener to become more compassionate and less reactive. Active Listening lowers anxiety and provides a platform for constructive progress. Also, the listener doesn't have to be 100 percent right in reflecting back what she hears; the speaker will correct it automatically, usually without annoyance since it feels so good to be attended to. In Shawna's case, her manager might reply, "No, I'm not angry at you, but I'm frustrated because I feel helpless. What we tried before didn't work, and I'm not sure I know how to help you." Or whatever.

A WORD ON COMMUNICATION

Here are some sentences people might say in the heat of emotion, and some Active Listening responses. Remember, reflecting the emotional process often involves educated guesswork, but this is really the more important component to reflect back, since it gets to the heart of the matter:

STATEMENT	ACTIVE LISTENING
This job sucks!	Sounds like you're feeling burned out and unappreciated.
I wish I'd known sooner about this. How am I going to squeeze this in?	Are you saying you feel pretty helpless?
Can you believe it? I finally made bonus!	It's a great feeling to reach your goal.
That Cara. She's so stuck up.	You seem resentful and a little envious.
Just once, I wish T.J. would get off my case. He treats me like I'm a kid.	You deserve respect and trust.

Now you try it. Imagine whatever voice tone you'd like for each sentence, and write an Active Listening response. Most such responses begin with phrases such as, It seems like . . . You're feeling . . . Are you saying . . . It sounds like . . . Sounds as if you . . . but since these become tiresome, just paraphrasing is fine.

SENTENCE	YOUR ACTIVE LISTENING RESPONSE
Oh my gosh! I didn't get hold of Ms. Collins at the bank, and it's after five. What should I do?	(Hint: Don't offer a solution or a suggestion. Tune in to the feelings.) _____ _____
Patrice! What's this I hear about you and David?	_____ _____
I really would like to implement your idea, but I'm afraid that there's just no money in the budget at this time.	(Hint: Two feelings. Can you reflect them both?) _____ _____

I can't do this job in two
weeks! What kind of extension could I get?

        _____
        _____
        _____

Your unit's performance is
finally starting to improve.

        _____
        _____

One problem people often have at the beginning of acquiring this skill is that it seems artificial, phony, or hokey to paraphrase what's being said. That's because we're not taught to communicate this way. Our cherished ways of communicating are founded on myths of mind-reading that just don't hold up at work. Of course it feels unnatural to begin to use Active Listening . . . at least to the person doing it. You will be amazed, however, that as you become more adept at it, your conversation mates will lap it up because the attention feels so good. They will not even notice that you feel awkward using it. Practice it at home and with your friends if you're not sure of yourself. In fact, the next phone call you get from a friend, just try reflecting the feelings and see if your friend doesn't smoothly keep up his/her end of the conversation. Your end will go something like this:

> Hello? This is she . . . Hi, Teri, what's up? . . . Really? When? . . . That must have been scary . . . Sounds like you put a lot of thought into it. Did you feel exhausted? . . . Oh, so it was more like tired but satisfied . . . It's a good feeling to know you could ask for what you wanted . . . I know, being kept dangling is nerve-wracking . . . So you were worried about how it would affect the team? . . . That's great that they were behind you. It helps with courage . . . Well, congratulations. I'm glad you pulled it off.

Notice the rhythm of the feeling words: scary, exhausted, satisfied, good feeling, nerve-wracking, worried, courage. That's easy. Let's take a more anxiety-provoking situation, and see how Active Listening might work when used to facilitate a thorny confrontation. Your co-worker, Jennie, was bypassed for a promotion in favor of Thomas, an ambitious rising young star who had one year less in your department than Jennie. Jennie, having just heard the announcement, comes storming over to your cubicle. No one else is within earshot.

> Jennie: Did you hear! Thomas got the promotion!
> You: I'm sorry, Jennie, you must be terribly hurt and disappointed.
> J: Hurt? Oh not really. Who cares anyway? Big deal. So Thomas can butter up the boss. Who needs it?

You: Sounds like it bothers you, but you're trying to figure out why Thomas got it instead of you.

J: I don't understand. I have a year on the guy, and I do good work. He comes along out of nowhere, and I know I'm next in line. The nerve! You know how hard I've worked. Don't you think they're wrong?

You: (Note: It's hard, but bypass invitations to take sides. Stay out of the middle.) You resent that your expertise and experience were overlooked.

J: Oh, it's more than that. It's a male/female thing. They had to consider me so they could say they *almost* put a woman in that position. I would have been the first, but no, that's too threatening for the good old boys.

You: It's such a powerless feeling to think you've been discriminated against. What are you going to do about it?

J: Do? What can I do? What would you do?

You: (Note: This is tricky. Do you tell her what you would do, what you think she should do, or dodge it altogether? You're on thin ice — this is a set-up. Stick to Active Listening, and elicit more information if you have to. Don't solve it for her, or you may be in trouble down the line if she quotes you.) You sound pretty upset to me. From what you've said, you have a number of feelings about this. What do you see as your options?

Active Listening coupled with good questions keeps the responsibility for solutions in the hands of the person with the problem. Even if you agree with Jennie, stick to Active Listening in the heat of emotion. When you've gotten some distance from the situation, you can decide for yourself if there's anything you want to do about it based on your own integrity and how such partisanship might affect you. If you were to express a concern or complaint, don't add fuel to Jennie's fire by sharing it with her. Go to the person who can be most helpful and enlightening to you — and be prepared for the consequences, if any.

In terms of straight content, use Active Listening: when you've been given directions (repeat them back, so both parties are clear); during performance reviews; when someone presents a new idea; when you find yourself beginning to feel defensive about something; in just about any situation you can think of, where a sprinkling of Active Listening here or there will add clarity. Do not underestimate the power of this tool. There would be much more understanding, and in the long run, much more efficiency at work, if Active Listening were used regularly.

Talking Sense, Talking Safely

The second topic, I-Statements, has to do with you as a speaker. (There are several variations on the format, so if you've already been taught a different structure, use what works for you.)

The basic I-Statement has three parts: a description of a specific behavior of the person; your feelings about it; and a basis for negotiation, usually a request for behavior change in the future. The intent of an I-Statement is to describe, not to blame, and to offer a foundation for a workable arrangement as an alternative to what has happened. It goes like this:

> When you _____ (describe behavior)
> I feel _____ (name your feelings)
> and I would like _____

The variations include explaining where your feelings are coming from (your own baggage), and naming a consequence which you will follow through with if the other person doesn't change. Here are some samples of basic I-Statements:

> Charlene, when you come up to chat with me and I'm working on the computer, I feel torn because I'd like to respond to you but I really need to get my work done. Would you please wait until I'm on break so I can be really available to you?

> Jake, when you said you'd find that legal precedent by Thursday and now it's Friday afternoon and you still don't have it, I heard it as a promise so I feel disappointed and betrayed. I would like to work out a better understanding of deadlines and commitment with you.

VARIATION I — Say where you're coming from:

> Bill, when you just walk in and look over my shoulder to see what I'm working on, I feel anxious because my dad used to watch me do homework and yell when I made mistakes. I know that's not what you intend, so could we just set up a time each week when I can bring you my projects to update you?

VARIATION II — Name a consequence:

> Eileen, when you make personal phone calls, you tend to have 20-minute conversations, and lately there have been two or three a day. I hate to set limits, but I'm worried because your last two articles were below your usual level of work. I'd like you to make per-

sonal calls from the pay phone on your break and be back at your desk promptly. If you are late five times in the coming month, I'm afraid I'll have to put you on probation.

Of course, in an ideal world, the person to whom you are addressing these will respond with Active Listening, and then you can both negotiate. Since life is not perfect, many people will hear I-Statements as threatening and/or blaming. All you can do is deliver them with a relaxed face, good eye contact, and calm voice tone. You cannot control how I-Statements are received, because each person is different. But making I-Statements is your contribution to a healthy communication system. Active Listening and I-Statements together are very powerful. You cannot control other people, but you can change how you communicate with other people to get results.

Applauseworthy Assertion

The third topic is assertion, which has to do with publicizing your boundaries. The dual aspects of assertion are a) asking for what you want, and b) saying "no" to what you don't want, without feeling guilty. Assertion is not about being rude, brash, or offensive. It is about being quietly firm. Assertion is nothing to be feared, since it can contribute to personal, mutual well-being.

You will need a partner for the following exercise. Get a trusted friend with whom you can be loose and playful. You will take turns asking for what you want with varying degrees of persistence, and refusing the request with various styles of negating. YOU CANNOT ACQUIRE ASSERTION SKILLS BY READING. YOU LEARN THEM IN RELATIONSHIPS WHERE YOU CAN PRACTICE THEM. The purpose of this exercise is to explore your own barriers to asking and refusing — and to find the assertion style that works best for you.

THE ASKING/REFUSING EXERCISE[1]
(You will need a friend and a three-minute timer.)
Part I. Decide first who will ask and who will refuse. At the end of three minutes you will reverse roles.

Asker: For three minutes, ask your friend anything you want, as long as it's something she could possibly give: driving you to work, helping with the laundry, a loan of $5.00, etc.

Refuser: Answer each request with a no, but give a phony excuse about why you can't do it, e.g., No, I'd like to, but my car is in the shop. (It is very important that you do not use actual excuses; you must lie, even if it's just a small lie.)

Set the timer and begin.

At the end of three minutes, reverse roles for another three minutes. At the end of the role reversal, spend a few moments sharing with each other how you felt about the exercise. Was it easier to be the asker or the refuser? How did it feel to make up excuses? Did you become better or worse as the exercise went on? Write down your observations.

Part II. Return to your original roles.

Asker: For three minutes ask for anything you want, no matter how ordinary or outlandish. When you are refused, badger your partner. Ask, why not? Ask the same question again. Try to persuade her. Try to talk her into giving you what you want.

Refuser: No matter what your partner asks, just say "no." (Sound like a familiar phrase?) No matter what your friend says or asks, only say the word "no." Do not say you're sorry, do not make excuses, do not say "No, thank you." Just say no.

Set the timer and begin.

At the end of three minutes, reverse roles for another three minutes. At the end of the role reversal spend a few moments sharing with each other how you felt about the exercise. What was it like to be pushy? How did it feel to only say "no"? What else would you have liked to say? Why? Record your observations.

Part III. Return to your original roles.

Asker: For three minutes, ask whatever you like, plausible or implausible. If possible, do not repeat any request, but you may badger.

Refuser: Either say "no" to each request, offering a true explanation (including "I don't want to") or simply say "No, thank you."

At the end of three minutes, reverse roles for three minutes.

At the end of the role reversal, spend a few moments sharing with each other how you felt. As the asker, are you getting better at asking? What still presents a barrier to you? As the refuser, how was this portion different from the other two? Which style of refusing works best for you?

Wherever you found your energy in this exercise, there lies your potential for asserting yourself. The impetus for being constructively assertive comes from knowing clearly what you want and don't want. No matter what position you hold at work, you will hold it with greater strength if you are assertive when necessary.

PART II

Your Spiritual Self At Work

CHAPTER SIX
Divine Discontent

Ouch! Physical ailments, even subtle ones, speak to us about how some types of work hurt our bodies. Emotional pain is signaled by the varieties of depression, anger, frustration or helplessness women may experience over their jobs. Career-related spiritual disorders, however, are much harder to diagnose. Losing one's spiritual connection rarely happens precipitously. Unlike Eve, few women have the experience of being born into Paradise, living there day after day after day . . . and then WHAM! losing it abruptly, which would be excruciating. Rather, the realities of life and work, the succession of daily decisions and distractions gradually erode a woman's spirit. Her pain may never fully emerge as a separate entity. It is more likely to be couched in the context of life's ups and downs, easy to overlook, bypass, ignore. This chapter is about the problems of spiritual pain and emptiness which can accompany women on the job.

It is essential, before describing the symptoms of an ailing soul at work, to acknowledge that a woman's career can be a source of spiritual fulfillment.

Many women find a freedom of spirit that accompanies the financial security of the paycheck and/or the liberation of getting "out of the house." They are not dependent on anyone; they have a sense of autonomy. For women whose backgrounds may have been narrow or rigid, work opens up a large worldview. For these women work is an education: as they meet new types of people and experience a range of human behavior, they expand their understanding of what it means to be fully human. They may acquire spiritual and moral maturity as they make personal choices based less on a rigid individual code of "shalts/shalt nots,'' and more on values grounded in the needs of the human community. Other women who believe that life comes with a responsibility to give to others often choose professions which incorporate an element of human service. These women, whose work integrates the larger good, have a built-in spiritual comfort that accompanies meaningful action. This is especially so if their work includes a community or team of people who share this value. They actively support each other in carrying out this vocation. Finally, there are career women whose work in its very nature is spiritual: clergywomen, theologians, spiritual healers, etc.

Just because a woman is performing spiritual work does not guarantee spiritual wellness. And millions of working women, regardless of their types of careers, are spiritually miserable!

"SPIRITUAL": NOT JUST ANOTHER PRETTY WORD!

By now some readers are asking, "Exactly what do you mean by spiritual?" There is a purpose behind the broad, descriptive context used in this chapter.

Many people equate spirituality with religion. When speaking of spiritual health or illness at work, it is more useful to think in terms of a quality which certainly includes religion, but which may also allow for agnosticism and atheism. Spirituality is a jewel with many facets. One need not be Buddhist, Jewish, Christian, Muslim, etc., to be a spiritual person.

In this chapter, and in Chapter Seven, the word "spirituality" is used inclusively to refer to a reverent and joyful sense of belonging to something larger than ourselves. We experience this at the very core of our being, what many people call the soul. As intangible as the word "soul" is, we recognize it as the aspect of ourselves with a faculty for communion: a quest for the meaning of life, harmony with nature, interpersonal connection, a sense of infinity, feelings about religion and God — these are all matters of the spirit. As one Jungian therapist said, "When you go all the way in to the still center of your being, you meet the part of you that is connected with the universe."

(Are you nodding your head because this is familiar ground, or are you shaking your head because this is not your thing? If the latter, rather than trying to force a fit, the authors won't be at all offended if, having read this far, you call it a victory and withdraw — at least from the rest of this chapter. It is important to acknowledge that life and work can be completely satisfying without trying to construct a spiritual sense where none exists. On the other hand, if this chapter opens a new door for you, or raises some self-doubt, perhaps it's time to do some spiritual exploring. In which case, read on.)

Members of recovery programs such as Alcoholics Anonymous (AA), Overeaters Anonymous (OA), Codependents Anonymous (CODA), etc., often use the term "Higher Power" instead of "God," in honor of the uniqueness of each person's spiritual quest. Since spirituality is an essential component of recovery programs, "Higher Power" is a perfect concept for women who don't believe in God as such. They may determine that their Higher Power is nature, the group, music, their inner desire for well-being — the possibilities are endless. In a sense, God or Higher Power is the largest umbrella under which everything else fits. Women who possess a wider perspective through a specific religious faith and/or an intuitive sense of transcendence derive great benefits from it, and this is what spirituality is all about. This chapter is concerned with spiritual wellness at work.

WORK: A DISEASE OF THE SPIRIT?

The advent of the Information Age held out the hope of a leisure revolution. Computers would assume the brain labor of human minds. Promises, promises. It hasn't happened. The arrival of a shortened work week is not just around the corner; it has apparently boarded an SST and headed for some other continent. If you worked only ten or fifteen or twenty hours and still made the same (or greater) income as you currently make, what would you do with your "free" time?

Many of us would hardly be at ease with ourselves. We would, truth be told, continue with Human Doings: extra cleaning, extra shopping, extra "leisure activities" (and doesn't that sound contradictory?) would emerge to fill our Day Planners. The fact that we are the only species to map and schedule each day may not exactly be an indication of "higher" intelligence.

The word disease is a perfect word for the void filled by work. Disease. Dis-comfort. Dis-content. It is difficult for many women, with time "on their hands" (as opposed to "during their lives?") to sit and just BE. To Be: at ease, comfortable, content . . . doing absolutely *nothing*? That, as Hamlet said, is the question.

Got an extra twenty minutes? If you are reading this book, the answer is YES. Want to try an experiment? Again, you wouldn't be reading this if you didn't want change, and all change is a laboratory for learning. Recent studies on people who meditate suggest that a minimum of twenty minutes of meditation is necessary to produce its beneficial effects. For now, just try this simple inner adventure in order to discover what twenty minutes of stillness brings.

Experiment directions: Get a timer that you can set for twenty minutes. It is important to use a timer, because if you begin clock-watching during the experiment you are *doing* something. (If it ticks loudly, put it in another room where you will still hear the buzzer or bell.) Set it for twenty minutes, then sit in a comfortable chair or on the floor. You may keep your eyes open or closed, whichever you prefer. Now do nothing. For twenty minutes, experience yourself. If that is too nervewracking and you feel like you're not doing enough, try to be conscious of yourself as alive and therefore good. You may end when the timer goes off.

Begin the experiment. Put this book down, and go do it. When the timer goes off, come back and resume reading.

Two questions to ask yourself after the experiment:

1. What are some of the various feelings I had? (Feelings may include silly, relieved, peaceful, uncomfortable, anxious, anticipating the timer, embarrassed, ashamed, contented, close to God, creative, excited . . . the list is endless.)
2. What did I believe about what I was doing? (Beliefs like: Well, this is only an experiment; It's okay to do this because the book told me to, but I could never do this in real life; This is stupid; I do this all the time anyway; This could be a good thing to add to my life, but I'd have to write it in my Day Planner; My friends would think I was crazy if they walked in the door right now; I would never do this at work . . . etc.)

Some feelings and beliefs are symptomatic of dis-ease. What patterns did you notice about your feelings and thoughts? Did you find the experiment challenging? Did it seem to drag on interminably? If so, you are not alone. Rarely are any of us taught how to be alone and do nothing. Wilderness stress/challenge programs such as Outward Bound often use a "solo" experience during which each participant is left isolated in the wilderness for several hours up to several days. When they return from the expedition, most participants look back on the solo as the high point — a peak experience. The majority, however, report that the absolute solitude was initially excruciatingly uncomfortable, even terrifying. While some of these feelings most certainly had to do with anxiety about survival, the simple position of having no one but one's self for company caused a most disconcerting situation! We are at dis-ease with ourselves, and we don't know how to become intimate with the ground of our being.

Dis-ease is the same as dis-spirit, a true allergy to solitude and leisure time. Consider the possibility that there hasn't been a leisure revolution because in our culture we busy ourselves with doings all our lives. We are allergic to be-ing, and much of this has its source in the Protestant work ethic (note the relationship to religion) and the Industrial Revolution.

Work has become a dis-ease. Authors in the Men's Movement, such as Robert Bly, have analyzed how men became separate from themselves, their loved ones, and their own spirits as a consequence of the Industrial Revolution and the rise of technology. It is a small step to understand that this is not a particularly masculine property.* Women who integrate the same career orientation into their lives fall prey to the same fate. This is a human problem, not a male or female problem. But it is the female spirit that suffers in a male work model and is the concern of this book.

Women at work may experience the adrenalin high of meeting deadlines and performing well under pressure. They may have the satisfaction of competent performance. They may possess the security of role definition and clear expectations. Those women, however, who take the time to be still and look inward are finding that despite these achievements, a chronic lack of *something* makes the rest seem somehow like a hollow victory.

Here are two examples:

> Rachel is a high-achieving consultant working for a Fortune 500 company. She was well on her way to partnership in the company when her divorce became an opportunity to evaluate what her life was all about. Besides examining her motherhood (she has two kids), her finances, her inability to choose men who are genuinely capable of intimacy, her long work hours and compulsive perfectionism, Rachel also began to consider the role of spirituality in her life. She had been raised by religious parents but in her early twenties had rejected the formal institution and rituals. Now, in her mid-thirties, she is seeking Paradise Found. She is learning to meditate, attending lectures on various philosophical issues, and reading books on feminist spirituality. The search itself is a source of renewal and inspiration for her. Even in the dark struggles of single parenthood, trying to limit how many hours she's willing to work, dealing with house painters who don't show up and a dog that gets sick on the new rug, she gains calmness and peace as she tells herself, "There's a reason for everything." This is more than an emotional reaction; this is a spiritual insight. Does she espouse a particular faith or religion? Not at this time. Does she see herself as spiritual? She is beginning to. Does this help at work? Yes — in more ways than she could have imagined.

> Or consider the story of Michelle. Born into a devout rural community, Michelle "backslid" when she moved to a Midwestern city where she obtained a secretarial position. Caught up in what for her was a glamorous social whirlwind, she found that her country-fresh

---

*Note: Certain aspects of the human spirit, as delineated by the Men's Movement, represent the "warrior": adventure, indomitability, conquest, protectiveness, etc. Such elements are experienced by women in their careers, since paid work is still primarily a male-created phenomenon.

friendliness and pretty smile made her a hit with her co-workers as well as among the singles at bars and parties. As the months expanded into years, Michelle felt a widening gap between the person she once was and the person she was becoming. She could not, however, articulate the source of her malaise. She felt emotionally fulfilled and monetarily secure, but this was not enough. She shared her discontent with her girlfriends, but they were of little help. Some instinct in Michelle argued against the advice of her friends to find Mr. Right and settle down. At 26 she had a strong desire for freedom and self-determination. But something was missing from her otherwise picture-perfect life.

Michelle awoke early one Sunday morning, feeling restless and lost. Without realizing what she was doing and with no conscious purpose, she went for a long walk and found herself at the steps of a neighborhood church. The sound of a hymn, one she remembered from her girlhood, brought a flood of tears. She later described the experience as "coming home to God." She went in to the service, tearful yet deeply happy. By some coincidence, the minister preached that morning on the lost sheep who is found again. Michelle felt as if each word was healing her. All that week at work, says Michelle, people kept remarking on how happy she seemed. To those who asked why, she simply responded, "Let's just say a private miracle happened."

This reply is not surprising. Spirituality is as individual and intimate as sex — and much less talked about! The norm of not discussing one's vision/faith/experience of soul-states creates the illusion that spiritual experience is reserved for a few saints and celibates. Nothing could be further from the truth! While not every personality type is given to mysticism, each woman cherishes in her heart moments of being carried outside her common reality, awed by a timeless moment of beauty or communion. (This is literally the meaning of the word "ecstasy": transported out of the ordinary place.) A rapturous symphony, a golden sunset, a soul-meeting gaze, a moving church service, a birth, a wedding, a funeral, lovemaking, a peaceful garden . . . these are experiences where a woman's connectedness to someone or something larger than herself gives life meaning and fulfillment. They may be accompanied by a sense that time is standing still or a feeling of becoming larger than one's body. These experiences are kept within for several reasons: they are hard to identify; they are even harder to articulate; and there is peer pressure (the group norm) *not* to discuss matters of an intimate nature — especially spirituality — in professional and/or social situations. Finally, it is a sad reality that many well-intended people can be righteous and judgmental about the religious and spiritual beliefs of others. Encountering someone like this once can poison the well and be an effective deterrent to sharing matters of the soul with other women.

To stimulate your own thinking about the state of your soul, especially with regard to work, grab a pencil or pen and do the following inventory. List the four headings on a sheet of paper, and check off the one that fits each item. Unlike research-oriented tests or surveys that tell you to answer whatever comes first to your mind, take all the time you like to reflect on each item. It is important that you be honest with yourself, but this is not an objective scientific test.

Always	Frequently	Occasionally	Never	
_____	_____	_____	_____	1. I feel as if I am in harmony with nature and the universe.
_____	_____	_____	_____	2. I feel as if my work benefits only the company's profits.
_____	_____	_____	_____	3. I experience a sense of awe and wonder at being alive.
_____	_____	_____	_____	4. I feel as if my existence is ultimately meaningless.
_____	_____	_____	_____	5. Most of my waking hours are filled with concerns about my job — even my non-working hours.
_____	_____	_____	_____	6. I attend religious services and find them fulfilling.
_____	_____	_____	_____	7. My career seems to fit well with where I'm going in life.
_____	_____	_____	_____	8. I've lost my idealism about life.
_____	_____	_____	_____	10. I increasingly find myself caught up in pettiness at work.
_____	_____	_____	_____	11. I don't have a clue what "spirituality" feels like.
_____	_____	_____	_____	12. I can connect so deeply with my partner/closest friends that time seems to become infinite.

Always	Frequently	Occasionally	Never	
_____	_____	_____	_____	13. I see my job as benefiting the well-being of others.
_____	_____	_____	_____	14. As a child, I felt close to God.
_____	_____	_____	_____	15. There are times on the job when I feel hopeless or cynical.
_____	_____	_____	_____	16. My boss only cares about the quality of my work, not about me as a fellow human being.
_____	_____	_____	_____	17. Each workday brings a new insight into the purpose of life.
_____	_____	_____	_____	18. My sense of myself as a human being is lost when I'm at work.
_____	_____	_____	_____	18. I can converse with my co-workers about spiritual matters.
_____	_____	_____	_____	20. If I'm truly honest with myself, I'd have to say my work seems meaningless.
_____	_____	_____	_____	21. I feel as though I've been given so much that I want to help make the world a better place.
_____	_____	_____	_____	22. There is no time or place for my spirituality at work.
_____	_____	_____	_____	23. Conversations at work seem to be about materialism, status, or negative feelings
_____	_____	_____	_____	24. I stop and reflect on what my life means.

Scoring: For numbers 1, 3, 6, 7, 9, 12, 13, 14, 17, 19, 21, and 24 score 2 points for each Always, 1 point for each Frequently, −1 for each Occasionally, and −2 for each Never.

For numbers 2, 4, 5, 8, 10, 11, 15, 16, 18, 20, 22, and 23 score −2 for each Always, −1 for each Frequently, 1 for each Occasionally, and 2 for each Never.

ADD THE TOTAL OF YOUR SCORES.

IF YOU SCORED:

48	Skip the rest of this chapter and Chapter Seven. In terms of spiritual fuel, you are running on a full tank. In fact, would you consider writing a book? You're a model of spiritual health on the job and off!
47 to 25	You're doing really well. Whether or not you consider yourself religious, you have a healthy spiritual cushion and can use it to help sustain yourself at work.
0 to −24	Your spiritual core is jeopardized by a shrinking perspective due to isolation, pressure, and distractions from the purpose of your life. A retreat would be a strategic restorative at this time.
−25 to −47	Do you ever wonder where your soul went? It may be a long search to reclaim her. If you don't even have the desire or energy to do so, you may need help.
−48	Get a spiritual director and a therapist as soon as possible. You are in a state of spiritual emergency — on the job as well as off!

Whether you are the picture of spiritual health, on the verge of collapse in relation to your Higher Power, or somewhere in between, chances are you contend with one or more of the specific ways in which work stimulates a woman's spirit. The remainder of this chapter describes the chief ways in which work is a Faustian arrangement for so many women.

THE SMALL PICTURE

The majority of working women have more than 40-hour work weeks which demand that they focus on the shortsighted pragmatics of the job. From the standpoint of profit and productivity, this is good. A packed workday, however, leaves precious little time to refocus, to consider where this job fits in one's life. It is as if we live to work, not vice versa. Ongoing concern over "How I fit in my job," as legitimate as that may be, robs us of a larger perspective.

Take Cheryl's case. Cheryl is a sixth-grade teacher who chose her profession out of love for children and the enjoyment of imparting knowledge. She is an atheist and is 46 years old. She has seen many changes in the field of education. In her urban school district, the demographics have shifted. Cheryl, besides teaching, is now also learning to speak Spanish to meet the demand for bilingual teachers. However, many of her students are handicapped by the language barrier, and there is tremendous pressure on Cheryl to produce high scores on her students' standardized achievement tests. Drugs are a growing problem among her students, as is violence. Cheryl is expected to identify and refer children at risk of dropping out, to report suspected physical/sexual abuse, to communicate with parents who are not available to attend school-hour conferences and to meet the needs of the gifted students and the learning disabled as well, since there is only one special education teacher. Many teachers in her building gripe or gossip in the teachers' lounge, so Cheryl finds no haven there. She frequently spends her lunch hour with a student who needs extra support. She says, "When I started teaching, I had stars in my eyes and love in my heart. I never wanted anything as badly as my certification and a chance to make the world a little bit better. Now I'm at my wits' end by three o'clock. I can't remember what it feels like to dream. I spend my days off numbing out and dreading Monday morning."

These could as easily be the words of a corporate executive or assembly-line worker as those of a human services provider.

While many women rethink their careers when they begin to reach spiritual burnout, the need for the paycheck also corrals their perspective. Most working women do not experience either the economic luxury or the freedom of spirit which would position them to be able to leave work without the apparent security of a job waiting in the wings. The mortgage or rent, the bills, the kids' clothes, car payments — providing all these basics keeps our vision focused on doing rather than on being. We are imparting the same handicap to our children, placing them in programs and classes as early as 18 months and plying them with material comforts. Perhaps there is a connection between what we feel we must do for our children, the message they receive about doing and deserving, and the growing number of diagnoses of Adolescent Narcissistic Personality Disorder in mental health centers and youth service agencies.

There is a tremendous paradox here: those who believe they will be provided for always seem to have enough — even if "enough" for one is bus fare and for another the monthly Corvette payment. We've all met women who, because of a basic spiritual security, remain upbeat and confident even when they are reorganized out of a position, or a budget cut forces a layoff. These women are aware of a larger picture and may even believe that there's a reason for everything. This vision sustains them through the bad times.

It is a blessing to enjoy the big picture. But the road to this treasure is blocked by a rock and a hard place: work itself may interfere with acquiring and keeping the vision; and without the vision, we can become increasingly embroiled in the demanding details of work. This, then, is the source of a vicious circle of becoming spiritual midgets because we work so hard, and then working harder because we're spiritually starving and work fills the void. The overall picture shrinks until we each need a microscope to see what our life's work is all about!

ALIENATION — OR AN ALIEN NATION?

The very structure of work can leave women alienated from their needs, desires, instincts, men, and other women. Alienation is not an emotion, like rage, glee, sorrow, or fear. It is a syndrome of the spirit, a tarnishing of the world-view. As such, it is nearly impossible to pinpoint, because it does not occur like a singular event: "Gosh, when I woke up this morning, I sure felt alienated." Rather, the gulf between identity and spirit is the result of an accumulation of choices, which some of us may unconsciously use to "fix" our sense of emptiness — but which camouflage, not cure, the problem. In fact, when we try to cope with emptiness by working, spending, eating, sex, whatever, we ultimately increase the pain.

The elements which separate us from our souls are often embedded in the framework of the job: schedules, hierarchies, communication, and patriarchal models of work behavior.

SCHEDULE

The notion of freedom of spirit implies flexibility as well as spontaneity. Most of us find that a reasonable amount of predictable structure lends stability and comfort in a life filled with surprising ups and downs.

If, however, you work a standard nine-to-five full-time job at *only* 40 hours per week, with three weeks off for vacation; and if you commute each way 45 minutes door-to-door, this comprises 40 percent of your waking hours (assuming that you get eight hours of sleep and don't bring work home or work on weekends). In other words, the biggest chunk of your time devoted to a single enterprise is rigidly structured. If, because of a life transition you're going through, you feel as though you'd like to work only three days and spend the off days on retreat for, let's say, a couple of months — you don't have the option. If you feel inspired to do volunteer work in a soup kitchen one day a week, don't think you can ask your boss for time off, even without pay! The daily or maturational events of your spirit's journey must be accomplished on your "own" time — whatever that is — even though our internal lives are not so compartmentalized or cooperative. And while it is true that even the great mystics had severely structured days, the purpose of the schedule was to free their minds (silence, meditation, chanting, manual labor), not to occupy them with new marketing strategies or a board presentation or ticketing passengers on airplanes or worrying about sexual harassment.

The spiritual bottom line here is this: if you don't free up prime time for your soul, it becomes impossible to recognize her. And if you feel as though you've lost your soul, you are not alone. A nation of working women are struggling to maintain their centers with schedules more burdened than ever.

PYRAMID POWER

There is a conventional body of wisdom on the abuse of power and the siren call of power itself. When a man abuses power, he may be labeled as dominant, militant, "high-power," aggressive, commanding. When a woman abuses power, the words applied to her are less ambiguous: bitch, shrew, henwife, hussy or four-letter obscenities. In the work world, there is a higher tolerance of male domineering behavior than of its female counterpart. But man or woman, the misuse of power — controlling, manipulating, using and intimidating others — corrupts the soul beyond measure. A position of power is as seductive a trap for women as for men, and it requires vigilance to use power as a servant, not as a slaver.

Furthermore, being the victim of a supervisor, foreman, principal, boss, CEO who is power-hungry is mortal for a woman's spirit. Many women, from girlhood onward, tend to internalize victimization, continuing to choose relationships in which they will be stifled or even battered. This is as true on the job as off — though the battering is probably emotional rather than physical. Whether she works for another woman or a man, a woman who is being treated as a cog in the wheel will lose her autonomy, a key ingredient in the human spirit. Room for self-determination is vital for creativity and generativity. Therefore, it is not only the individual women who suffers. The entire organization is hurt when the soul is unrecognized — or worse, brutalized.

Besides the formal organizational chart, every company has its share of status and sexual issues. Both of these are dehumanizing. Women who are savvy about these issues either learn quickly how to play the game, or how to maintain integrity in a straightforward way. Playing the game, while it ensures one's survival in the company, has a cost. You must relate to other human beings as objects, just as they are relating to you. This is, whether you're conscious of it or not, an abuse of your own power. As for integrity, there may be an initial price to pay here as well. Many organizations will scape goat members who live and work with autonomy, freedom of thought, honesty and morality — no matter how gentle or soft-spoken the scapegoating may be. Sometimes the situation becomes intolerable, and the healthiest choice is to leave the job. The good news is that women who are spiritually healthy begin to meet others in the career networks like themselves. Patience and faith reward the seeker with a more compatible environment.

THE MEANING OF IT ALL

Joseph Campbell, in his work on mythology, coined the phrase "Follow your bliss." There is a promise and joy implicit in these three words:

Follow The leadership, the road signs, the beacons in the night are all there if we take the time and the solitude to discern them. It can be so simple!

Your Not someone else's; not your mother's, your boss's, your lover's, your children's, or your friend's; your *own*, which feels so right to do!

Bliss Happiness; what you love; your inner wisdom and spirit of play!

Work is meaningful to the extent that it is what we love, and that in some respect it meets our need to be altruistic. Since serenity is a vital component of a healthy soul, genuine satisfaction with one's position, whether president or receptionist, is diagnostic of spiritual wellness. Each woman deserves a job in which her work is a creative expression of who she is.

Take a few moments to reflect on who you are. Write your answers to the following questions.

At the core of your being, what gives you the greatest peace when:
  a) you are alone?
  b) you are with a man you love?
  c) you are with a woman you love?
  d) you are with a child you love?
  e) you are with your parent(s)?
  f) you are doing a task you love?

Are there any patterns, or common elements, in your answers?
How many of these patterns or elements are present in your job?
If not, why not?
Do you believe you deserve a career in which you would be paid for following your bliss?
If not, why not?
What would you be willing to do to change this?

DON'T THROW STONES

At work, glass walls often exist between colleagues when it comes to spirituality. We don't talk about this with each other.

To begin with, some women have a problem recognizing and trusting what is genuinely spiritual in themselves. Feeling good, as in "If it feels good, do it," is not necessarily spiritual. In fact, sometimes anguish and grief are deep expressions of the soul. The phrase "altered states" is associated more with drugs than with endorphins, yet nature has provided us with access to an organic mind/time/space expansion system. Learning to discern what is and is not unique to your spirituality and how to tap into it is the first hurdle.

The second hurdle is language. The language of spiritual experience is one of poetry, symbolism, myth, and metaphor. This is not the language usually spoken at work — unless your work is theology, philosophy, or the arts. We simply aren't able to put into words what we know really happened to us. "I felt like time stopped and I became one with everything"; "I was suddenly filled with a tremendous assurance, and I felt so loved"; "I felt like I was a conduit, and energy was flowing through me like light." These words are pale reflections of the reality they attempt to convey. When we try to verbalize our spiritual experience, we become discouraged by the "language barrier." Gender-exclusive language, which refers to the Divine as only male, is also linguistically limiting.

The third obstacle is the group norm. Norms are implicit or explicit precedents of behavior that operate like rules. They are never written, but everyone in the group could identify them with a minimum of thought. We learn as much from what is not done as from what is done. The communication norms in most workplaces prohibit soul conversations; in fact, they exclude genuinely intimate communication, both in terms of time constraints and expectations about personal honesty being kept to a dull roar.

Yet we have an instinct and a hunger to share, to affirm our spiritual needs and experiences. This is how we gain confidence and know we are not alone. This is how we identify and sustain our vision, serenity, and patience; how we encourage each other to take time, reflect, discern; how we enhance each other's growth and well-being. Work is the single greatest place where we spend our prime hours and energy. Work, more than our marriages and parenting, receives the numerical majority of our prime waking hours. Yet, for most of us, our jobs are where we spiritually hunger.

It behooves us, when we work in "glass houses," to put down our stones: isolating, complaining, gossiping, using or manipulating others. We deeply desire to be rid of glass walls — which is what throwing stones is really all about. But when we toss rocks out of frustration, alienation, and hunger, we only do damage.

In some cultures, women were literally stoned for committing adultery. As women, we are frequently more critical of the shortcomings of our sisters, as though we pass judgment on their spiritual adultery, than we are of men's foibles. When glass walls exist among ourselves, first use the wall as a mirror. Take a look at your spirit reflected in your feelings toward your colleagues. (Why do you think the most important spiritual act is called "reflection" anyway?) Then, find a way through or around the wall to build a supportive team to keep your soul alive and radiant at work. Chapter Seven will present concrete steps for achieving spiritual wellness at work.

Finally, as women, let's acknowledge Eve for introducing us to the knowledge of good and evil. When any aspect of your life is not working in the way that is right or best for you, and you take steps to realign it, you are much less likely to take the result for granted for having known the pain. When, because of your own healing choices, you achieve greater health, sanity, joy, you are more likely to value your attainment because you earned it. Paradise, the Promised Land, lies ahead. When you are committed to the pilgrimage, you can appreciate youself for every step you take. Have faith that you are not alone on the journey. You are surrounded by others moving in the same direction, many of them unknown to you. Chapter Seven will present concrete measures to restore your own spiritual wellness at work, and ways to meet and join your fellow travelers.

CHAPTER SEVEN
The Spiritual Bottom Line

What a fascinating, intricate being a woman is! That which affects a single part of her body affects the whole. Conversely, when a woman experiences a broad life change, each single component of her self is affected. Even at the biochemical level, our cells are microcosmic communications factories; information on the impact of an event, relationship, or situation is swiftly carried throughout the body so particular systems can respond accordingly. For example, when you cut your finger, your entire immune system is mobilized and information on the need for blood-clotting agents at the specific site of the cut is dispatched.

This tightly interwoven network is absolutely miraculous. Taking steps toward achieving physical and emotional well-being at work will generate an unexpected harvest of benefits. A woman who begins a practice of deep-breathing breaks at work (see Chapter Eight for breathing techniques) will also think more clearly and respond more calmly to that aggravating co-worker. Thus, by doing something physical, she has taken a concrete step toward emotional well-being. And then . . . surprise! During one breathing break, on an inhale, she experiences a sense of oneness with the universe — something she wasn't seeking, but a gracious gift nonetheless. She is on the road to an increase in spiritual health, and she wasn't even seeking it! She may not be looking for Paradise, but Paradise is looking for her.

The multitude of conversion or spiritual-awakening stories told by women documents how often the cycle of spiritual growth begins with the unexpected: a brush with death, a new love, the realization that one's children have grown up, a trip to Yosemite, taking a course in journalism . . . the variety of spiritual experience has no limit.

Wouldn't it be wonderful if the act of implementing physical and emotional well-being at work could also guarantee spiritual initiation or reinforcement? Certainly, our bodies and brains know when we have chosen to slow down and breathe, when we are strong, flexible, open, grounded. Our bodies know when we are ready to move to the next level of growth. While everything in this book so far will create a context or opportunity for the well-being of your spirit, why wait for the unexpected? This chapter offers a deliberate "training program" in having a healthy soul on the job — as well as in all areas of your life.

Think about this: if you wanted to have a fabulous meal with your closest friends next Saturday, would you decide on a menu, shop for food, spend Saturday cleaning and preparing the food and setting the table . . . and then hope they showed up? Ridiculous! At some point, you would issue an invitation, whether by mail, phone, or in person.

That's what this chapter is all about. The previous chapter contained important preparations to make sure you had all the ingredients and a clean house for a feast with your soul. "The Spiritual Bottom Line" means actively putting out the word that you are ready for the guest of honor: your own soul. Prepare to enjoy the banquet!

A MESSAGE FROM THE AUTHORS

Earlier in this book, "spirituality" is used broadly, referring to a sense of being a part of something larger than ourselves that gives meaning to life and engenders reverence and joy. Spirituality is the most intimate area of a woman's life. As with all tender spots, each woman has strong and protective feelings about this — and so it should be! History is littered with tales of crusades, persecutions, and inquisitions based on "true" religion, as one group sought to control the spiritual life of another. As sad as these debacles were and are (in many parts of the world religious persecution lingers), it is a grim testimony to the capacity for such intense feelings about the correctness of a given theology that torture and death were the hideous results.

Each woman must develop her own spiritual practice. Because many women are increasingly sensitized to the use of non-exclusive language regarding the gender of God, this chapter uses a variety of names for the Higher Power. From time to time, we may refer to God, The Great Mother, The Divine, The Ground of Being, and so on. On the other hand, there are many women who may not relate their spiritual practice to a "God" concept at all. For them, as well as for many atheists/agnostics, they may draw their spiritual experiences from some aspects of nature, meditation, music, or anything that gives them spiritual rewards. We ask that each reader keep an open mind and an awareness of womankind's luscious variety of knowledge, experience, devotion, discipline, and relationships that go into conceptualizing The Divine.

Finally, we will maintain the broad connotation of spirituality developed in "Divine Discontent." Universally, the relationship of an individual to a larger, intuited Be-ing, whether Personal or Impersonal, is experienced as a source of meaning, perspective, energy, and often love. For many women, organized religion facilitates this relationship, but not all women find it through religion; for some women, religion may actually interfere with it.[1] But spirituality is not necessarily religion. It is not simply an intellectual and philosophical phenomenon, and it is deeper than feelings. While it involves both intellect and emotionality, it is recognized as a separate category of human experience. The most fitting word for it is *soul* or *spirit* — take your pick, or give it your own name. Whatever you call it, our goal is to provide you with a menu as comprehensive and specific as possible, so that you will bring to your career a spirit as whole as your body and your emotionality.

AN APPLE A DAY . . .

Medical science had its origins in curing disease and thereby prolonging life. In today's world, the medical profession has increasingly espoused prevention, wellness, and holistic health. Note the shift in emphasis from disease to wellness. The timeworn "An apple a day keeps the doctor away" demonstrates how long the prevention model has been around, and now M.D.'s are also on the bandwagon. Thanks to advances in this century, it is not only popular but also possible to stay well and thus live a long *and* fruitful life.

In the Old Testament, "an apple a day" represents the beginning of spiritual ills. And who gets the blame for taking the first bite? A woman! Whether or not it's fair to pin the corruption of Adam's soul on Eve, it is important that each person, male or female, is responsible for reclaiming his/her birthright of spiritual health. Spiritual wellness is characterized by:

1. A regular practice of reflection/prayer/celebration
2. A sense of communion with the Divine, self, and others
3. Sound moral values (ethics)
4. Action consistent with ethics (integrity)
5. Confidence that one's life is meaningful
6. Shared responsibility for the welfare of the planet
7. Continuing spiritual growth (evolution, process, searching — it's never done)

Review your results on the spiritual wellness questionnaire from Chapter Six. How did you score? If your soul's pulse is weak and fading, don't despair! For many women, the spiritual emergency of realizing how far they've strayed off the path is the first step toward spiritual emergence — a new beginning, a rebirth. Look at the similarity between *emergency* and *emergence*. Both words have the same Latin roots: *ex*, or "out of," and *mergere*, "to immerse." Finding yourself immersed in spiritual need calls for immediate action. This action, in turn, helps your spirit out of the murky swamp in which your soul is sinking and into plain view.

MIX INGREDIENTS, STIR WELL

Many writers, including sociologists, psychologists, philosophers, and theologians have commented on the instant-gratification mentality of American culture. Our vocabularies are peppered with such phrases as "labor saving," "quick fix," and "efficiency control," implying that we should spend no more time than is absolutely necessary to achieve a goal. You can take Interstate 678 to the Kennedy Airport, hop on an SST, use your calculator to compute the cost of your vacation to France, slide your credit card into a slot to make a phone call while you're in the air, continue reading *One-Minute Manager* when you hang up so you can finish your MBA in 18 months instead of two years, and sit back with a glass of champagne to encourage a leisurely state of mind before you land in Paris.

Whoa! What you're about to read is antithetical to the efficiency mentality that pervades our businesses, schools, homes, and even vacations. The care and feeding of the spirit is paradoxical: on the one hand, there is a goal of spiritual health; on the other, there is no results-oriented timetable for getting there.

Our recipe for the health of your soul at work has five main ingredients: reflection, relationships, location, celebration, and giving (donation). This chapter will present each of these elements relative to your workday, although they are all components of integrated spiritual practice at any time. Following this recipe in the proportions that are right for you will enhance the well-being of your soul on the job — but exactly when, how, or where will be idiosyncratic. Factors such as your previous experience, age, personality, self-discipline, etc., will determine your progress.

Read through the entire chapter before you decide what appeals to you as a starting place. Begin slowly, with one small, concrete step. It takes 21 days to break a habit; it takes 21 days to establish a new habit.

THE SPIRITUAL BOTTOM LINE

When you embark on a new spiritual practice, give yourself three weeks of one small, manageable daily activity. If you are solid in it at the end of 21 days, add a second, or deepen the first. Thus, you will keep your spiritual growth incremental yet consistent. Eventually, you will find the blend that's perfect for you.

SOLUTIONS: REFLECTION

If there is one essential ingredient in a healthy spirituality, it is interiority. Approximately seventy-five per cent of Americans are extroverted;[2] they relate primarily to the outside world of people, ideas, events, and things as sources of data, energy, and action. Reflection can be difficult for extroverts. It means not speaking, sitting still, and going to the center of one's self. It means taking time out of the "productive" mode to become aware of and restore inner vision.

Women who work full-time in a business or company have breaks provided in the workday structure (although compulsive, workaholic women often disregard them and work straight through). Women who work part-time or are self-employed, especially at home, will have to experiment with daily structure to commit to a program of reflective breaks. The practical aspects of commitment will be discussed later. For now, this chapter offers a range of resources for reflective breaks, beginning with inspirational tools and gradually deepening into meditation and prayer.

A Glance in the Mirror

The word "reflection" implies seeing ourselves — who we really are, not who we wish we were. Time to pick up your pen or pencil, and take a little challenge. In fifty words of less, write a description of yourself, talking about your roles, relationships, physical characteristics, possessions, and accomplishments. For instance, "I am a 45-year old, 5'4" mother of three children living in Los Angeles; I am divorced, have a B.A. in English, and work as an administrative assistant for a midsized corporation. I am a Virgo, and in my free time I go antiquing." Now write your description. Who are you?

I am _____
_____
_____
_____
_____
_____
_____

Do it again, but this time, avoid any words that describe roles, relationships, physical characteristics, possessions, hobbies, and accomplishments. Answer as if none of these existed. Write a description of who you are at the core of your being:

I am _____
_____
_____
_____
_____
_____

Most women find the second description of self more difficult to write than the first. The first is concrete, rote. It is the identity we have put on, and the external world is the mirror that confirms it: yes, you are a teacher; yes, you have two kids; yes, you do needlepoint.

When we look in the inner mirror, we have less external validation — at least initially. The major source of affirmation is your own inner self. This can be disconcerting and uncomfortable, especially in a world that lavishes reinforcement on outward achievements, belongings, and roles.

The purpose of taking reflection breaks on the job is to recover the core sense of self intrinsic to spiritual growth. Remember: while you're earning your daily bread you could just wait hopefully for an act of grace to collide with you. But if you want your soul to thrive at work, it is crucial that you place yourself in the path of enlightenment. Pausing to reflect is a deliberate act of becoming still and open. It is an opportunity to quiet the chatter of your conscious mind, remove your external mask, and become inspired.

(A note here to those for whom this isn't making sense: there are countless women who choose to consider work as a separate domain from the rest of life. For these women, when they work they want exclusively to do the job, to occupy their minds and hands with the necessary tasks. They are not looking for or desirous of time for spiritual caretaking; they would find it too complicating in their workday. They may wish to allocate other time during the week for matters of the soul, or they may not be interested in spiritual life, period. If you count yourself among these women, that's fine. You may or may not wish to continue reading this chapter. What is important is that you know yourself and do the right thing for you.)

What comes to mind when you see or hear the word "inspiration"? Perhaps you think of an artist, poet, or musician receiving a brilliant flash of creativity, or a holy person having a vision. The word actually refers to breathing, to the inhalation phase of a complete breath. As in breathing, your soul is learning how to draw into itself the new life of spiritual energy. You will, later on, be instructed in working with your breath as a physiological preparation for spiritual work, and as a point of focus to open your awareness to regions of consciousness which are eclipsed when your conscious mind is dominating your workday.

Mental inspiration is the food which will nourish your spirit at work. The more you use regular work breaks to stop and reflect, the greater facility you will develop for allowing wisdom, peace, and bliss to enter you. This, in turn, will eventually amplify your knowledge of what work you really love to do, and the creativity, commitment, and energy you will bring to it. If you are unhappy in your current work, doing spiritual exercises will either give you the "oomph" you need to leave it, or the inner peace to surrender and thus find harmony within it. Either way, you win!

The Tools of the Trade

If self-reflection is new for you, we are providing you with twenty perforated Daily Questions in Appendix III. Detach these, and place five of them in your purse or a drawer at your work place. These cards can be used flexibly; you might want to try a four-week cycle of one card per day for each five-day work week, or they can be used as you wish — randomly, in combination, twice a day, five days on the same question — whatever. We suggest using them as a springboard for beginning structured introspection. Stack them in order; take five minutes of your morning work break, beginning with Question One on day one. Each card reminds you to take three deep, cleansing breaths before reading the question. Then read the question, allowing your conscious mind to answer it first; most women find it difficult initially to flip a switch to a different mode of consciousness, the better to "speak your mind" to yourself. Then let your conscious thoughts about the question fade away, and continue to breathe slowly. Keep your eyes on the Question Card, and allow other images and feelings to come to you. Try to get to the deepest, most honest reality in the present moment. The purpose is not to become a great philosopher (although who knows — you might), but to access the core of how you are at that given moment and accept yourself just as you are.

If you already have a regular reflection period in your day or week, you may determine that the Daily Questions are an adjunct to what you already do — or that they are irrelevant at this time. Your own judgment on this matter is your best authority and ally!

Think of the possibilities for enriching and deepening your connection to your Higher Power, and thereby amplifying your peace and inner security if you substitute collectedness for caffeine, devotion for donuts, serenity for cigarettes. The Daily Questions are aimed at taking spiritual inventory: what's working, and what isn't. It is perfectly normal for these cards to stimulate emotions and physical sensations. Spirituality uses whatever it needs to get our attention once we start opening up. Each of us is an integrated totality. Trust your body as well as your mind to guide you. If you are honest with yourself, you'll become adept at recognizing when you are avoiding reflection or letting yourself be distracted, whether you are in poor physical shape or staying up so late that you fall asleep when you reflect, or when you are genuinely available for the messages from your soul.

Besides the Daily Question Cards, Appendix III contains twenty different Affirmation Cards. They do not correlate in any particular way with the Question Cards, and are also meant to be tailored to your own needs. The purpose of the Affirmation Cards is to establish a foundation of consistent hope and positive outlook toward developing yourself spiritually. While this approach may not work for everyone, it is based on the theory of behaving "as if" something is true so that it becomes true! The act of validating oneself repeatedly can empower a woman to believe in her spiritual capacity. It is a great help in following through with a commitment to a program of spiritual wholeness.

Directions: Use an Affirmation Card in the same way you do the Question Cards. Begin with five minutes during your morning break. Sit quietly, follow the instructions to breathe and focus on the Affirmation. Use your conscious mind first; then release your conscious awareness, and allow images and concepts to fill you with inspiration.

What if you are focusing on an Affirmation or a Question and your mind's inner dialogue objects? For example, you have just read Affirmation #9, "I am making a positive contribution in my work or career," and that little nagging voice in your head says, "No you're not! Are you kidding? You're just in it for the money, and even *that's* lousy," etc. Obviously, it will be difficult to move more deeply into a spiritual moment, especially if you suspect that voice is right.

Don't panic. This doesn't mean the Affirmation is wrong. Perhaps your greatest contribution to your career at that point is to begin to think of changing it. Perhaps you and your career have burned each other out. It is just as much a spiritual insight to realize that your soul is depleted as it is to be grateful that it is brimming! The most important thing is to accept your experience without shaming or berating yourself. Then get your Daily Question Cards, and pick out numbers 1, 3, 6, 7, and 11. Use these cards for a two-week cycle, and stay calm. Allow answers to come to you. Thank your conscious awareness for confronting you with your dissatisfaction; then ask it to be content that it has done its job, and let other facets of your mind do theirs. Try extending your reflection to 10-15 minutes per day, and keep a log or diary during this time. Remember: enlightenment comes in unexpected ways! And do affirm yourself for having the courage to face your pain.

Daily reflections on probing questions and/or affirmations is the primary tool for spiritual health on the job. But don't neglect weekends, holidays, and vacations. It is crucial that you set aside some time each day, however brief, to devote to reflection.

Sacred or Religious Writings

When women first had time off from obtaining and preparing food, bearing and rearing children, etc., they had time to think and share. Although the majority of sacred writings appear to be male-authored, we will never know how many good prophets had a woman behind them! In any case, the historical sacred writings from many cultures are readily available to us: the Bible, the Baghavad Gita, the Koran, the Tao . . . the list goes on and on. More recently, the writings of holy women are gaining popularity: The Gnostic gospels, Hildegard of Bingen, Terese of Avila, Catherine of Siena, and Therese of Lisieux, to name a few. If there is a women's bookstore in your area, spend some time discussing your needs/desires with the proprietesses. You will find empathy and understanding as well as valuable recommendations of reading material.

Pocket-sized Inspiration Daily Books

Hazelden Books puts out books for daily reflection and meditation. Books like *Day By Day* and *Keep It Simple* are spiritual in nature since they were designed as tools for people on twelve-step recovery programs from addictions, such as Overeaters Anonymous; all twelve-step programs depend on spirituality for healing. You don't have to be an addict to find these books of great value — just substitute "my problem" (or whatever) for "addiction" in the text of these books. You will be amazed at the results in terms of the well-being of your spirit! Especially recommended, for working women who have trouble saying "no," is Anne Wilson Schaef's *Meditations for Women Who Do Too Much*.

There are other types of inspirational books — collections of sayings or thoughts that may move you at the core of your being. They also often contain lovely art to engage and please the sense of sight and provide a visual focus. "The eyes are the windows of the soul" means two-way access: they reveal a woman's spirit, and they admit soul-stirring visions inward!

Most inspirational or daily meditation books are printed in formats small enough to fit in a purse, pocket, or desk drawer. When you find one you like, keep it on hand.

Poetry and Music

Some women find that the language of poets and poetesses speaks to their innermost selves. Check out the poetry section of your local bookstore. Be discriminating; much of 20th-century poetry deals with parched spirits, alienation, existentialism — you may find it bleak rather than fulfilling.

Another wellspring of inspiration is music. Marcy, a career counselor, carries a small cassette tape player and a favorite tape or two in her purse. When she catches herself losing touch with her center, she waits until she can clear five minutes, closes her door, and lets the sweet melody do the work of centering for her. With eyes closed, she can open her heart and breathe deeply with the music. It is a tangible, sensate anchor that works for her. It calls her back from the scatterings of paper work and other people's problems. Having taken the time during weekends or evenings to select music that works for her, the few minutes during the day actually spent listening to music through her earphones provide her with hours of calm happiness and tranquility during her work day. Doesn't that sound wonderful? The investment required includes a tape player with headphones, a search for music, and 21 days (consecutive if possible) of "training" for five minutes a day.

If this method of spiritual safeguarding appeals to you, check the Resources in Appendix IV for music with a soul-opening quality. Or use what you already know will work for you. Practice at home before you try this at work so it will be familiar to you. Headphones are recommended for being least distracting to others and making you less distractable.

Begin listening to the piece, close your eyes, and take three deep breaths. Then breathe normally, allowing yourself to let go of conscious thoughts. The music will care for you if you surrender into it and will bring you images of reassurance if you let it. To deepen the experience, picture or imagine your Higher Power. On the inhale, picture yourself opening up to your Higher Power, requesting to be filled; on the exhale, picture yourself surrendering or letting go of your own agenda. Float; let the music carry you.

If nothing happens, do not despair. Two possibilities exist. Either a) you are a newcomer to this type of experience, and will need several tries to recognize the sensation of surrender, (so don't give up); or b) you are a personality type that is wonderfully concrete and down-to-earth — the type that helps keep visionaries' feet on the ground. If so, using music as a launching pad may require so much effort on your part that you would be better off turning to something more tangible, such as a mentor or a journal, as a tool for spiritual wellness. Refer to the appropriate sections in this book for tips in these areas.

Art

Several years ago, the Museum of Contemporary Art in Chicago sponsored an exhibit on art and spirituality. Since it was arranged more or less in chronological order (historically), it was fascinating to see how the use of art to depict fusion with a god/goddess has evolved in the Western world. From specific representational pictures of humans in luminous moments to abstract expressionism, the exhibit ran a gamut of styles. The representational art conveyed a sense of recognition: "I've been there; I've had that experience!" The abstract art, in some cases, actually occasioned an experience of unity right then and there on the part of those who were gazing at it.

Art can be used as both a stimulus of collectedness and an expression of one's spiritual experience. In Eastern European cultures, gazing at an icon meditatively is transformative, bringing the meditator to a transcendent sense of union and perspective on life. In other cultures around the globe, mandelas or circular paintings and symbols are used the same way, providing focus and drawing the viewer out of the conscious mind. Art is a shortcut; in a single image lies a universe which the brain apprehends even before it can formulate words. Thus, a common spirit can infuse a piece of art and effectively communicate an experience beyond ordinary, daily realities, even beyond the senses. Representational art can bypass the intellect entirely, as in the case of surrealism, which engages the onlooker's worldview with supernatural events and relationships — the improbable. There is nothing rational or logical, per se, about the mandela; it is an abstraction that transcends feelings, thoughts, sensations. You can imbue it with meaning from your own experience, and in turn allow it to knock on the door of your own soul.

If you have wall space at work, consider becoming a spiritual decorator. Prints, posters, paintings that calm your spirit, move you to ecstasy, or focus your attention are necessary distractions from your tasks. When your attention wanders, let it repose in contemplation of a scene or symbol on your wall, and empty your mind. You will return momentarily to your work, but with a sense of the bigger picture. Let the image do the work of tapping you on the shoulder to remind you of the presence of the Divine in your life and work. And if you can't put something on the wall, how about a card to carry in your purse or wallet?

Finally, you can personally use art to express your spirit, much as you can with feelings. Find a way to keep art materials accessible on the job. An inexpensive set of pastels and a blank notebook or sketchbook are all the materials you need. When you are feeling lost or alienated, draw the feeling; when you are blissful, or in a state of creative vision or flow, draw it. You need not be realistic — in fact, the more abstract, the better. Choose a color, close your eyes, and let your hand wander around the page. To deepen the experience, use your non-dominant hand, and trust it! Art has been as effective throughout history in showing the spiritual agonies and dilemmas of human beings as it has in imaging rapture and transport, which words alone can never fully capture.

TAKING THE PLUNGE: MEDITATION

Many excellent books are available on meditation, written by both men and women. A six-month sabbatical to delve into this subject would still only scratch the surface; think of men and women who are called into a monastic life, and spend years and years learning to meditate! Obviously, most of us are not meant for this total dedication. However, learning to meditate to whatever degree we are capable is entirely worthwhile. On the physical and emotional planes alone, meditators derive great benefits in terms of physical healing,[3] mental clarity, and psychological stability.

This chapter so far has encouraged taking time for reflection each day. Obviously, a job is not the place to begin a devout meditation practice. There are too many disruptions and distractions; insufficient breaks do not permit disciplined growth in meditation. Only retreats or monastic lifestyles guarantee a structure to nurture this. But rest assured: it is possible to maintain enough of a meditation practice at work so that you can derive the full richness of this technique.

Adelaide Gardner, in *Meditation: A Practical Study* differentiates among concentration, meditation, and contemplation.[4] According to her, concentration is the use of one's will to keep the mind consciously focused on one thing. Meditation means placing before one's consciousness a subject of spiritual meaning and allowing that subject to reveal its full richness in all its facets until some inner significance becomes clear (which is the experience of enlightenment or inspiration). In other words, concentration is a necessary seed; meditation is the blossom. And Gardner says very little about the phenomenon of contemplation, which is the level of spiritual experience hardest to communicate, since we have poor words for communion, ecstasy, rapture, or mystical oneness . . . whatever the term, it's like the proverbial wisdom about orgasm: if you don't know what it is, you've never had one.

At any rate, here is a simple progression of exercises, beginning with concentration, and progressing through several varieties of meditative methods.

Concentration

In the section on reflection (Question Cards and Affirmations), the emphasis was on self-examination and validation as an aid in experiencing the aspect of yourself that is hungry for meaning and higher values, that longs to love and be loved on a level called communion, that is the spark of the Divine in each of us.

Concentration is a step in that direction. Most women at work have a vast number of stimuli bombarding them during the day. You may begin to focus on one task, but thousands of interruptions — from a crisis at work to a phone call from home to your own daydreams — can intrude. The act of concentrating is a precursor to meditation. Try these simple exercises.

> *Object Concentration:* Take three minutes of your morning break to gaze at a simple, meaningless object (one about which you have no particular feelings, such as a pencil, paper clip, cup, etc.) Without forcing it, keep your attention on the object. If you find your mind wandering, go backward through the sidetracks to return to the object, and continue to focus on it until roughly three minutes are up.

For example, if you're gazing at a pencil, you may realize that it needs sharpening; this reminds you that the pencil sharpener is near the co-worker whose guts you hate, which leads you to think about an incident two weeks earlier, and you begin a diatribe in your mind about what you wish you'd said! Then you realize you're off track from the pencil. So you retrace your steps from the imaginary putting-her-in-place to the incident to the co-worker to the pencil sharpener to the dull point to the pencil itself.

Try this exercise in mental discipline for three weeks, and see if you can begin to focus on an object for as much as five minutes. This is a learned skill.

> *Concentration In the Moment:* This exercise will bring you even closer to spiritual awareness. Simply keep your attention on whatever you're

doing from moment to moment. If you are tightening screws on an assembly line, try to be aware of your hand, the tool you're holding, the screw and its size, color, hardness; how you feel about doing this, where you're standing, how you're balanced, etc. Keeping your concentration in this moment, fully and openly, is a building block for what is to come.

In both these exercises, gaining insight is much less important than training your mind to say focused. Meditation is about discipline. A regular time, a daily commitment, a "boot camp" for the muscles of the unconscious — harnessing your conscious mind is a requirement. However, you are not a drill sergeant. Do not force your mind to cooperate. Coax, encourage, be consistent . . . but do not demand. You will find that eventually your throught processes catch on to your desire and begin to give you what you want.

Beginner's Meditation

Breath, posture, and relaxation are essential for spiritual as well as physical and emotional well-being. In this beginner's meditation, you will be working with your breath. In subsequent meditations, we will offer variations.

Before beginning, here are some things you should know. Meditation affects you physiologically. While you meditate, your heart, breathing, and metabolic rates slow; you use oxygen more efficiently, your autonomic nervous system is more stable. During and after meditation, your powers of recall are more acute; your blood pressure decreases; your reaction time is greater, your senses are sharper. Emotionally, meditation results in higher levels of job satisfaction, improved relationships with supervisors and co-workers, and increases in productivity of job performance.[5] Notice: these effects are not the result of simple concentration, but of meditation! As was stated earlier, meditation, as we're using the term, is the deliberate act of presenting your mind with a spiritual or meaningful concept, such as the integrity of your love for your Higher Power, letting every component of your awareness savor the richness of the true nature of the subject, and allowing some felt insight to present itself specifically to you.

It should be obvious that concentration is a prerequisite for, but not the sole determinant of, meditation. Reflection is a look in the personal mirror; concentration is a peek at reality through a narrow slit; and meditation is a broad view through the cosmic window. You may catch a glimpse of yourself in the glass, but keep looking outward. Eventually, inspiration tailored for you will return to you. Trust in the process; during meditation, a person tunes out external stimuli, yet remains absolutely alert. This enables the meditator to become receptive to other "wave lengths" of information. Try it and see for yourself.

A Beginner's Meditation: The Goodness of Life

To prepare yourself, you need 1) a quiet place, 2) where you're not likely to be interrupted for ten minutes or so, and 3) where you can sit comfortably erect, either on a chair or on the floor. It might be more effective if you first learn this technique at home, preferably in the morning before you leave for work. Later you can find a way to incorporate it at work — even in the bathroom, or outside in your parked car, weather permitting! Beginners in meditation are encouraged to practice in the morning before breakfast and late afternoon before supper, according to many spiritual traditions. However, there is no evidence that meditation will be any less beneficial if performed at other times of the day. Our advice is to integrate it at work if possible, and initially to have a fixed daily time. The morning break seems most logical, since most women are generally alert and motivated around this time. If you work a late-afternoon or night shift, simply adapt to your own rhythms to find the time that's best for you. By all means, however, don't attempt meditation when feeling rushed, pressured, or irritated.

Here comes the tricky part: it is counterproductive to read instructions on meditation and try to meditate at the same time. Therefore, please do one of two things with the following directions. Either read them through several times until you feel you are absolutely sure of them, or make a tape of yourself reading them aloud, with thirty-second pauses where the ellipses (. . .) occur. You can always remake the tape if you want the pace faster or slower. Once you've got the instructions down pat, you won't need the tape. Some women have a remarkable ability to sense time, and know when ten minutes are up. If you are not constituted this way, get a quiet timer or alarm. If at any time during your practice you are interrupted, try to remain seated and take a few deep breaths before you respond. Avoid abrupt, jarring endings, as these may leave you feeling restless and incomplete. If you have been practicing relaxation exercises, consciously relax yourself at the beginning of your meditation.

Directions:
  1. Set your timer or alarm for ten minutes if you are using one . . .
  2. Sit in a chair or on the floor in a balanced, upright position — whatever is comfortable for you. Make sure your sitting bones are

grounded, and your shoulders relaxed back and down. If you want back support, use it. It's important to feel comfortable . . .
3. Close your eyes in a relaxed way. Inhale slowly and deeply. Exhale slowly and completely. Repeat a little more slowly, releasing tension on the exhale. Then breathe normally, allowing your mind to become clear and open . . .
4. You are going to focus your mind on life's goodness. Simply let your mind hold the concept of life's goodness. As you inhale, mentally say, "Life is —" and on the exhale, think to yourself, "good." Continue this throughout the meditation period . . .
5. Allow yourself to experience the silent goodness and new life energy flowing in and out of you . . .
6. Let yourself believe in the true nature of this idea: Life is good. Let understanding fill you. If other ideas/thoughts/feelings/images enter your mind, recognize them and gently usher them out. Do this for several minutes . . . (if you are taping, leave about six minutes of blank tape here.)
7. Begin to bring your awareness back to the present moment, to your body position, to the light in the room, to any outside sounds . . .
8. Open your eyes, and take three slow, deep breaths. When you are ready, slowly shift to a new position that feels right to you.

Pay attention to how you feel at the end of each meditation. No two days are alike. Do this beginner's meditation for three weeks, preferably twice a day. Gradually extend the time to 20 minutes during these three weeks. If you prefer, you may substitute other sentences for "Life is good"; try "I am loved" or "Receive and let go." This is a meditation that works with your own breath, so any idea with two parts, one for the inhale, one for the exhale, will work. The repetition of mental words helps minimize distractions since it keeps your conscious mind occupied. What you are striving for is the openness of your unconscious mind, which will comprehend the whole idea and present you with insights and inspirations. It is good to work up to 20 minutes, since the human organism seems to need that much time to still itself and access other elements of awareness.

Mantra Meditation

Some people meditate with a mantra, usually a word or a phrase which they mentally repeat or verbally chant, at a speed which may or may not correlate with their breath. Often these mantras are in another language, such as Sanskrit, since they are drawn from venerable non-Western traditions. The purpose of a mantra is to keep the mind free yet focused. An analogy can be drawn to the concept of white noise which, while not consciously registered, blots out other audible distractions. A mantra need not have a specific sacred meaning; even a neutral word, uttered with respectful intention, could be effective. Furthermore, mantras need not coordinate with the breath, as in the Goodness of Life exercise. Simple mental repetition of a meaningful syllable, word, or sentence can liberate the mind to plumb the depths of a spiritual concept. You can create your own mantra by choosing a word or phrase that captures your basic personal beliefs, such as "oneness," "mystery,' "ohm," "have mercy," "I search." If you wish to try meditation with a mantra follow these directions:

1. Set your timer if you are using one . . .
2. Sit in a comfortable, balanced upright position . . .
3. Close your eyes. Take two or three deep, cleansing breaths, and relax on each exhale . . .
4. Breathe normally, and begin mentally repeating your mantra at a rate that feels comfortable to you. (Some women establish a rapid, chant-like repetition; others work with their breath, uttering the mantra on the exhale. Or anything that feels right to you . . .)
5. Focus your conscious mind on your mantra. If other ideas/thoughts/feelings/images come to you, acknowledge them and let them float away . . .
6. Trust that your subconscious mind and heart are opening up to your connection with all that is. Continue for several minutes . . .
7. At the end of your meditation period, keep your eyes closed, end the mantra, and take three deep breaths. Before you open your eyes, let your conscious mind become aware of the present moment, how your body feels, and where you are. Then open your eyes.

If this method suits you, gradually increase to 20 minutes over three weeks.

Breath Meditation

You can use your breath as an anchor for a wordless meditation. The following exercise can act as a prelude to two other experiences. The first is the use of visualization, which will be dealt with in greater detail later in this chapter. The second is the experience of communion with or intuition of a larger force, which many women find calming as they feel a part of something interconnected and timeless. If you attempt this method without "success" (which is impossible since you "succeed" each time you meditate no matter what does or does not occur), wait to try it again after the section on visualization. Again, either read the following directions until you are familiar with them, or read them into a tape recorder with thirty-second pauses at the elipses. Do not set a timer for this. The first time you do it, you will probably take five minutes or so. You can later expand it to a greater amount of time.

1. Sit quietly and comfortably, eyes closed. Relax as you take two or three deep, cleansing breaths, then breathe normally . . .
2. Place your awareness at the center of your breathing, wherever that is for you. Feel yourself as a small point of consciousness at the center of your breathing; feel your breathing surround you, with you at the center. Don't force your breath. Just be aware of it surrounding your consciousness.
3. Now, staying where you are, imagine that your breathing is slowly expanding until it is the size of the room. Stay in the center, but feel the room all around you breathing . . .
4. Staying where you are, imagine your breathing is slowly expanding until it is the size of the entire building. Stay in the center, but feel the building all around you, breathing . . .
5. Continue to allow your breathing to expand until it is the size of your town or city. Imagine the whole town breathing, with you at its very center . . .
6. Stay in the center, and expand your breathing until it is the size of the planet. Keep your awareness focused, and feel your breathing as big as the planet, all around you . . .
7. And now expand your breathing out into the universe, until it is as big as the whole cosmos, with you at the center. Feel it all around you, filling the universe, and breathe. Let whatever happens, happen. Accept it. Stay there for several moments . . .
8. Now gradually begin to reduce the size of your breathing, taking as much time as you need for each step. From the cosmos, bring it down to the size of the planet . . . then to the size of your town . . . then to the size of your building . . . then to the size of the room . . . then back into your own lungs, with your awareness at the center of your breathing . . .
9. When you feel ready, bring your awareness back to your entire body . . . to your position . . . to the sounds around you and the feel of the air in the room . . . and when you are fully back open your eyes.

If this meditation works for you, it is a very comprehensive package. Physiologically, your breathing rhythm will automatically slow down and deepen, which is an important element in stress management — very healing! Emotionally, you will become tranquil. Psychologically and philosophically, your perspective on life enlarges; problems no longer seem mountainous, and your capacity for joy is amplified. And spiritually, the wordless inspiration creates faith that everything has a place, and hope that all is well. It has the added nonverbal and nontheological advantage of working for religious believers of all faiths as well as for nonbelievers.

PRAYER

Prayer is the deliberate initiation of communication with the Divine. While it seems logical to assume that this entails belief in God, apparently this is not necessarily so. The January 6, 1992 issue of *Newsweek* reported a survey in which nearly 20 percent of atheists say they pray![6]

Prayer is the opening of one's mind and heart to a Higher Power. Traditionally, there are four attitudes of prayer: contrition or atonement, petition, gratitude, and praise. The first, contrition, is the sincere expression of sorrow for having made immoral or sinful choices of action or omission, and for which one is willing to make amends. Contrition presupposes the intention to do better next time. The second, petition, means asking God or a Higher Power for that which is in her nature to grant. As children, we usually asked for tangibles which were not in our power to obtain: a new doll, that mom and dad stop fighting, that Grandma recover from cancer — as though God were a wizard with magical powers. As we mature in faith, conscience, and understanding, however, prayers of petition evolve from "magic thinking" into personal responsibility. Adult prayer of petition has more to do with asking for the grace or ability to do or not do something, as in asking for support: "Kind and loving Mother, give me the wisdom and motivation to continue my job search," rather than, "Please give me a job." The third type of prayer, gratitude, speaks for itself. While there are many things we appreciate, or should appreciate, the utterance of a formal thank-you to God is a humble yet happy acknowledgment of each gift that comes our way — including wisdom, peace, a favorable resolution to an argument, a raise, etc. And finally, prayers of praise or adoration are simply a way of saying to Motherspirit, "You are wonderful!"

Prayer is personal in the sense that it is unique to each woman who prays, and is directed toward a Consciousness that we assume can understand and help us as human beings. Since most of us were taught to pray when we were children, with words that we may have long forgotten or that have lost their meaning, we have had some experience with placing ourselves in the presence of Loving Mystery. Even if we pictured God as an old sort of grandfather with a long white beard living up in the clouds, we still had a sense of awe, majesty, and hopefully, love and mercy.

Prayer is possibly the simplest practice of spirituality on the job. You can find books of formal prayers already composed, or you can just speak in your own words or silence. You can pray for five seconds or twenty minutes. If you have never prayed, or haven't for years, it can seem like a crazy monologue at first — is anyone really listening? Even people who have been devoutly praying throughout their lives experience "dry spells" during which no one seems to be out there. But if you have patience and pray daily, you may find that it becomes an indispensable activity sprinkled throughout your workday.

Women who pray find frequently that they receive what they ask for, though often in a form different from what they imagined. For example, one woman noticed that when she began praying for the courage to stand up for herself, she suddenly found herself in almost daily situations in which people intimidated her. She later said, "It was as if I had asked to be more muscular, and then someone started handing me weights." People who don't pray tend to dismiss the claims of those who do with such statements as "Well, you were looking for it to happen, so you read into events that God had done thus and so." Who cares? There is an overwhelming body of evidence that spirituality changes people and their lives, and there are too many stories of the power of prayer to worry about the causality of it. When it comes to wellness on the job, our motto is, "If it works, do it!" If prayer gets you through the day, the week, the year . . . then it is a viable spiritual tool.

A Brief Restorative Prayer

If you feel unsure of yourself in beginning to pray at work, here is a suggested format which incorporates the four postures of prayer:

Begin by placing yourself in the presence of your Higher Power, whoever or whatever that is for you. Take a few silent moments to breathe deeply and be aware of the presence of the Divine.

Now think of one thing you've done recently that you regret or feel sorry for. Sincerely, in your own words, offer a mental "I'm sorry" to your Higher Power. Tell her what you intend to do to make up for the act or omission. Let yourself believe that you are loved and forgiven.

Now ask, again in your own words, for some quality you need to become even better than you already are. Let yourself believe that you are loved and provided for.

Next, focus on one thing for which you are grateful today. Offer a prayer of thanksgiving. Let yourself believe that you are loved and appreciated.

Finally, feel the wonder and greatness of the Holy One. Let the mystery and grandeur fill you. If you wish to use mental words, do so; or simply feel it — that is enough. In this moment, your very existence gives glory and praise to That-Which-Is-Greater-Than-All.

Prayer From Other Cultures

We are at a point in history in which we are coming to grips with the earth as a global village. We have access to the religious practices of many other peoples with whom we share the planet, as well as the venerable traditions of cultures from the past. Many women are disenchanted with religious heritages which are predominantly masculine in their orientation. Therefore, increasing numbers of women are investigating nontraditional, Eastern, pagan, tribal, and New Age spiritualities, to name just a few. The prayer objects of other cultures include prayer wheels, incense, drums, herbs, fire, bells, chimes, various figurines or images of the Goddess or God — some of which can be very alarming to people who have been taught to associate such objects with satanism or other dark forces. We encourage you to practice prayer in whatever form is right for you at work, including the use of sacred objects which are meaningful to you. You will have to find a balance of doing what's right for you and knowing your environment well enough not to make it harder on yourself than it already is to integrate spirituality in the workplace. Later in this chapter, building a spiritual community at work is discussed; sharing and support are so helpful for spiritual growth. At the same time, however, discretion is more important if you know that you will become the object of someone's "God-given crusade" to convert you away from your "heathen ways." Some journalistic elements reflect cynicism and even hostility toward the practice of nontraditional spirituality (and by nontraditional we mean other than the Judaeo-Christian heritage most Americans embrace). Please: do not set yourself up for attack. This defeats the purpose of spiritual well-being. If you know you work in an unreceptive environment, having a boundary to protect your privacy will be a much more constructive choice than going public. It's pretty hard to sit in your cubicle, burn sage, and drum without creating an uproar!

VISUALIZATION

Visualization is another "menu item" to try out for your spiritual banquet. Basically, most visualization for this purpose begins with the conscious creation and control of images but it somehow takes on a life of its own. Thus, our unconscious minds, generally more open to intuition of other dimensions of reality, can provide us with direct access to spiritual experiences, nurturing, and problem-solving — often allegorical, symbolic, or full of visual puns, just as our dreams are.

Take the story of Chris, a married mother of two with a solid research position. Chris had read Jean Shinoda Bolen's *Goddesses in Every Woman*, a Jungian approach to self-understanding through mythic archetypes. She also attended a workshop in which the presenter introduced the participants to visualization. Chris, on her own, developed an inner dialogue with the goddesses from Greek mythology that represented aspects of herself. She had a distinct image of each goddess: Athena, Hera, Aphrodite, Diana; she would make a private time, close her eyes, and picture a council of her goddesses with herself present. Chris's marriage had become rather stale, and she had met a man with whom she experienced a strong and vibrant mutual attraction. They shared many intellectual and emotional interests. Chris, who never thought she'd be capable of having an affair, found herself sorely tempted! She felt her sexuality compelling, but this was in conflict with her moral beliefs. What to do? Chris decided to summon Aphrodite, the goddess of love, to discuss the problem. In her visualization, she explained her dilemma to Aphrodite and asked her to moderate her influence in Chris's life. To her astonishment, Chris found Aphrodite abrupt and testy: "I don't do moderation!" huffed the goddess. "Go talk to one of the others who does!" Chris was stunned because this reply was not of her imagining! So she called the entire council, and, while the love goddess was less than enthusiastic about the council's decision to refocus on the marriage, she did point out to Chris that she had been ignoring and denying her sexuality for too long. At that point, Chris knew what was the right thing for her in terms of revitalizing her marriage.

Another anecdote brings visualization closer to the subject of spirituality. Carol, a never-married successful real estate agent in her late forties, became acquainted with visualization while in therapy to deal with her disappointment at not having a family. In her early use of visualization, she encountered a Mother Teresa-like woman who always gave her a great sense of peace and love. She subsequently began to turn to her more and more as she grew beyond her grief and loss. In her mind's eye, she experienced the calm wisdom and faith of this archetypal crone who seemed to have great love for and confidence in her. When Carol would go to her with a problem or need, more often than not the ancient one would hand her a small symbol: a seed, a gem, a bone — things that sometimes had a clear meaning for Carol and sometimes seemed as arcane as an oracle. Eventually, Carol found herself becoming deeply intuitive and completely comfortable with the flow of life. Inexplicably (or so it seemed to her) she became content in a way she had never been, and her life and work acquired a sense of meaning: she saw herself as helping people find homes they would love and be at peace in and thus somehow increase the well-being of the planet. She also found people relating to her with new respect, seeking her out when they themselves felt troubled. She said, "I was never particularly religious as a child, and my parents were twice-a-year Protestants — Christmas and Easter. Now I feel as if I've become a minister of sorts, even in my sales. I don't really believe in a specific God, but it's clearer to me that there's a loving force we can trust that will work through us if we let it. For the first time in my life, I am truly happy."

The beauty of visualization as an aid to spiritual well-being is this: a picture is worth a thousand words. The use of images is the most precise and concrete way to access what our souls know, but which is generally obstructed by the business of working. Furthermore, since the mind bypasses linear, verbal thought during this process, it can present the unexpected. There is a saying: When the pupil is ready, the teacher will be there. You may not always recognize when you need to grow spiritually, yet if you let your unconscious mind take over, you will find that the essential message comes through loud and clear.

The Inner Guide

With visualization directions, you have three choices: 1) read the entire explanation several times until you are sure of the steps, then do the visualization with your eyes closed; 2) make an audio tape of the directions, with approximately thirty-second pauses at the ellipses; or 3) follow the instructions one at a time, closing your eyes for the practice of each step, then opening them to read the next step once you've gotten a solid image. If the picture is clear, you will return to it upon closing your eyes again. You will probably do these in a sitting position, but if you have the luxury of a place to lie on your back and sufficient energy to avoid dozing, that is also fine.

1. Close your eyes, settle yourself in a comfortable, aligned, grounded position. Take two or three cleansing breaths, relaxing as you exhale. Then breathe normally . . .
2. Allow your mind to let go gently of cares, worries, relationships, work. Let your consciousness discover a safe, temporary emptiness . . .
3. Now picture yourself on a beautiful, warm beach where you are safe, your skin protected from the sun, and you are alone . . .

4. Notice the lovely details of the sky . . . the water . . . the color of the sand . . . the shape of the shore . . . any nearby plants or birds. . .
5. Pay attention to the sounds . . . the colors . . . the smells . . . the temperature of the air . . .
6. Notice your position, and the feel of your body . . . what are you wearing? . . . how do you feel? . . . if you are feeling strange or awkward, change the image as you like, to feel more comfortable . . .
7. Now, looking up the shoreline, you notice a calm person approaching you from a distance. Somehow you know this is a very wise and gentle person. Just observe the person as he/she draws near . . .
8. When this wise person arrives at the place where you are, he/she sits down in front of you. Notice who this is, and the details of her/his face. When you gaze into this person's eyes, you feel very calm and cared for, as if you can trust this person completely . . .
9. You sit together in silence for awhile, then you realize there is something you wish to ask or say to this person. Let yourself do that now, and listen to the response . . .
10. Now you notice that this wise person has a small pouch. She/he reaches into it, and hands you an object with a special meaning just for you. Receive it, and look at it closely. What is it? . . . What meaning does it have for you and about you? . . . You find that you also have a small pocket or pouch to hold the object. Place it there and thank the person . . .
11. Now it is time for this person to leave. Say goodbye in whatever way you wish, and then watch as the person stands up and slowly continues down the beach . . .
12. When the wise person is out of sight, take a deep breath, and pay attention to how you feel and what insight you have gained. Then slowly let the beach fade away, returning to your own consciousness . . .
13. Pay attention to your breathing until you are back to where you began. When you are fully back, open your eyes and breathe normally.

If you had difficulty with the images, don't give up. Try it again in a week or two before you judge whether or not visualization is right for you. Everyone is different, and certain personality types can access visual data more readily than others. If this is not your cup of tea, by all means don't force it! Simply use whatever works for you. If you have a desire for spiritual integration at work, you will find the tools that are right for your needs.

On the other hand, if you found yourself getting into the process, take charge of creating whatever scenes you like. These are your own special places, and you can make them be what you'd like. Some women find that a mountain, meadow, or forest feels safer than the beach. Some women find that imagining themselves on a path to find the wise person is more comfortable than letting the person come to them. The important factors in creating your own precious scene are:

1. Pay as much attention as possible to the details of the image as well as what you feel during it, and
2. Let the images come to you. Don't try to consciously control them. Trust the process.
3. When you find a place and an Inner Guide who speaks to you, return frequently for advice, consolation, appreciation . . . whenever you feel at a spiritual ebb. With practice you can achieve the ability to contact this person swiftly, for a "quick refresher" on the job, even when you're under pressure.

The Inner Sanctuary

You can use visualization to construct an inner room or temple where your spirit can find a serene haven. You can use it just for a quiet visit, or you can spend your entire meditation there. The mind has powerful abilities. Think of all the illusions you've talked yourself into throughout your life: I have enough money to buy this dress; he really loves me; my thighs are three times the size of anyone else's; and so on. Why not use "illusion" constructively? If you practice this repeatedly, three to five times a week, you will find that whether you've built a cathedral or a fire ring, you can visit your inner temple at any time, without leaving your chair!

1. Close your eyes, settle yourself in a comfortable, aligned, grounded position. Take two or three cleansing breaths, relaxing as you exhale. Then breath normally . . .
2. Allow your mind to let go gently of cares, worries, relationships, work. Let your consciousness discover a safe, temporary emptiness . . .
3. Picture yourself in a sacred, silent place. It could be the church of your childhood, a very famous structure, ancient or contemporary, a cathedral of elms with long angles of sunlight filtering through, a small chapel, a cave with primitive paintings on the walls; it could have candles and incense, or stained glass, or no walls at all; notice if there's a focal point, such as an altar, or if

it's an unstructured space. Stay with it as long as you need, to let it becomes exactly what you need . . .
4. Take a few moments now to pay attention to the details that your senses gather: the sights . . . sounds . . . smells . . . quality of light and darkness . . . temperature . . .
5. Let yourself be surrounded by the holiness of this place. Feel the presence of your Higher Being, and stay for as long as you like . . .
6. When you are ready to come back, let the image softly fade away. Gradually return your awareness to your present reality . . .
7. When you are fully back, open your eyes, take a deep breath, then breathe normally . . .

(You can deepen this visualization by inviting the presence of your Higher Power into your sanctuary. Picture this in whatever way is right for you.)

Remember: if you are interrupted by a phone call, a knock, whatever, don't jerk your eyes open and immediately move. Take a few silent seconds to readjust so you don't jar your system. Your spirit is more important than any intruder.

Become aware of spiritual desire and encourage it. Many psychologists have suggested that women are closer to their own spirituality than men because we are generally more intuitive, sensitive, and tuned in to the cyclical, creative nature of life. This may be so but is never to be taken for granted. Some women just naturally seem to be more mystical or joyful than others, but most women must cultivate spiritual wholeness.

This raises the issue of commitment to spiritual growth. In a sense, the workplace can provide, if you use it to your advantage, a safeguard for your spirituality simply because it is probably the most structured time of your waking life. Even centuries ago, the most contemplative orders of nuns had to participate in the daily bread of life, and the majority of daylight hours went into physical labor to maintain the convent. Nonetheless, the daily ritual of regular respites for prayer guaranteed spiritual opportunities. Your job can work for you in the same way. Daily use of at least one break is all you need to revive your soul. Use the following headings on a pad, and answer the questions honestly by checking off the heading that fits:

	Yes	No	Don't Know
1. Do I believe spiritual wellness is important?	☐	☐	☐
2. Do I currently see myself as spiritual?	☐	☐	☐

THE SPIRITUAL BOTTOM LINE 155

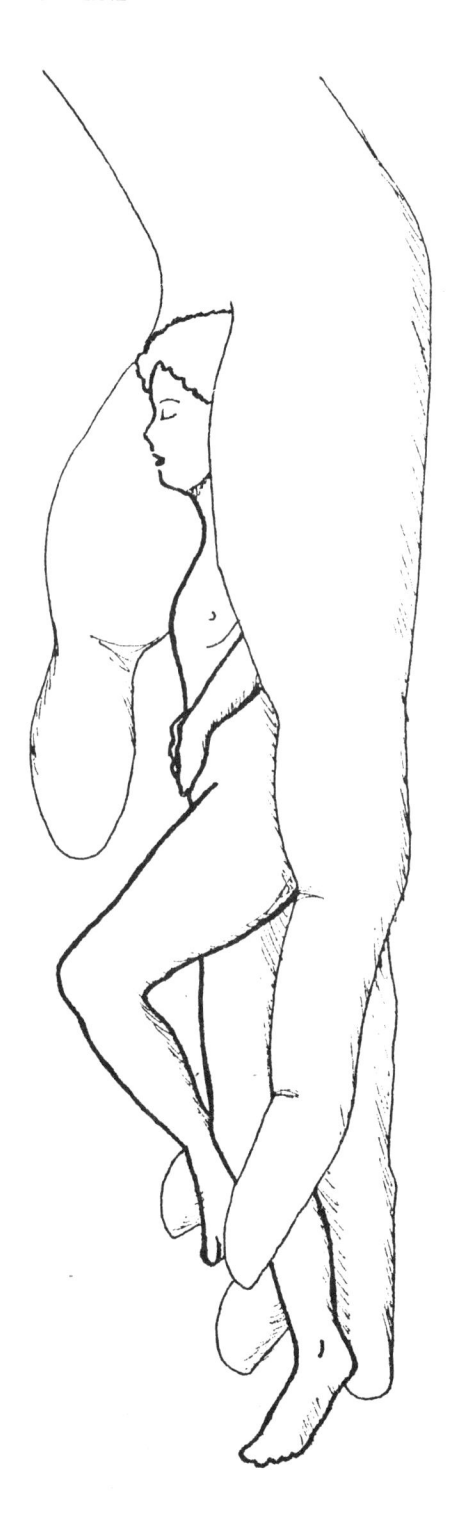

	Yes	No	Don't Know

3. Do I currently have a spiritual practice?
4. Do I believe I am capable of spiritual growth?
5. Am I willing to designate a 6-week period to explore the tools suggested in this book, or other techniques I know?
6. Am I willing to commit to a regular 20-minute period each workday to deepen my practice?
7. Will I place this time above other priorities, even when the "crunch" is on?
8. Will I follow through with my practice even on the days when I just don't feel like it?

If you have at least five "yes" answers, you have the desire and capacity to begin a spiritual program at work. Each day is an investment in your level of commitment; each day of sincere practice reinforces beliefs. And when inexplicable coincidences and even small miracles begin to occur, not only your attitude but your entire perception of life will begin to shift as you feel the creative forces of the Great Spirit at work in you and all around you.

SOLUTIONS: RELATIONSHIPS

Think of the times in your life when the presence, words, touch, or love of another person brought you joy. Think of the words of many popular love songs that incorporate images of a world beyond our world: heaven, an angel, an eternal flame, eagle's wings, stranger in paradise . . . The notion that each of us participates in bringing heaven to earth, or incarnating the love of the Goddess, is one common to most religions. The power of relationships to influence individuals is recognized in psychological and sociological theory (not to mention biology and physics) which are peppered with such expressions as systems theory, group dynamics, peer pressure, winning friends, influencing people, and so on. Whether we are amenable or not, our wills are daily modified by the feelings, beliefs, values, and behavior of those around us.

The act of utilizing people-power that already exists for spiritual well-being is comprised of three levels of relationships: communication, mentoring, and community. Each of these is available to you, in greater or lesser degree depending on your circumstances, at work. It's up to you to take advantage of the potential that surrounds you in the form of your colleagues. And it's worth it to take the risk!

Chucking the Chit-Chat

Marissa began working right after high school as a secretary in a large downtown corporation. It didn't take long to meet the other young women, all clerical, who generally congregated in the vending-machine lounge on break. Their conversations hung in the air with the smoke from their cigarettes: I had a fight with my boyfriend last night — he's such a jerk! I LOVE your shoes — where did you get them? Did you hear? — Sherrie's engaged and wait till you see her ring! My mother is so ignorant — she treats me like I'm 12 years old. What are you doing this weekend? So what did you do over the weekend?

As Marissa matured, advanced, changed jobs, got married, had kids, changed jobs, advanced some more, it seemed as if the content of her conversations at work changed, but the basic process remained constant. Where to shop for what, the really great sales, a smattering of the latest political scandals or candidates, husbands, children . . . all quite superficial, unless the occasional outburst of someone's emotional pain took the talk a little deeper. There were times when Marissa was goaded by a little thought that there must be more to communication than this, and lurking beneath that thought was the feeling, too terrifying to explore, that she was desperate for something she couldn't name. But she quickly discarded the thought when it bobbed up and thereby kept the terror at bay.

There is a fierce norm or unspoken rule that personal spirituality be banned from the common traffic of life, not to mention the board room. Yet support if crucial is you are serious about the wellness of your spirit. With the exception of a very few yogis and hermits who exist in absolute silence and isolation, the rest of us need some type of community to affirm, model, and celebrate our progress. If you are part of a regular spiritual community, that may be sufficient to sustain you throughout your work each week. However, there is no reason to disregard the additional benefits of a spiritual "buddy system" at work. Sometimes just knowing that you *could* lean on someone when you've had an overdose of the crass superficiality or dehumanizing moneygrubbing around you is enough to turn your attention back to the need to nurture your own soul.

Is it a risk to begin a deeper conversation? You bet! Chapter Six explained the obstacles to communication about personal spirituality, which bruise our tender spirits and distract us from our essential holiness. Each of us is good; yet if we measure self-worth exclusively in terms of paycheck, power, and six-month reviews, we lose sight of the worthiness that is our birthright. Each of us is a speck of sacredness and can give and receive that for each other.

In the face of all these hurdles, though, who in her right mind (or soul) would share with another her desire to be more spiritual at work? To be honest, an element of discretion is most advisable. Before suggested conversation openers, here are a few cautions:

1. Be observant. Notice who seems chronically manipulative, domineering, greedy, lustful, parasitic, extremely needy, reactive, fearful. We all have our feelings, but when you see a suspicious pattern in a person — even a person who talks about religion, God, or spirituality — avoid revealing your soul. There is danger waiting there, just like the wolf awaiting Red Riding Hood!
2. Spend at least six weeks conducting your own private spiritual program at work before you approach someone else. Get grounded! If, during this period, someone should notice a difference in you and comment or ask you about it, trust your judgment and utter a silent prayer for guidance before you respond. If you take a moment to center yourself, you will probably accurately recognize whether that person is sincere or has ulterior motives (refer back to point number one).
3. Evaluate the role of other sources that bolster you: weekly worship services, a women's group, reading, etc. If your life is already full and there's plenty of spiritual nourishment, you may decide to cap it off where it is for now.
4. Are you an introvert or an extrovert? Extroverts do much better with sharing as a source of support than do their inner-directed sisters. If you know you're an introvert, you will probably do just fine without spiritual colleagues at work.

As with everything in this book, use your own best judgment. Just because it's in black and white doesn't mean it's right for you!

Now, how about some snappy spiritual one-liners? Something like, "Say, who was that old soul I saw you with last night?" Assuming you do, indeed, meet a co-worker who, like still waters, seems to run deep, how do you initiate a conversation to check it out? Think of yourself as a pilgrim seeking the Holy Grail. The best way to uncover a fellow seeker is to be straightforward, and to do it one-on-one. No more bush-beating; be direct. "Roxanne, I don't know you very well, and I'd like to ask you something. I'm struggling with being true to myself spiritually, and you seem to be happy and peaceful a lot. I like your integrity. It seems to me that you don't do much game-playing. Could we talk over lunch sometime?" Or more simply, "Cathy, there's something about you that seems really spiritual. Could we talk sometime?" (The worst that can happen is a no, and if it does, don't take it personally! People have many reasons that have more to do with themselves rather than with you when they reject an invitation. It is a form of narcissism and grandiosity to assume, "Gee, it must be me," if you're turned down. So erase that thought from your mind, and continue your pilgrimage!)

Sometimes serendipity may play a part in bringing you together with a soul-mate, but more likely you will have to make a deliberate first move. Beginning a spiritual conversation may have awkward, even embarrassing, moments. Be honest with yourself and the other person about your feelings. This, in itself, is morally as well as emotionally healthy. Don't be afraid to say, "This is hard for me to talk about. I want support, but I've never done this before and I don't know if there's a 'right way' to do it." Chances are the other person feels the same way. The potential for nurturing each other's spirits is a juicy carrot that will draw the relationship forward.

A word of warning: The conventional wisdom on opening spiritual conversations is to choose women and men toward whom you do *not* have sexual attraction. By so doing, you'll avoid confusing the two, especially for personality types who are easily "charged up" by exciting relationships. Such traditions as the ancient Tantra recognize the often-fine line between spirituality and sexuality. Do not dualize body and soul; they are one being. Respect this, and you will avoid a messy manipulation of spirituality. Be self-aware, and honor the communal wisdom on this subject.

Spiritual Support

Assuming that you are able to connect up with at least one other person who feels as you do about integrating her spiritual vision at work, you can agree to utilize this relationship in whatever way is right for you. Some women simply meet occasionally over lunch to ask how it's going. Others literally work out specific individual plans of spiritual practice and then hold each other accountable, which may add an element of gentle confrontation. Others choose to structure time in which they meditate together or go for a silent walk on break. Take some time to think through what you need/can offer by way of support:

WHAT KIND OF SUPPORT WORKS BEST FOR ME?

___ An empathetic listener
___ A regular meeting time to talk
___ Reading/discussing books together
___ Learning from someone with a different practice from mine
___ Meditation/praying together
___ Being asked how I'm doing
___ Being reminded/confronted when I'm apathetic or bored with my practice
___ Talking about who/what the Higher Power is to me
___ Just knowing I'm not alone
___ Other

WHAT KIND OF SUPPORT CAN I OFFER?

___ Being honest and open about myself
___ Encouraging someone to keep going
___ Being a good listener
___ Being willing to explore a new spiritual method
___ Acting as a gentle confronter
___ Taking the initiative to check in frequently to see how the other is doing
___ Affirming the other's experience even if it's not mine
___ Other

Mentors

A system of learning a skill or trade that is rarely used today is apprenticeship. This involved a contract that for a fixed period an experienced person would provide training and sustenance for a pupil in return for a fixed period of paid labor after the training. The advantage to the apprentice is obvious: the undivided tutelage and guidance of an expert.

A mentor is more than a teacher, although that is the largest proportion of such relationships. What distinguishes a mentor from a tutor, however, is the rest of the relationship, which involves trust, friendship, and inspiration as well as guidance or education. A mentor's wisdom is shared in the context of reciprocal affection, thus blurring the professional emotional boundary which delineates such relationships as teacher/pupil, therapist/client, or spiritual master/disciple. There is an emotional connection and commitment which characterizes mentoring. In a sense, then, a mentor is an inspiring friend who is able to communicate a method of growth.

There is no formula for recognizing and acquiring a mentor. However, if you know someone on or off the job who seems to have integrated spirituality into her life's work, and you feel drawn to this person, don't hesitate to begin tapping into this resource. It could even be a member of your own family: a grandmother, aunt, sister — even your own mother. A connection may develop between the two of you unlike that with your other friends and teachers; you may awaken one day to the realization that you have a mentor. It is a very special feeling to know that someone is in your corner in a uniquely loving and helpful way — that she is there for you. Do not make this person your Higher Power, but let the relationship be a living metaphor to help you understand that the Divine does for you what you cannot do for yourself.

Throughout the process of seeking co-workers with whom you can share your spiritual journey, or hoping for a mentor, remember to use your inner blessings: patience, trust, belief that you will be given the relationships you need to reinforce you in your search. Ask your Higher Power for help with this: that the appropriate people cross your path, that you will recognize them, that you'll have the courage to take a risk and speak up. If you have faith in this process, you will be amazed to find how well it works.

Creating a Community

All Western religions are based on worship/support communities. Unfortunately, all too often these begin as fervent basic communities but gradually become encrusted with the trappings of institutions: written codes of behavior, economic issues, the politics of inclusion and power, real estate, fixed meeting times. Even though much of this is necessary, sometimes members become so caught up in the machinations of these factors that they are spending more psychic energy with gobbledygook than with "God"!

You don't need numbers to have community. As you encounter two or three trusted spiritual friends, introduce them to one another. At intervals, and/or when the timing spontaneously makes sense, meet together to compare notes, encourage each other, share what has worked, and brainstorm ideas for further direction. The more support you build in for yourself, the more likely you are to protect your spiritual well-being. Also, there is greater probability that your workplace will shift in terms of being a meaningful part of your life. You will renew your enthusiasm for going to work and revitalize your ability to discern what is and is not right for you at work. Thus you will see benefits in other arenas: your productivity will increase without undue effort; your emotional health will improve, your relationships with superiors, subordinates, and peers will be less contaminated with baggage — thereby earning you greater respect and likability.

Think about it. You will have begun a positive spiral of spiritual health. (See illustration.) Notice that the spiral widens and narrows, representing the reality that sometimes we're really "on" with our spiritual well-being; at other times we are lazy, interrupted, closed, etc. No one can maintain a perfectly consistent practice. But adding the community element helps get you through the lean times, just as you will be helping others do the same.

Initially your "community" may meet in the cafeteria over lunch or breaks, but you will probably eventually experience a desire for privacy. If you can arrange that, great! If not, continue as you are doing. You can always meet occasionally outside of work, on an evening or weekend. As you generate ideas for integrating spirituality into your career, your group may evolve into a team for implementing them. In other words, there is strength in numbers, and you can therefore approach your management to lobby for what you want: a contemplation room, a staff retreat, inservice presentations on spirituality in the workplace, time off to do volunteer work, etc. When you and your co-workers demonstrate commitment and performance in alignment with your job descriptions, you are more likely to be taken seriously. You can use the research done by Denniston & McWilliams[7] to support your position that productivity increases and work relationships improve when such practices as meditation are incorporated into the workplace.

And do remember to temper your enthusiasm with moderation. No one appreciates people they perceive as fanatics, especially religious ones! If you are overly zealous, you may end up losing more ground than you gain.

To summarize guidelines for forming a community of spiritual support:

1. Begin with one other person; expand later.
2. Be honest with each other about your search for spiritual integration.
3. Commit to supporting each other.
4. Meet regularly.
5. If your numbers grow, use teamwork to lobby for structural support from your company: geography (a room), a time (paid/unpaid leave for workshops/volunteer efforts), and money (tuition reimbursement; inservice training; decorating a quiet room).

Spiral Diagram (text labels, from bottom to top):

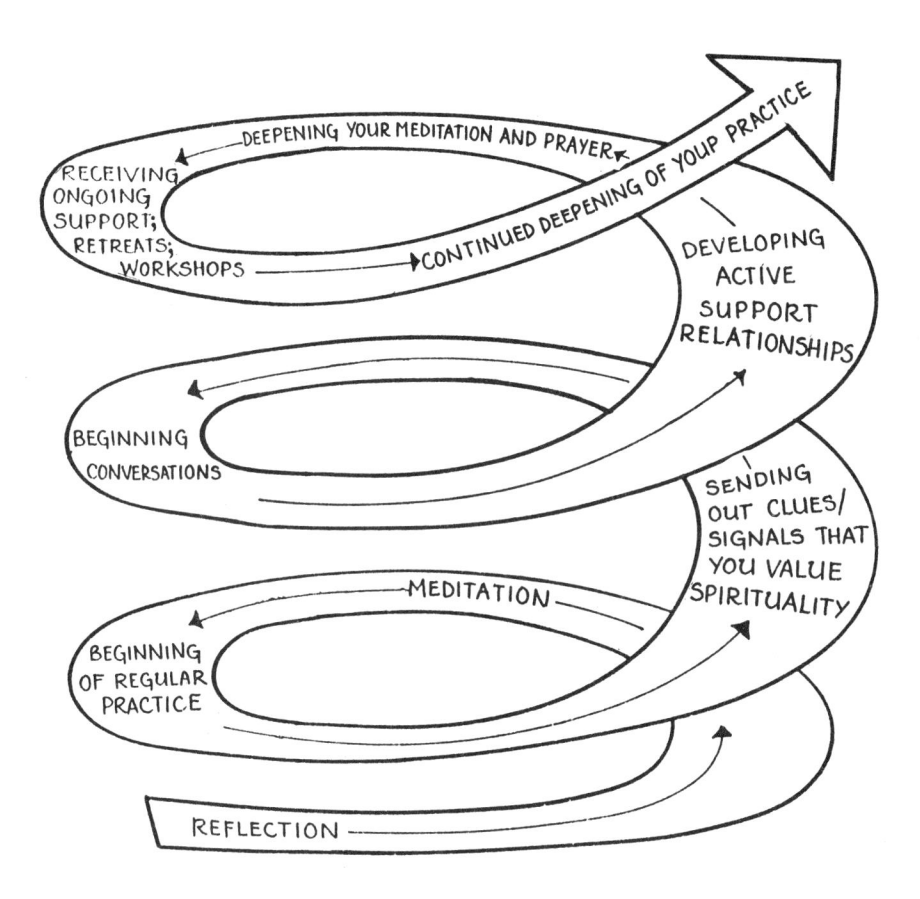

REFLECTION

BEGINNING OF REGULAR PRACTICE — MEDITATION — SENDING OUT CLUES/SIGNALS THAT YOU VALUE SPIRITUALITY

BEGINNING CONVERSATIONS — DEVELOPING ACTIVE SUPPORT RELATIONSHIPS

RECEIVING ONGOING SUPPORT; RETREATS; WORKSHOPS — CONTINUED DEEPENING OF YOUR PRACTICE

DEEPENING YOUR MEDITATION AND PRAYER

SOLUTIONS: GEOGRAPHIC

A Place of the Spirit

As pointed out earlier, you can create a soul-enriching atmosphere around your own work space; symbols and art, fresh flowers, a candle, even incense if it doesn't bother others, can add a tranquil, sensate connection to the Holy Spirit. You can create a desktop sanctuary of your own design. There are even little Zen gardens, or sand-and-pebble arrangements, available through catalogues (see Resources in Appendix IV).

Many suburban office complexes are being constructed in the midst of woods, or with an atrium or outdoor pool or fountain. If you don't have a quiet corner or room indoors, why not take a few still moments outside if you're lucky enough to work near a natural setting. Many spiritual traditions in tribal (microcosmic) societies are fundamentally rooted in the connection to the rest of nature. Like the stone pillars and flying buttresses of Gothic cathedrals, tree trunks and angled, interlaced branches draw our perception heavenward, yet remind us of how small we really are. And the stillness of woods, meadows, and mountains muffles the clanging stimuli that clamor for our attention, so you can listen to your own holiness and worthiness. If you indeed work in the midst of natural beauty, have you become habituated and immune to it — are you taking it for granted? Open your senses once again to what is around you. Even if you work in the city, there are minute miracles of nature available to you: look closely at the sky, the quality of light, a weed that refuses to be deterred by concrete, a bird, animal, or insect that has adapted to urban life. Look for what is transcendent about nature in the city.

Sadly, relatively few working women have access to a beautiful location and a climate conducive to consistent spirit-breaks outside. Many mid- to large-size corporations are beginning to provide on-site health clubs, massage, and child-care; why not on-site contemplation rooms? A simple room with soft lighting, carpeting, a banner or Japanese flower arrangement, a few chairs and floor cushions where employees could touch base with their inner selves (not to mention their Higher Power) would eventually enhance several factors, all of which are desirable and make good business sense: ethics, morality, integrity; individual productivity; alignment of individual, corporate, and global purpose; pleasant, respectful relationships; decision-making and problem-solving. An executive secretary at Xerox Corporation, which has a reputation for taking good care of its employees, was asked if her company provided such a room. "I never heard of such a thing — but I would certainly use it!" she stated emphatically. Most hospitals have chapels, but they are primarily visited by worried patients and their loved ones, not by the overworked doctors and nurses. Ultimately, the addition and use of one room would have relatively vast consequences for not only the individual but also for the company. This is where the advantage of having allies, or your spiritual cohorts, becomes clear. One person alone asking for such a space is highly unlikely to bring it about. Use the strength that abides in numbers, and be tenacious. Though an initial request is often rejected, like water dripping on a rock you can wear a groove in even the hardest surface if you gently persist.

Some words of advice from a former CEO of a hi-tech corporation: if you are going to advocate for such space, start with language that the company speaks. Even though you will be asking for something qualitatively distinct from a library or think-tank, explain that you want a room with a contemplative atmosphere that can be used to alleviate stress and promote problem-solving, a room with not only minimal distractions but a lovely atmosphere. Be clear from the outset what such a room might cost, including soundproofing, carpeting, lighting, the dimensions of the room, paint, furniture, decorations. You can be budget-minded and still present plans for a room of quiet beauty. Be aware that words like "prayer" or "meditation" are controversial for most corporations and may set off alarm buzzers in the mind of your listener. Aim to be diplomatic and pragmatic, but keep your own vision clear. The more people you have on your side who also understand the need for discretion, the greater the probability of getting what you want.

Another geographic solution to the problem of being spiritually healthy lies outside the workplace altogether. Retreats abound and are steadily gaining popularity as a sort of booster shot for the soul. Retreat centers exist in urban, suburban, and rural locations, and generally offer non-denominational as well as denominational experiences. Just look up "Retreat Facilities" in the Yellow Pages. If you belong to a church/synagogue/temple, contact your spiritual leader or the person responsible for adult education for a calendar of upcoming events. Also, make a specific request for a day of recollection, or an afternoon workshop on spirituality in the workplace. If you begin making the need apparent, sooner or later someone will respond to it.

Increasingly, monastic "vacations" are also a choice for many harried executives and workers who are soul-starving. The use of precious vacation to cloister oneself in the convent or abbey away from material influences is really quite revolutionary! The simplicity, structure, and silence are so healing for wounded spirits; the instruction in reflection, meditation, and prayer provide, for many participants, a more dramatic "get-away" than if they leave Alaska in January for a week in Tahiti! And yet it's not a get-away at all; it's a "get-to"! *Get to* your soul, *get to* your Higher Power, *get to* be who you really are — instead of letting things *get to* you! What you will bring back from such a trip is much more than a souvenir. It's an investment in the life of your soul.

Finally, a new product is beginning to appear in the spiritual marketplace. Weekend workshops and ongoing support groups are being specifically designed to integrate career and spirituality. In Chicago, for example, two women (Robin Sheerer and Marsha Haake) who run a business called Career Enterprises are offering a weekend experience, *Contribution, Leadership and Grace*. Their brochure describes this as, "A course for individuals who have answered the most fundamental questions about career direction, and are now ready to expand their contribution both inside and outside of work, and to express their spirituality in their everyday life." The development of such workshops is a response to a very real need into which women evolve as they become more fully developed and aware persons. In your area there may not yet be such workshops. If you are interested and want to find out, begin with calls to career consultants and retreat centers. If you don't find the resource, but you find someone in your calls who sees the need and is enthusiastic about the idea, ask that person to design and pilot one, with free or nominal tuition for yourself and whomever you would enroll. How many thousands of years ago did one of Aesop's fables illustrate that necessity is the mother of invention? If you don't find it, create it — or find someone who will! (See Resources, Appendix IV, for the number of Career Enterprises if you wish to network with Robin and Marsha on this.)

SOLUTIONS: CELEBRATIONS

No one knows who painted the Lascaux Caves, or carved the Venus of Willendorf, or began the observance of annual harvest festivals. It could as likely have been women as men; some would say even more so, since women's own bodies more clearly mark cycles and therefore are more evocative of repetition, which is what ritual is all about.

We observe many, many rituals: on daily, weekly, monthly, annual, and life's-milestone bases we mark and stabilize various kinds of passages. Putting on a mask (makeup) and shield (power clothes) for the tribal dance (monthly board meeting) is a way of showing a rich harvest (annual profits graph) to pay homage to the gods (president) and win favor (a raise). While many rituals are so pedestrian as to be overlooked, we also use elaborate, myth-laden customs inherited from our blood and cultural ancestors to celebrate the major events of life: births, weddings, comings-of-age, new jobs, purchasing homes, deaths, holidays, holy days, birthdays, anniversaries . . . on and on. We are creatures of ritual and repetitions and through these we anchor emotion, meaning, purpose and perspective — all elements of spirituality. Through symbol, myth, and rite we keep our feet on the ground through our senses while we transport our heads and hearts into the clouds of awe, mystery, and intensity. So, how do we incorporate ritual into work without creating . . . more work?

A Personal Symbol

If you are old enough to remember the "Ben Casey" TV series, you may recall Sam Jaffe, week after week, drawing five simple figures on a chalkboard, saying solemnly with each: ♂ "Man," ♀ "Woman," ∗ "Birth," + "Death," ∞ "Infinity." Each figure is abstract; that is, it doesn't look like what it represents, but has been assigned a meaning. A symbol is a figure that stands for or means something other than itself. A very powerful symbol would be one that not only represents something but conveys to the viewer an experience of that thing, or feelings about it. Symbols take on shared meaning only by common use and agreement. Without explanation we don't automatically understand the symbols of another culture — which is why archeology, which deals with artifacts of peoples long extinct, can be subjective with various interpretations and full of educated guesses. So a symbol is a creative shorthand that can evoke an internal experience but its meaning is not necessarily self-evident. Here are a few symbols identifiable by most American adults: the American flag, Santa Claus, a dollar sign, a jack-o-lantern, the Playboy bunny logo, a shamrock, a heart, a cross. As you read the list, some symbols are probably more meaningful for you than others. Some may have positive connotations; others, negative ones. But most people can name feelings that accompany each of these symbols. They evoke more than intellectual recognition; they are not neutral.

For purposes of maintaining a spiritual foundation, symbols can be effective aids. Placing a "power object" on your desk or hanging a religious symbol at your work station won't guarantee the automatic vitality of your spirit. But it will function as a reminder that there is more to you than your job. If you're the type of personality that thrives on newness and becomes easily bored, change the symbol(s) every couple of months to keep your own attention focused with variety.

There are many shops and catalogues offering spiritual/religious objects and symbols. Or, you can create your own personal symbols. If you're drawn to Native American spirituality, for instance, you can attend a workshop on making your own shield or drum, especially if you live in a major urban area where such resources exist. Or if you have an idea for a symbol that is perfect for you, expressing your connection to the Goddess, sign up for a painting or sculpting class with your local adult education district. These classes are inexpensive and are usually taught by competent professionals. Even if you judge yourself to be not very artistic, you will be surprised at your undiscovered abilities when you are under someone's tutelage.

Rituals of the Spirit at Work

Repetition, constancy, predictability — these characterize ritual. If you were a visitor from another solar system and you dropped into a child's fifth birthday party, you would have no way to distinguish it from any other daily occurrences. You might report back to your own planet, "Earthlings spend their time in groups of eight, wearing colorful hats and making a lot of noise. They choose one among them to receive gifts from the others; they are served by larger earthlings who bring them sweet food." You, an observer, could not recognize this as exceptional, commemorative behavior without a much larger sample and basis for comparison.

Ritual is different from the repetition of ordinary routine in the amount and kind of preparation that goes into it, and the quality of meaning that transcends mundane realities but can make those realities more meaningful. For example, a couple can live together, and even consider themselves committed, and be quite content. If, however, they decide to formalize their commitment with marriage, several things frequently happen:

1. The marriage preparations take on a life of their own. Quite often, more money is spent than was budgeted, more time is spent than was anticipated, even to the point of exhaustion, and fights break out, usually between the bride or groom and her/his parents — to the consternation of everyone, since "weddings are supposed to be happy occasions."
2. The bride and/or groom may experience doubts, even panic, leading up to the event.
3. The actual exchange of the vows imbues both bride and groom with a tremendous sense of love and empowerment.
4. In the weeks and months afterward, the new wife and husband may awaken in the morning filled with a sense of wonder — if not an out-and-out identity crisis.
5. The marriage vows sustain them through conflicts which might otherwise be the end of the marriage.

Such is the power of ritual to affect us before, during, and after an event such as marriage: the preparation, the evoking of positive and negative feelings as we clarify our own commitment and intent, the gift of meaning and empowerment to carry it out, and sustenance through the hard times. Ritual keeps us going.

In the workplace, each of us is a gift to our employers, as well as to ourselves. It is important that the work we do has purpose and meaning for us, and that we are a good "fit" for the company's needs. That is why companies interview several candidates for a given position; they are seeking the best match and good chemistry. (Caution: it is also important to keep in mind that unhealthy, dysfunctional organizations also seek a "good match." They hire unhealthy individuals who will tolerate

THE SPIRITUAL BOTTOM LINE

the corporate abuses!) Assuming that you possess reasonable self-esteem, are suited for your work (appropriateness), and the work suits you (pleasure), you indeed have reason to celebrate, affirm your commitment to your job, and deepen your purposefulness on the planet! That is what the creation of ritual is for.

Individually, you have the ability to construct private rituals on whatever scale you deem best for you. For most of us, simply following through with a commitment to take a daily meditation break, but adding to it a lovely flower in a bud vase, a lighted candle, or a special location may be ritual enough. Anything to which we ascribe a special meaning, for which we deliberately prepare, and which we repeat . . . is a ritual! By constructing rites which also incorporate more than one sense — music, incense, art, movement — we further amplify the "sacred space" which the ritual defines.

Stephanie, a clerk at a California university, uses her lunch break twice a week to sit under a fragrant eucalyptus tree in a remote corner of the campus. She describes her ritual as ". . . my private time to remember who I am and what I'm doing here. It's always the same — this probably sounds so boring — but I take the same route to my tree, sit in the same way in the same place with my back against the trunk, on a special mat I bought just for this purpose. Then I close my eyes and breathe, trying to feel the air, to smell it, to hear the birds. I try to feel the life of the tree at my back, and I ask God to help me at work to be true to my nature, like the tree. Then I open my eyes and try to appreciate whatever I see. After a while I eat my lunch and head back. It absolutely revives me and keeps me sane."

Just in case you're thinking, "Well, heck, that's California! Anyone can do that out there, but not where I work," take the case of Carmen, who is a floor manager in a large department store. Carmen is a devout Catholic, age 25, and single. As a member of an ethnic minority, she feels she frequently has to deal with others' prejudices: "It makes me tough. What do I care what people think? I am a good person, a hard worker. Every day, on my break, I sit on the bench in the ladies' room and say my rosary. Ladies go in, go out. I don't care what they think about what I am doing. I don't make a big show of it, I just say my rosary and a couple of prayers that I will find a good husband. Then it's back to the floor. I can take the bad attitudes of others when I am close to God. Otherwise I think I would be, you know, a bitch."

Ritual can be shared with others. Three women who work for a mid-sized production firm spend their lunch hour together twice a month. They have all read the same book or article which one of them chose, and they use the time to discuss it and swap insights. The criterion for selecting the reading material is that it pertain to spiritual, not necessarily religious, ideals (they are not all of the same religious faith). Each month one chooses the material, one brings the lunch, one brings flowers for the table. These contributions rotate, which gives some variety, but the basic structure remains constant. They find that other people are very respectful, curious, and sometimes even envious — though no one has asked to join them, nor have they invited anyone else. Says Penny, "It took us long enough to find each other, to get comfortable with this. It was a complicated thing to work out. It's good and safe; for now, that's enough."

You can also simply transfer the accoutrements from familiar religious rituals to your job. The seasonal observances of most holy days are replete with their own sacred objects, music, and art. Use them to your advantage: decorate your cubicle, wear a special item of clothing, eat the traditional foods. You don't owe anyone an explanation or apology! You have the right to nurture your soul; the more you do it, the less the opinions (real or imagined) of others will matter.

SOLUTIONS: GIVING

Altruism is both innate to our species and connected to a higher purpose. Some sociobiologists have suggested that evolution has selected for unselfishness by enhancing the chances that in lean times, those who have been recognized as generous and willing to share are more likely to be given access to communal resources than those who weren't, and thus those people survive and procreate. This may be so and certainly sheds a pragmatic light on altruism. In a visionary light, the act of giving ourselves is transformational. We feel good when we give; humans don't like to say no to need. We literally experience a dilation of the region of the heart when we know we have been genuinely helpful and are appreciated. The greater the lack, the more rewarding the act of providing. Most of the time, the feeling of having been appreciated, like an arrow, points us in the direction of our own gratitude. When we are generous, we recognize that we have received much, too. This is spiritually healthy: to recall the times when we were in need, and someone responded, reached out, replenished.

As with all the subjects in this book, a word about balance: give, give often, give even when it hurts — but *don't* run the tank empty! So many of us grew up in families where proverbs and aphorisms were drummed into our heads. "Company first." "Do unto others as you would have others do unto you." "Don't hurt Aunt Tillie's feelings." "Think of others first." "Don't be selfish." It's no wonder that our own inner authority was eroded — the authority that comes from listening to and trusting our own feelings and experiences. Add to the equation our religious and moral training, and you have the makings of a martyr . . . but *not* in the saintly sense. Martyrs (or co-dependents or rescuers — pick your favorite word) notoriously manipulate others through obligation, guilt, and fixing. But when others can't keep up with the martyr's needs for control and self-esteem, they abandon the martyr, who then burns out and collapses, and plays "poor me." No one likes martyrs. They give to meet their own need for self-esteem. Healthy women, on the other hand, possess self-esteem and are therefore free to give. In order to donate yourself, you already have something there in terms of your own wholeness. Mother Teresa gives prodigiously because she is brimming with confidence and faith in God. She, like everyone else, has probably had her moments of discouragement and exhaustion. But something empowers her to continue indefatigably with the poorest of the poor; she is, in the truest sense of the word, a holy woman, a rare incarnation of the possibilities of divine love.

(Author's note: Mother Teresa or not, each of us must be true to ourselves in weighing out what we have to offer, what we are called upon to give. Years ago, Karen had a dream that she was Jesus in the garden of Gethsemane on the night before the crucifixion. "I was, literally, Jesus Christ in agony, knowing that I would soon be tortured and die, dreading sunrise with mortal terror. Never had I experienced such dread, but I kept trying to pray, 'Father, please if there's any other way out, let me have it. Yet, if not, help me to do your will.' And so it went through the night, the disciples snoring nearby, and me nearly vomiting with fear. Near dawn, I saw coming up the hill the torches of Judas and the soldiers, and suddenly I knew what I had at do! I stood up, threw off my cloak, and began to run away as fast as I could. Over my shoulder, I looked up at the dawning sky and yelled, 'FIND ANOTHER SAVIOR!' Even though I felt awful for being such a coward, I was *so* relieved. Now, so many years later, I still love that dream. I no longer feel guilty when I know clearly that even if the situation calls for a savior, I'm not it.")

Well. Few of us are called to till the same vineyard as a messiah, or even as Mother Teresa. Each of us must work the fields at hand, cooperating as best we can in bringing heaven to earth. Gifting and blessing others as you are blessed is as much a part of spiritual health as daily reflection, and so is self-knowledge regarding your limits.

The Little Things

It is in the context of our mundane realities that most opportunities to extend blessings occur. A word of support, a smile, an act of kindness, a sympathy card, a listening ear . . . each of these, so simple in itself, is a donation of self. Spiritual wholeness guides us to wisdom: there is no reason to withhold charity from anyone. We experience degrees of learning in this. The women who were so overextended with generosity that they gave away their wellness may go through a clumsy period of healing, wrapped in new knowledge of their wounds, during which they will be irritable, arbitrary, angry — awkwardly learning to assert themselves and establish boundaries, sometimes bruising others' sensitivities in the process. Recalling that no spiritual change occurs quickly, it is esssential to let the ideal of charity guide us like a beacon over the reefs of personal development.

This will be a lifelong juggling act. Extending unconditionally to others while making healthy choices for ourselves will proceed smoothly during some years, bumpily during others. On days when you just don't have it, don't paste a phony smile on your face and try to force yourself to give. In fact, perhaps this will be your day to receive from someone else, and let her have the reward of feeling good that she could be of service.

This is why it is vital to maintain a daily spiritual practice. It will keep you honest with yourself, prolong the vision and purpose of giving to others, and gradually reinforce the ability to recognize needs, however tiny, and respond caringly. Acts of kindness make the workplace more pleasant for everyone and gradually draw others into the circle. Sometimes you will give too much and wear yourself out; other times you will give too little and regret it later. Take advantage of feedback loops and work out the balance that is right for you.

Thinking Bigger

Once you feel as though you are an active and gracious contribution to the well-being of those around you at work, and that this flows from having a perspective on your place in the universe (or whatever meaning comes to you in your meditation), you may begin to look for larger opportunities to be of service. This may arise as a desire springing from your spiritual practice, or it may be an understanding leading to an act of will and commitment. And if not, that's fine, too, so long as you are generous with yourself from day to day.

There are so many needs around. The obvious ones include AIDS victims, with numbers growing at an astonishing rate; the chronic homelessness in our own nation; the problem of hunger on the planet; and the planet itself, increasingly wounded so as to be unable to sustain this precious life she houses. It is very rare for employers to allot time, even unpaid time, for volunteer work on the part of their employees. And, while some corporations exhibit a social conscience through their business conduct and methods, they are still a tiny minority.

If, however, you are one of the women whose spiritual integration at work flowers into a larger consciousness, follow your heart as well as you can. Whether that means lobbying for change within your company, or using your own time to volunteer outside the bailiwick of work, if you have the time and energy — do so. You are needed, and whatever your abilities and material resources, when you give you make a difference. Believe it.

Will you still have to struggle with balancing priorities? Yes. Will there be trade-offs? Yes. Will you have cycles in which you regress into pettiness and nastiness? Of course. You are human, aren't you? Sometimes the healthiest thing you can do will be to mentally yell, "Find another savior!" But the overall value of giving to others is ultimately a gift to yourself: a peaceful, satisfied spirit, knowing that you are instrumental in revealing the love and mercy of the Divine, which is the birthright of each of us.

PART III

Your Physical Self At Work

CHAPTER 8

Your Well-Working Body

In this chapter, we're going to take a special, direct route on the treasure map to paradise via the body. Using current research, this chapter will show you how to avoid many of the physical problems inadvertently brought about by typical work situations. What can be foreseen can be prevented. And where damage is occurring or has already occurred, simple techniques to restore and maintain physical comfort will be spelled out. There is little excuse for having to pay a high physical price for earning your daily bread when, with a little knowledge, desire, and self-discipline, you can actually make deposits into the bank account of your health. The serpent gets our attention through our bodies: Tight shoulders? Spreading flab? Eyestrain? It could be better . . . It could be better . . . It could be better. . . .

Animals instinctively know how to care for themselves. Besides licking their wounds, they change position when they are uncomfortable, eat when they are hungry, stretch their muscles to relieve tension, and curl up to take naps when they are tired. If only we could tune in more to our "animal" instincts! Most jobs do oppress our bodies and our natures by requiring long hours in uncomfortable positions, by dictating short periods of time when we eat even if we are not hungry, and by reinforcing bad habits with caffeine/sugar/fat breaks.

The biochemical effects of physical stressors rob us of our Edenic birthright; the interrelationship of lack of exercise, poor diet, and artificial environments can be downright infernal! How does the body respond to chronic strain? What adaptive mechanisms are utilized, and what are the short- and long-term effects of calling on them?

STRESS: BEAST OR FRIEND?

Our remote ancestors who lived in caves were faced with constant life-threatening situations. Each of us carries within herself a primal and autonomic nervous system set up to increase the odds of survival. Remember earlier in this book the ancestral woman suddenly accosted by a fierce wolf? Let's call her Ena. A number of physiological and chemical changes affected Ena's digestion, circulation, breathing, perspiration, muscle tension, and secretion of sugars, fats, and various hormones into the bloodstream. In a flash, she was braced for fight or flight in what is called a stress response. Her subsequent physical activity served to "burn off" or rebalance the chemicals accumulated during the crisis.

Stress is defined as your physical and emotional reaction to change. The wolf's presence abruptly changed Ena's situation and resulted in stress in her body. A stressor, on the other hand, is what stimulates us to change. For Ena it was the wolf. For us the morning alarm, the honking traffic, the memo from the boss — these are our *stressors*. Our physiological and emotional response to them is *stress*. How we perceive and respond to the demand determines whether the stress is positive, that caused by a pleasant challenge like getting a promotion, or whether it's dis-stress, from hating your job, for example. We all need stressors in our life or we'd cease to exist. We need to feel hunger to remind us to eat. We need our physical, emotional, sexual, and spiritual selves aroused to satisfy their needs. So what we are saying is that a certain level of positive stress creates a fulfilling and healthy life. However, chronic emotional stress, the result of helplessness and frustration in the face of unpleasant stressors, including our own beliefs, is what damages us over time. Eve found having to make the decision of whether or not to bite into the apple a negative stressor. And in her case, so the story goes, her choice resulted in chronic distress — to say the least!

Hormone Havoc

We, too, are faced with daily stressors ranging from minor to major, depending on how we view them. When the "cave woman" within feels threatened, our brain pushes the emergency button and our adrenal glands respond by releasing adrenaline, while our sympathetic nerves release noradrenaline. These two hormones, called catecholamines, act like Hans and Franz, the two characters on the "Saturday Night Live" TV program whose motto is, "We are here to pump you up!" These stress hormones increase your heart rate and blood flow by pumping up to five times as much blood per minute (Wow!), dilate your blood vessels, increase your blood pressure, increase your respiration, slow your digestion, contract your muscles, release stored fat for energy, and sharpen your senses. To keep you "pumped up," your adrenal glands also secrete cortisol, which prolongs the effects of the catecholamines, but which undermines the body's own self-protection during periods of prolonged distress. (This could be equally true whether the distress is from months of fearing a layoff or months of working tediously at a REALLY BORING JOB!) However, our amazingly efficient hormonal system does work beautifully in acute, short-term crises, enabling us to help ourselves in situations where we might act out a "fight or flight" event. For instance, if you could punch your boss for laying you off, your body would be primed for that. Or, if you wanted to sprint five miles from your job when it drives you crazy, your body would have the resources to help you run. Obviously, neither of these options is realistic or appropriate.

So what do we do with our "pumped up" body that is ready to take action? If the physical or emotional threat is still perceived as real and won't go away, our body remains "pumped up," alert and ready to fight or flee. Without a healthy outlet, this stress can become chronic and play havoc with our health. If the stress lingers for days, weeks, months . .

it inevitably leaves some chemical scarring, especially from the effects of the cortisol on your immune system. If we continue to respond negatively to stress, our bodies can suffer. "Stress-related disorders tend to show hyperactivity in a particular preferred system, such as the skeletomuscular, cardiovascular or gastrointestinal."[1] It appears that just about every internal system can be affected by stress ranging from suppression of the immune system, which makes one vulnerable to sickness, elevation of blood pressure combined with increased cholesterol levels, which contribute to potential heart disease, and increased fatigue and depression, which affects how you respond to your life on an emotional and physical level.

Just as your brain can summon your "fight or flight" forces to create a heightened state, it can also call upon your biochemical processes to relax and calm you. If your body and mind no longer feel threatened, your brain will no longer send out emergency signals. Within a few minutes to hours, the hormones and chemicals that prepared your body for a "fight or flight" syndrome will be metabolized, and your body's chemistry will return to normal. It is our goal throughout this book to help you develop a healthy response system to your daily stressors at work so that acute stress will be dealt with in positive ways, thereby preventing chronic stress from setting in. The same techniques you'll learn to use on the job will be useful in all other areas of your life. It all interconnects.

Different Ways to Meet the Same Challenge

Here is Carol's story: "By the time I got to work my nerves were fried. I had wanted to get up extra early to go over my notes for my presentation to the big new client we wanted to get. But because I had stayed up late preparing, I was too tired to get up when the alarm went off. So I ended up oversleeping. I then rushed out of the house with no time to eat. I got stuck in traffic and thought I'd go crazy as I watched the time slip by. Once traffic cleared, I nearly rear-ended someone in my hurry to get to work on time. I had five minutes to go when I waited for the elevator. I was frantically pushing the call button, knowing it wouldn't make any difference. After what seemed like an eternity, I ran panting into my office — trying to make myself look somewhat together (in my rush I got a run in my stocking and stepped in a puddle of water). I plastered what must have looked like a half-crazed smile on my face and ran into the conference room. I felt so out-of-control by the time I got there that I forgot to say the important things and mainly jabbered. I was trembling by the time I finished. Now I doubt if we'll get the client."

Here is Pat's story: "By the time I got to work I felt so together. I got up extra early to go over my notes for my presentation to this big new client we want to get. I purposely went to bed a little early so I'd be able to get up extra early. In order for me to function well, I need close to eight hours of sleep. That extra time in the morning allowed me to go over my report. I made my favorite breakfast to make me feel good. I did get stuck in a traffic jam, but I wasn't too bothered since I had plenty of time. Actually, that gave me the opportunity to rehearse my presentation. Once at work, the elevators seemed to take forever, and I was beginning to feel a little anxious. So I used that waiting time to practice some relaxation techniques to calm me for my presentation. By the time the elevator delivered me to my floor, I felt ready and raring to go. My presentation went well, and I'm almost positive we got the client!"

Pat turned a potentially stressful situation into a positive experience. She planned her time well and nourished herself through food and rest. She used a traffic jam as a time to rehearse instead of futilely honking her horn. Instead of panicking when the elevator was late, she saw it as an opportunity to relax.

Pat was able to see her stressors not as burdens, but as opportunities to use to her advantage. Carol, however, didn't plan well, causing herself to get caught up in a series of downward-spiraling events, which continued to reinforce an already stressful situation. Both stories show how we have within ourselves the ability to respond positively or negatively to stress. Do we create a heaven or a hell? It's almost scary to begin to understand how much potential we have to choose.

There are an infinite number of causes of stress, each an invitation to the body to gear up for action and adaptation. In fact, if we allow it, everything within our life can be viewed as a potential stressor, from waking in the morning, fixing a meal, choosing what to wear to work, and making the bed, to changing jobs, getting into a fight with a co-worker, being fired, or even getting a promotion. There are positive stressors such as holidays, vacations, and raises, as well as negative ones. Little things can be just as stressful as big ones. For most of us it is the daily accumulation of the little stressors, good and bad, that can begin to cause us wear and tear. The big ones just don't happen that often.

STRESSLESS SOLUTIONS

Just as there are many causes of stress, there are also many antidotes. In the pages that follow, a variety of suggestions for managing physical stress, all of which are interrelated, will be presented. Try each one and give it a bit of time to see how it feels to you. Then practice the ones that make the most sense to you and seem to be more effective than others.

Breathing With Awareness

Most of us don't realize the profound effect our breathing style has on our physical and emotional well-being. When done with awareness, breathing can be used as a natural tranquilizer; it is always available to us, is easy to use, and has only positive side effects. But when performed incorrectly, our breathing can have just the opposite effect. When we are fearful, tense, or angry, we tend to hold our breath, gasp and/or breathe quickly and shallowly, all of which serve to intensify stress and cause fatigue.

Cleansing Breath. Before you continue reading, take a quick breathing break that will help to illustrate clearly the profound effect your breathing has on how you feel. After reading the following instructions, put this book down in order to do the following exercise: Take a good deep breath in through your nose and gently sigh it out through your mouth. Notice how the sighing out affects how you feel. Most people agree that it gives them a good feeling — one of releasing tension. With that awareness, repeat the previous breath exercise but this time, as you exhale, make a nice easy moan or groan sound — exhaling out all the day's tensions in both your body and mind. A gentle moan or groan with the exhalation often encourages an even deeper feeling of relaxation. Do it once more and let your body feel at home, centered, relaxed.

The wonderful thing about our breathing is that it is our only physiological function that we can either do automatically or by our own conscious control. Because we usually breathe on automatic pilot, we don't think much about the quality of our breathing. It's the intent of this section to make you more conscious of what most of us take for granted — our breathing. Thus, you'll be able to use your breath more positively and more productively.

Physiology of Breathing. Understanding how breathing works will help you keep in mind what's happening in your body and the kind of physical and emotional impact breathing has on you.

The diaphragm is your breathing muscle. It is a dome-shaped muscle that lies underneath your rib cage, and it separates your chest from your abdominal cavity. As you inhale, the diaphragm contracts and flattens downward toward the abdomen making more room in your chest for your lungs to expand. As you exhale, it relaxes upward, helping to push the air out of your lungs. Diaphragmatic breathing also involves

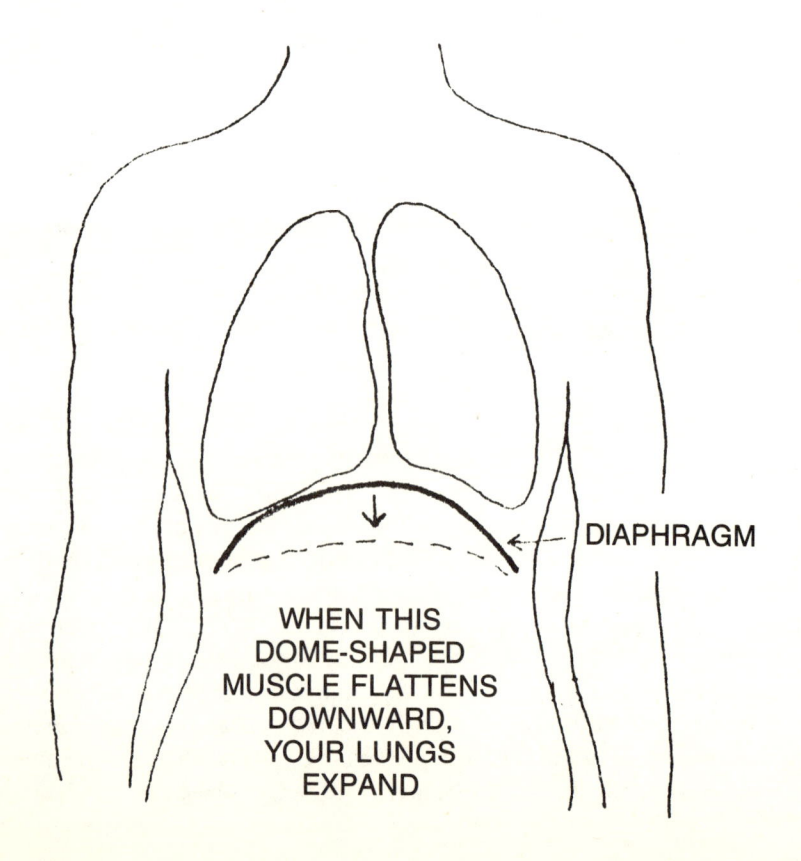

DIAPHRAGM

WHEN THIS DOME-SHAPED MUSCLE FLATTENS DOWNWARD, YOUR LUNGS EXPAND

YOUR WELL-WORKING BODY

the use of the abdominal muscles. As the diaphragm moves downward during inhalation, the abdominal muscles release outward. When the diaphragm relaxes upward during exhalation, the abdominal muscles contract inward.

Abdominal Breathing vs. Chest Breathing. Even though diaphragmatic or abdominal breathing is the most efficient and healthy way to breathe, many of us have shifted to chest breathing (the reasons will be explained in the pages ahead). In chest breathing the dominant movement is in the chest rather than the diaphragm.

> Chest breathing fills the middle and upper portion of the lungs with air but is not so efficient with the lower portion. When the body is upright, however, most of the blood is in the lower, gravity-dependent areas and so air is not mixed as thoroughly with blood if breathing is done by expanding the ribs. Chest breathing also requires more work to accomplish the same blood-gas mixing than does slow, deep diaphragmatic breathing, and since more work is required, more oxygen is needed, resulting in one's taking more frequent breaths. Finally, more blood needs to circulate through the lungs, requiring more work from the heart. How much work the cardiovascular system must do, then, is directly related to how efficiently we breathe.[2]

Just think: the very act which nature provided to energize and nourish life can actually add to your work load on the job if done improperly! In fact, it can affect your professional performance over time, not only putting you at risk physiologically, but interfering with your ability to deliver quality service!

> When an insufficient amount of fresh air reaches your lungs, your blood is not properly purified or oxygenated. Waste products that should have been removed are kept in circulation, slowly poisoning your system. When your blood lacks enough oxygen, it is bluish and dark in color, and can be seen in a poor complexion. Digestion is hampered. Your organs and tissues become undernourished and deteriorate. Poorly oxygenated blood contributes to anxiety states, depression, and fatigue, and makes each stressful situation many times harder to cope with.[3]

You become less able to enjoy your work; your employer becomes less able to enjoy you. Everyone suffers.

We are born breathing with our bellies. If you have babies or small children, notice when they are quiet that their bellies move in and out as they breathe. Why, then, as we grow up do we tend to breathe with our chests? There are many factors that can influence how we breathe. Posture is one. Little girls are often told to hold their stomachs in. How many of us wore girdles during adolescence to make our stomachs flat? Binding your belly doesn't make it easy to do abdominal breathing! As we enter the adult work force, we carry our learned posture with us. Sitting for hours at a time at work only encourages our posture, whether good or bad, to worsen. (For a more complete discussion of posture, read on in this chapter.) Tension and anxiety will also promote chest breathing because under stress you may gasp, hold your breath, and/or breathe shallowly with your chest.

A Simple Test. A simple breathing exercise will help you to understand diaphragmatic (abdominal) breathing. Read these instructions thoroughly and then practice them. Lie flat on a bed or on the floor. Bend your knees if you have back discomfort. Place one hand on your belly and one hand on your chest. Close your eyes and mentally observe your breath for about one minute. Notice which hand is moving. If you are breathing diaphragmatically, the hand on your belly should move up as you inhale and down as you exhale. If, instead, the hand on your chest is moving up and down, you are a chest-breather. If you have discovered you are already a belly-breather, then continue to keep your eyes closed and focus your awareness on the gentle movements of your belly rising and falling. You'll most likely find this exercise to be quite relaxing.

If, on the other hand, this exercise has taught you that you are a chest-breather, don't worry, because with practice you will change your

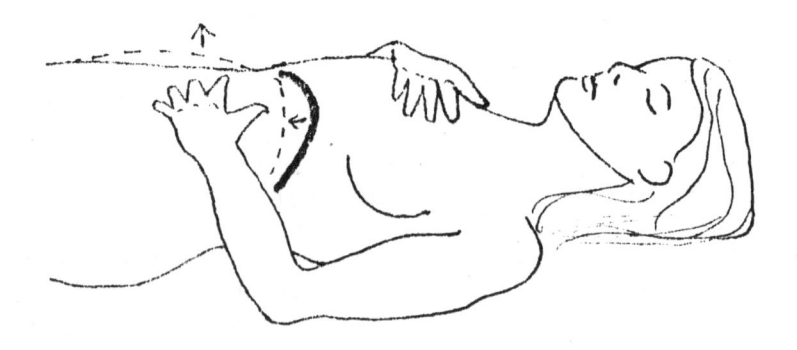

ABDOMINAL (BELLY) BREATHING:
YOUR ABDOMEN WILL GENTLY EXPAND
OUTWARD AS YOUR DIAPHRAGM
FLATTENS TOWARD YOUR ABDOMEN.

shallow breathing habit. Continue to keep one hand on your abdomen with the other on your chest. With your eyes closed try picturing your abdomen as a balloon. As you inhale think of filling the balloon with air (notice your hand and belly rising); as you exhale think of the air escaping from the balloon (notice your hand and belly relaxing down). The hand on your chest shouldn't be moving at all. Does this feel artificial or forced? That is normal at first. Just continue this exercise for at least 30 or more breaths. An excellent time to practice this breathing exercise is when you're going to bed. After a few of these conscious breaths, you'll probably drift easily off to sleep. When you feel you've perfected this exercise in bed at night, perform it in the morning while sitting in a chair and then while standing up. Begin incorporating it into one break at work each workday and once during each weekend morning. It may take a few weeks for diaphragmatic breathing to progress from a conscious breathing exercise to an unconscious habit. With patience and practice you'll eventually realize that you've switched from an inefficient habit to a beneficial one.

Breathing Techniques to Help You Cope Effectively With Stress

1. *Conscious Breathing*. Conscious breathing will most likely become your best "friend" and ally in helping you to find your calm within to handle stress. Conscious breathing is extremely simple to do because all you have to do is observe your breath. Before attempting conscious breathing, read these instructions so that you completely understand the concept of conscious breathing. To practice, get into a comfortable position, close your eyes, and for a minute or so begin to observe each breath you breathe. Focus your awareness completely on each inhalation and exhalation. See if you can feel a subtle, cool sensation as your breath enters your nose and a subtle, warm sensation as it leaves your nose (or your mouth, if you are unable to breathe through your nose). Begin to notice the movement of your abdomen — feeling it gently rise and fall as you breathe in and out. As you exhale, can you begin to notice how your body's muscles are able to soften? And can you feel a sense of heaviness and warmth envelop your muscles? As you exhale, can you also allow any thoughts in your mind to float out with your breath? Just taking two minutes to do conscious breathing can do wonders for your body and mind. Once you are familiar with conscious breathing, you can do this with your eyes open and use it to keep yourself relaxed, alert, at peace, throughout your day. It's especially helpful to use in stressful situations at work. If you are in a situation where you are angry, frustrated, intimidated or fearful, you can do the following:

- Before responding to either the person(s) or situation, tune into your breath (either with eyes closed if you have privacy or with eyes opened if it's more appropriate).
- While responding to your challenging situation, continue to keep focused on your breath.

By doing the above you'll be able to diffuse some of your negative emotions which will allow you to become centered, permitting you to respond in a more rational and effective way.

2. *Cleansing Breath*. Repeat the earlier instructions for doing a cleansing breath. Whenever you are feeling stressed, do one or two cleansing breaths.

3. *Complete Breath*, or three-part breathing, fills your lungs completely to energize you when you are feeling tired.

    a. Sit upright in your chair with a straight spine.
    b. Close your eyes and place one hand on your abdomen and the other on your chest.
    c. As you inhale, feel your belly go out, then continue to breathe into your chest, feeling it lift as your belly flattens somewhat; then continue to breathe all the way to your collar bones. Exhale by feeling your collar bones relax downward, then your chest, and finally your belly.
    d. You can repeat deep breathing two or three times. Repeating it more often could lead to hyperventilation or over-breathing, causing dizziness, lightheadedness, or tingling in the fingers and toes.

4. *Alternate Nostril Breathing*. This is a modified version of a yoga breathing technique called Nadi Shodhanam, which is best learned under the instruction of a qualified yoga instructor. The simple modified version that follows can help to calm and relax you. The technique in this breath-awareness exercise is to breathe in one nostril and breathe out the opposite one. It may sound strange to you, but go ahead and try it, because once you get the hang of it, it can have profoundly relaxing effects.

    To prepare: Using your right hand, place your ring finger against the left side of your nose while your thumb rests against the right side of your nose. (If you are left-handed, you might want to use your left hand instead.) Let your breath be calm, quiet, and even.
    To breathe: Close off your right nostril by gently pressing your thumb against it. Breathe in through your left nostril. Close it off with your ring finger and exhale through your right nostril.

	Inhale through your right nostril, exhale through your left, then inhale through your left nostril, exhale through your right. Continue breathing in this alternate way for at least two minutes.
Hint:	Some peole find that breathing in and out to the count of four helps their focus by keeping the inhalation and exhalation equal. Be certain to let your breath flow naturally — not breathing too slowly or too quickly.

THE ART OF RELAXATION

"You act as though you're wound up tighter than a spring. Why don't you just relax — get a little 'R & R,' " said Justine to her workmate, Laura.

"Yeah, that's a good idea," thought Laura. "I really want to, but how?"

When told to relax, most people understand the concept, but don't know how to implement it. It's kind of like playing a board game where the goal is always to get to the jackpot, but with every throw of the dice you end up back in "jail." Even on a well-earned vacation, many of us have a hard time unwinding from the rigors of our lives. Some women create structures so full when they're on vacation that they might as well be back on the job! The goal of this book is to help you have moments of "vacation" throughout your workday, little oases, islands of paradise. Deep relaxation has beneficial side effects: your heart rate and breathing slow, your muscles relax, your mind rests, and your whole body is encouraged to go "on a cruise." If you've ever taken a trip to a Caribbean island or other site of gentle, breezy warmth, you probably saw the natives saunter, not stride; you may have felt your muscles let go, your skin and hair blossom, your breathing decelerate. You can have this at work, and you don't even need palm trees and a shoreline! (But that would be nice, too.)

To obtain the best benefit, the following relaxation techniques are divided into two parts. The first part will be the long versions which are to be practiced at home. The second part consists of short relaxation techniques which will be useful at work. We urge you to practice the long versions at home so you'll have a thorough understanding of the exercises. Then you'll be able to apply the short techniques easily to your work situation.

The following methods are based on the understanding that relaxation is simply the ability to let go — to let go of fears, thoughts, and anxieties in the mind along with tension, strain, and nervousness within your body. And all these methods begin with breath awareness, which you have already practiced. It's worth restating that breath awareness and relaxation must work together to be effective.

As with all the exercises, it's recommended that you either have someone read the following script to you or, better yet, make your own tape so you'll always have it available for practice. (To purchase ready-made relaxation tapes, see Appendix IV.) Read the instructions aloud in a slow, calm and pleasant way, allowing for pauses when appropriate. When practicing each of the following relaxation techniques, make yourself comfortable, either in a sitting or prone position. Ideally, use pillows under your knees and a pillow under each arm to help relax your limbs. Make certain your head is supported.

Progressive Relaxation

Way back in 1929, a medical doctor named Edmund Jacobson wrote a book called *Progressive Relaxation*. The book's premise was that the human body responds to stress with muscle tension. His method for relaxing deeply involves first tensing a set of muscles while observing if the tension wants to spread to other areas. Then with awareness, let go of the tension while feeling the muscles totally release. Here are the instructions:

> Think of taking a journey through your body from one muscle group to the next until you've gone from top to bottom. You will first tense a set of muscles and then relax them. Throughout your journey tense each set of muscles for about five seconds. Note whether the tension wants to spread to other muscles. As you relax each set of muscles, become really aware of the feeling of releasing tension completely. You may find it natural to want to hold your breath while tensing your muscles, but always breathe as you relax them.
>
> Close your eyes and take a couple of deep cleansing breaths. Observe how you feel. Notice your forehead. Raise your eyebrows as high as you can, but keep the rest of your body relaxed. Hold the tension in your brow, noticing how that affects your head, and then slowly release. Good. Frown. Squeeze your eyes shut and hold for five seconds. Does the tension want to spread? Release the tension as you feel your face soften. Clench your jaw by biting down on your teeth and purse your lips — be aware — then release.
>
> Press your tongue to the roof of your mouth; hold and release. Press your chin down to your chest and release. Now just observe how relaxed your head, neck, and face feel.

Continue your journey by shrugging your shoulders up toward your ears. Hold, observe, and then let them release downward. That's right.

Now make fists with your hands — and then release. And now squeeze all the muscles in your arms and relax. Notice how your arms and hands feel. Notice your breathing.

Squeeze your shoulder blades together — be aware of tension spreading — and then release them. Round your shoulders forward toward one another and then release. Gently arch your back without straining and then release. Notice how your chest and back feel.

Tighten your abdominal muscles — be aware — and then let them go soft. Squeeze your buttocks together and then let them go soft. Squeeze your pelvic floor muscles and release. Observe how your entire pelvic area feels. The entire upper half of your body should feel a comfortable sense of warmth and heaviness. Observe your breath. Good.

Let this wonderful sense of relaxation continue to spread downward to your legs by squeezing your thigh muscles and pressing them toward one another, observing what the tension does, and then release them. Gently point your toes to pull tension into your calves but not to the point of cramping, and then release. Then pull your toes in toward your nose and relax.

Your entire body should now feel relaxed. If you are aware of any remaining tension, first tense the area and then completely relax it. Allow your body to have the pleasure of feeling limp, loose, and heavy. Luxuriate in this great moment of total relaxation. (Pause for at least 60 seconds.) When you feel ready, begin to bring the energy back to your body by taking two deep, cleansing breaths. Think of breathing in new energy while breathing out, feeling totally refreshed. Begin to gently move your fingers and toes and gently stretch out your arms and legs. Open your eyes and smile as you slowly get up. Feeling — shall we say — divine?

Passive Relaxation

Passive relaxation involves you in taking a journey through your body and mind, relaxing them together. It is based on a tradition of yoga-like relaxations. You don't have to do anything except experience the marvelous feeling of letting go of tension. Make certain you are comfortable and the environment is conducive to relaxation.

Script

After making yourself comfortable, take three cleansing breaths. With each inhalation focus on breathing in a sense of peace and calm to your entire being; as you exhale, feel any tension, fatigue, or negativity leave with your breath.

And now think of traveling through your body, being aware of all your muscles. Begin with your head and your face, noticing your eyes. Allow them to close; that way you might find it easier to focus on your body. Be aware of your breath and, with your next exhalation, begin to feel your eyes sink deeply down within their sockets. Let them fall even deeper. Become aware of the space between your eyebrows. Are you frowning? See if you can let that space grow wider. Good. And feel your cheeks and your forehead grow soft. And now become aware of your jaw. Allow it to release so that your lips become slightly parted and your teeth do not touch.

Now continue on to your neck and your throat, feeling your neck grow soft, and see if you can allow your throat to feel larger. Feel your shoulders grow heavy: just let them drop down — even more. And from your shoulders, breathe down and out, through your arms, your hands and fingers, releasing any tension with your breath. Notice how your breath is very easy, very gentle, going in and going out, making a circle with your breath, one breath flowing into the next.

And now, continue your awareness to your chest and feel it grow heavy. Be aware of your abdomen, feeling it grow soft. Observe your breath and notice how it causes your abdomen to move gently, a very subtle movement of rising and falling — perhaps just like the waves of the seashore, very gently going in and going out.

And now, be aware of your back, feeling it sink into the chair, the bed, or whatever is supporting you. Visualize your spine, seeing all the vertebrae, and relax all the muscles on either side of your spine. With your next exhalation, feel your back release even more, as though you're melting onto whatever is supporting you, just as butter might melt in the warm sun.

Continue now to your hips and buttocks, allowing them to feel heavy. Allow your pelvic-floor muscles to release.

Now notice your legs and let go of any tightness in them by exhaling out the tension, down your thighs, your knees, your calves, your ankles, your feet and toes.

Your entire body is completely and totally relaxed. If you should be aware of any remaining tension, bring your awareness to it and release it with your next exhalation. Your breath is very gentle, and your body has a pleasing, warm, limp and heavy feeling.

Now that your body is relaxed, allow your mind to relax as well. Visualize in your mind's eye a very special place, one that will give you a feeling of peace and tranquility and one that enables you to feel very safe and at ease. Perhaps it's your favorite vacation spot, like a beach, an island, the mountains, a waterfall, or maybe it's simply a beautiful garden, a single flower, sleeping in your backyard or in the park under a tall shady tree on a warm summer day. Or you might like to create your own special place — perhaps it's an image of beautiful colors — whatever comes into your mind's eye; just allow it to be. Visualize all the details: see all the colors, hear any sounds that might be present, smell any aromas that might be there, and feel any sensations. If there's sun, feel your entire body basking in its heat. If there'a a gentle, warm breeze, feel it caress your skin. See yourself feeling very safe, very secure, and totally at ease. Breathe in this wonderful feeling with each breath. Breathe out feeling completely at ease. (Pause for one to two minutes.)

When you feel ready to leave your special place, begin to deepen your breath and take two cleansing breaths to bring energy back to your body. Begin to move your fingers and toes slowly. Gently stretch your arms and legs and feel the energy return. Open your eyes and smile. Keep this good feeling with you as you roll to one side and slowly sit up.

The Relaxation Response

Dr. Herbert Benson, a cardiologist and associate professor of medicine at Harvard Medical School, wrote *The Relaxation Response* and a more recent book, *Beyond the Relaxation Response*. In both books, he talks about the powerful effect that quieting the mind and body has on our general well-being. His method of relaxation is a synthesis of Eastern practices of meditation and Western scientific research. To elicit the relaxation response is rather simple:

1. Sit quietly in a comfortable position with closed eyes.
2. Deeply relax all your muscles from feet to head.
3. Breathe consciously, and each time you inhale concentrate on a single word such as "one," or whatever you'd prefer.
4. Remain passive as you practice this for 10–20 minutes two times daily.

RELAXATION "QUICKIES" TO USE AT WORK

You wouldn't last long at your job if your supervisor kept finding you lying in the aisle or on the floor of your office listening to 20-minute relaxation tapes when deadlines had to be met. The value of practicing at home is that the effects linger, and the same principles for a long relaxation apply to short ones. The following techniques are easy to do, require no props, can be done while at your desk (or anywhere else); and, most importantly, no one will even notice you are doing them.

Cleansing Breath to Clear Tension Away

Think of your breath as a filtering system. As you breathe in, breathe in positive new energy to fill every cell in your body. As you breathe out, think of letting go of any negative "stuff," whether it be fatigue, frustration, tension, or anger. You might want to imagine breathing in a beautiful color to lighten up your entire being while imagining breathing out a smoky color to rid yourself of any "pollution." Take several cleansing breaths throughout your day, especially when feeling tired or under stress.

Tense to Relax

To facilitate relaxation it's often helpful to consciously tense the body to exaggerate any tension that's already there and then, with awareness, to release the tension. You can tense your whole body or just the area of your body that needs to relax.

> *Whole Body:* Tighten your whole body from your toes to the top of your head. Hold the tension, and now with your next exhalation completely let go. Feel the tension ease on out. Repeat.
>
> *Face:* Squish up your face, frown, tighten your jaw. With your next exhalation, completely let go, feeling your face become soft. Let your jaw drop down, let your eyes sink back. Repeat.
>
> *Shoulders:* Shrug your shoulders up to your ears. Hold the tension. With your next exhalation, let them drop down. This one is most important to do because our shoulders tend to hold a lot of tension, especially if you work at a computer or sit for long periods of time.
>
> *Arms:* Make fists with your hands and tighten all the muscles in your arms. With your next exhalation let your arms go completely heavy. Repeat.

Pelvic area: Squeeze your pelvic-floor muscles (Kegels), abdominals and buttocks — hold and release with your next exhalation. Repeat.

Legs: Flex your toes up, extend your heels, pull tension into your calves and thighs — hold and release as you exhale. Repeat.

The Countdown Breath

Counting your breath down, from the number 10 down to zero, can be extremely effective for diffusing stress — especially that caused by anger and frustration — or during a confrontation. It can be done quietly so no one even knows you are doing it.

1. Begin with a couple of cleansing breaths.
2. Mentally say "ten" with your first exhalation.
3. Then say "nine" with your next exhalation and so on until you reach zero.

With each exhalation, focus on feeling your entire body grow heavy, allowing the stress to release with your breath. By the time you reach zero you should feel calmer.

Escape-Hatch Breathing

Visualize a hole in the top center of your head. Using a cleansing breath, think of breathing your breath in through the top of your head and all the way down to your toes. As you exhale, bring your breath from your toes all the way up your entire body and out the top of your head.

In other words, feel as though you are "sweeping" your body with your breath — inhaling a calm energy while exhaling emotional debris.

Autogenic Suggestions

This technique involves "talking" your tension out of your body. For instance, if you feel tension in your shoulders you will focus your awareness on your shoulders and with each exhalation you will mentally say "My shoulders are relaxed," "My shoulders are relaxed," "My shoulders are relaxed." Or you mentally say, "My shoulders feel loose, warm, and heavy." Repeat each phrase three times.

You can "talk" like this to any area of your body to release its tension. You can also talk to your emotions by saying, "I feel calm, my mind is quiet, and my body is relaxed."

Yawn and Stretch Relaxation

The following instructions are adapted from Adrienne Lieberman's book, *Easing Labor Pain* (Harvard Common Press, 1992). In her description of yawning to release tension, she says that it "causes your lungs to expand, stimulates your heart, and charges your blood with oxygen."[4] Yawning also provides gentle exercise for the facial muscles.

You most likely don't need a how-to on yawning. We've all done it since infancy, usually when we need a good dose of oxygen. This time, however, you'll do it with more awareness. As you inhale on your yawn, stretch your arms out as though you were a bird stretching its wings and, as you exhale your yawn, feel your whole body release.

VISUALIZATION

Mental Movies

Visualization is the art of using your imagination to create a picture in your mind's eye or a sensation within your body to achieve a desired effect. Chapter seven spoke about using visualization for spiritual well-being; now you can use visualization to ease stress, promote relaxation, and set goals.

The use of positive imagery has been effectively used by the medical world for healing and pain relief. Stephanie and Carl Simonton, along with James Creighton, wrote *Getting Well Again*, which explained their use of visualization as part of their treatment for terminally ill cancer patients. More recently Dr. Bernie Siegel, surgeon and author of *Love, Medicine and Miracles* and *The Leading Edge: New Visions of Science, Spirituality and Society*, writes extensively on the healing powers of our imagination. Laboring women use imagery to help ease pain and to speed the process of birth. Olympic (and other) athletes picture themselves performing their events in perfect form, over and over, before the actual competition. They imagine the sounds of the crowd, the contest itself, where and how they will begin and end . . . as many details as they need. Research has demonstrated that visualization actually improves success, with or without actual physical practice!

Most of us enjoy going to the movies or watching videos at home. Think of visualization as a readily available and easy way to watch mental movies that can make you feel good and perform your best. Or think of it as structured daydreaming. In any event, dim the lights of your mind and get ready for a simple demonstration of this technique. Do it slowly, and pause after each sentence to "see" clearly. Don't move on until you have a definite image: Picture a large, bright, juicy yellow lemon . . . What does it look like? Is the skin smooth or textured? . . . Now picture yourself cutting the lemon in half — notice the inside — then can you see the thin membrane that encases the pulp? . . . Can you see the thick white part of the skin? Notice it clearly . . . Now cut it into quarters. Can you see the juice? . . . Can you smell the fragrance? . . . Let your senses remember what a lemon is like. . . . Experience it. Now picture yourself picking up one of the quarters and imagining a nice big bite into the lemon pulp.

So, what happened? Anything physical? Did it get your "juices" flowing? You may have actually salivated; perhaps you felt the pressure on either side of your tongue or an involuntary urge to pucker. This sneak preview is a great example of the powerful mind/body connection.

As you experience the following visualizations, be sensitive to the fact that not everyone is visually attuned. Some people might prefer listening to music or use another method of relaxation. If you find it difficult to visualize, or it's not effective for you, that's okay — there are many other relaxation tools to use.

Using Positive Imagery to Transform Tension into Comfort — A Structured Experience

(Read the instructions first; then do the exercise from memory.)

Instructions: Take two or three cleansing breaths as you settle into a comfortable position. Close your eyes and take a moment to relax your body as you've previously learned. Imagine before your mind's eye a big chalkboard. See it as it would be at the end of a school day — covered in chalk dust. Imagine yourself using a big wet sponge to wipe the board. Wipe all the dust off to leave a wet, clean surface. See the moisture evaporate, a dry clean board emerging. Allow each of the following images to appear on the chalkboard. When finished, erase it, go on to the next "movie," and so on. Or, if you don't like the image of the chalkboard, see your mind's eye as a large video screen where you can view each image clearly.

Tense Situation: See yourself feeling tense as the elevator you are riding gets stuck between floors.
Visualization to Ease Tension: See the doors slowly open upon a beautiful garden filled with all your favorite flowers and beautiful birds.

Situation: Hear the high, shrieking sound of the drill at the dentist's office.
Visualization: Allow the sound of the drill to become your favorite musical instrument making music you love to hear.

Situation: See yourself falling from a cliff.
Visualization: See yourself become weightless as you land on cloud-like layers of warm, soft, billowing down comforters.

Situation: Feel yourself scratch your fingernails against a chalkboard.
Visualization: Let the chalkboard turn into a soft, sensuous, warm substance like a nonsticky putty or soft, warm jello.

Situation: See a bright, irritating light shine in your eyes.
Visualization: Allow the light to become a beautiful, soft, warm, comforting color that embraces your body.

Situation: Smell a foul-smelling odor like sewer gas.
Visualization: Let the smell turn into your favorite scent. Inhale, smelling the wonderful fragrance.

Now that you've got the idea, apply your vision to your workplace:

Visualizations to Use at Work

Extinguishing a "Brush Fire"

Situation: You are in a "hot" situation at work. Someone's angry at you; you made a major blunder, or you are angry at someone else.
Visualization: Imagine smelling smoke at work. You notice a very small fire. You know there's no need to panic because you know exactly where the fire extinguisher is. Quickly, but calmly, you fetch the extinguisher. You see small flames. In slow motion you are able to extinguish all the flames without the fire ever getting out of control. The fire is safely out, and there is nothing left to clean up. The situation is back to normal, and you feel good about having put the fire out.

Easing Physical Tension

Situation: Your shoulders are rounding as though they are collapsing from bearing the weight of the world upon them.
Visualization: Imagine a crane that carefully and safely lifts all the weight off your shoulders. Allow a warm pair of hands to gently massage any tension away.

Situation: You feel a tension headache coming on, or you already have a headache.
Visualization: Visualize the space between your eyebrows widening. See a pair of cool hands smooth away any wrinkles in your forehead. Imagine your hair being washed professionally or by someone you love. As the soap is washed away, feel all the tension and pain go down the drain with the water.

Situation: You feel the need for overall relaxation.
Visualization: Refer to the earlier Passive Relaxation section for details on "special place imagery."

YOUR WELL-WORKING BODY 195

**VISUALIZATION:
LET YOUR MIND TAKE
YOU TO MAGICAL, SERENE PLACES.**

Apply the art of visualization to any work situation that may be challenging to you. It can be a creative outlet for you. You may not always be able to control your work situation, but in your mind's eye you will always be the producer, editor, and director of your "mental movies." You won't win an Academy Award, but you'll surely receive the satisfying reward of true relaxation.

MASSAGE: KNOW WHAT YOU "KNEAD"

While working at her VDT, Consuela was completely unaware of her shoulders creeping slowly up to her ears as the tension of meeting a deadline increased. Suzanne's lower back ached from having sat too long at her desk reading reports. Mary's neck felt tight from having cradled the phone against her ear to free her hands for taking notes on the conversation. And Elaine, with a furrowed brow, felt her tension headache intensify while concentrating during a meeting where major decisions had to be made.

Unlike our emotions, the feelings in our muscles can't be hidden. They talk back to us in many ways. Whether under physical or emotional stress, they can communicate their need for attention by tensing, aching, or even going into spasm. In fact, our muscles mirror our emotions. When we are calm our muscles are calm. When we are tense our muscles are tense. The expression "I'm all tied up in knots" clearly is a reflection of how our body responds to our emotions.

An effective and wonderful way to ease muscular tension and smooth emotional calluses is through massage. Touch is a basic human need that nourishes our body just like food, water, and rest do. And the right kind of touch can erase tension in our muscles, calm our minds, and soothe our souls. The act of touch and its therapeutic benefits, however, have often been overlooked. As Ashley Montague so aptly said in his book *Touching*, "Touch is the parent of our eyes, ears, nose, and mouth. It is the sense which became differentiated into the others as the mother of the senses."[5]

Therapeutic massage is given by trained massage therapists who have completed several hundred hours of schooling at a certified school. They are thoroughly trained in anatomy and physiology and learn a variety of massage techniques ranging from classic Swedish massage to Shiatsu, an oriental method of massage that works with the body's energy flow. There are subspecialities, such as sports massage for athletes and on-site massage for the working weary. Enlightened employers who understand the value of massage therapy to ease stress provide their employers with on-site massage. A trained practitioner comes armed with either a portable massage chair or table in hand and gives a 15-minute invigorating "tune up" to those who make appointments. Patricia Deer, a massage therapist who is the director of Energy Breaks in the Chicago area, says: "State-of-the-art coffee breaks don't come in paper cups." She goes on to comment that, "On-site massage is like the water cooler and pop machine. It used to be a luxury, but is now considered commonplace." Patricia Deer said that one of her clients, an executive

YOUR WELL-WORKING BODY 197

secretary, claims that since receiving on-site massage every two weeks she's become more aware of her posture while working at her computer and, as a result, is more productive. Her boss even noticed the difference and congratulated her on a job well done when they were racing to meet a deadline.

Most on-site massage is done in a padded chair, which is angled so the client can sit in a restful position while leaning forward onto it. A massage chair provides the massage therapist easy access to her client's neck, shoulders, and back. If this special chair isn't used, then a portable

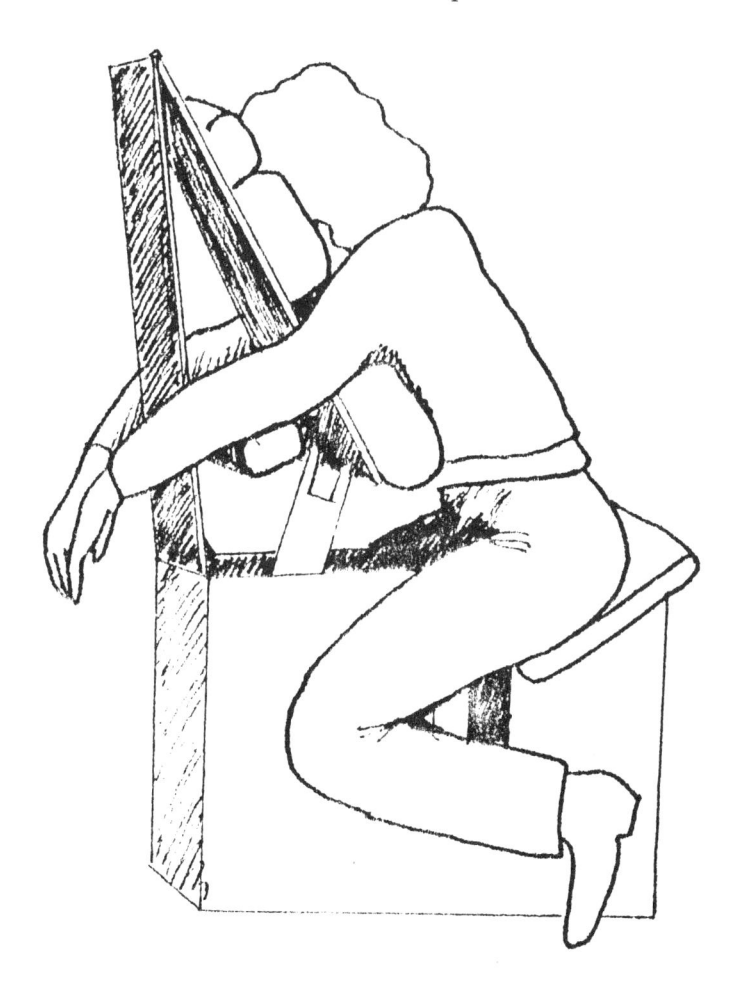

THE MASSAGE CHAIR:
PORTABLE, ON-SITE STRESS RELIEF

table would be provided. Clothes are left on but shoes are taken off, and belts are loosened. No oils are used as in traditional massage but, depending on the individual style of the therapist, relaxing music might be played and lights dimmed. Most companies set aside a conference room to provide privacy or, if they have the luxury of a fitness center, a room for massage will be set aside.

Iris Lee, administrative director of On Site Enterprises, offers workshops for massage therapists on the technique of on-site massage. Since 1986 they have trained over 2,000 practitioners in their method. Iris Lee likes to emphasize that on-site massage doesn't leave the client feeling so relaxed that she wants to just go home and take a nap. (Not a good way to get a promotion!) She claims that clients, ''. . . after receiving an energizing massage at work, will feel relaxed in their musculatures but revitalized in their body.'' In addition, the focus of On Site Enterprises is on prevention and not treatment.

Hundreds of companies, ranging from large corporations to hospitals and small companies, have provided their employees the service of massage. The fee is usually 10 to 15 dollars for a 15-minute session. Some companies pay the entire fee, while others may split the cost or provide the service at the employee's expense. One sales division in a company in Chicago has offered free massage as a perk to salespersons having the highest sales each month. The administration wanted to show their employees their appreciation in healthier ways than the usual rewards. So instead of taking them out for drinks to celebrate, they offer massage. The original idea was to be on a trial basis, but it was so well received that it's now done regularly — on the last Friday of each month in a reserved conference room. The company pays for those sales people with the highest sales, but other employees are invited to make a 15-minute appointment and pay the fee. One recipient said, "Just the act of lying on the massage table helps me to relax. I know that the next 15 minutes are just for me — to receive. It's the one time in my job when I don't have to be 'on.' I relish every second of my massage."

Getting Your Hands on On-Site Massage

If your workplace doesn't provide on-site massage, you could present the idea to the appropriate person or department that would handle such a program. It could be attempted on a trial basis to see how it works out. On Site Enterprises has a national referral system. Just call 1-800-999-5026 to get referred to a practitioner in your area. Companies that make the service available as a benefit for all employees, regardless of title, can use the program cost as a tax deduction. But, if they aren't willing to pay for it, they could make the service available at the employee's expense.

Self-Massage

Whether or not you are able to receive on-site massage, you can respond to your body's tension by doing self-massage. It won't be as relaxing as receiving a massage because you are having to contract certain muscles in order to give a self-massage. But it's certainly better than nothing, can have positive effects, and can easily be done at work in your chair, lounge, or bathroom. (See Appendix I for self-massage techniques.)

HUFF AND PUFF TO BLOW YOUR STRESS AWAY

Try to picture Eve donning an athletic bra and brief, pulling a T-shirt over her tousled locks, grabbing a rumpled pair of running shorts, lacing up her cross-trainers, and pushing her hair off her face with a sweatband. She is not getting ready to take the garden by storm; now that she's been banished, she needs to keep herself healthy. Lucky Eve! She has signed up for a low-impact aerobic program.

A complete fitness program for dealing with stress and maintaining good health requires some form of aerobic exercise. Aerobic exercise involves continuous work that elevates your heart rate to 60–80 percent of your maximum for 20–30 minutes. As explained earlier, chronic stress has a profound effect on our body's physiology. Stress prepares our body for that famous "fight or flight" action. It's been primed for a long run or a hard fight. In order to diffuse its alarmed state, you actually have to engage in a physical activity that simulates a "fight or flight" action. Otherwise your body stays "pumped up" which, as discussed previously, can have deleterious effects on your health.

Aerobic exercise revs up your body; you'll huff and puff for 20–30 minutes; you'll break a sweat and your heart rate will increase. Endorphins (your brain's natural tranquilizers) will be released, giving you a natural "high." The sum of such a workout helps to facilitate the return of your body to an unstressed state. An easy way to understand the need for consistent aerobic exercise is to use the analogy of car care. In city driving where we are consistently stopping or starting and rarely accelerating over 35 miles per hour, carbon builds up in the engine (similar to stress within our body) and negatively affects the car's performance. The remedy is to drive the car at a consistent speed for a period of time to properly heat the engine and rid it of excess contaminants, just as aerobic exercise rids the body of pollutants caused by stress. If you are fortunate and work in a large company that has an on-site fitness center, make good use of it. This means you will have to either make the time to arrive early to exercise before work begins, use the time from your lunch break, or stay after work. If a fitness center is not available, there are a variety of alternative private fitness clubs, park district programs, YWCA or YMCA facilities; you can also rent or buy a video for home use, swim, jog, and/or do fast walking outdoors, or buy affordable fitness equipment for home use.

Making a commitment to physical fitness is a pledge to good health. If you are already "hooked" on working out — Super! If not, know that it may take a few weeks of diligence before you experience that aerobic "high" people talk about. There are different guidelines for aerobic fitness, but for the purpose of maintaining fitness and using exercise as a stress releaser, we recommend the following:

1. Before committing to aerobic exercise, it's always wise to consult with your doctor. If you have any medical conditions, especially a cardiovascular problem, diabetes, arthritis, etc., it's mandatory that you first seek medical advice.
2. Choose a form of exercise that you enjoy. Some people love an aerobic class for the high energy and group experience, while others may prefer a solitary aerobic experience such as a fast walk. For fitness success it's vital that you delight in what you are doing; otherwise it becomes too easy to stop.
3. Be patient with yourself. Allow time to build up your endurance and confidence gradually.
4. Work up to engaging in aerobic exercise three to five times a week for at least 20 minutes per session.
5. Set a goal of doing 20 minutes of continuous aerobic exercise with your heart rate at about 60–70 percent of your maximum. Use the following formula or abide by your doctor's recommendation. Subtract your age from the number 220. Multiply the results by 60 to 70 percent to find your target heart rate. For instance, if you are 40 years old:

    $$220 - 40 = 180 \times 70\% = 126 \text{ beats per minute.}$$

    If you are 40, your heart rate should be approximately 126 beats per minute. This formula may need to be adjusted for individual needs, especially if you have a medical condition and/or are taking medication. If this is your case, consult with your doctor. An easy way to obtain your heart rate is to take a 10-second pulse and multiply the number of beats by 6. Your 10-second pulse reading would be 21 beats to reach your target of 126 beats per minute.

An equally effective and less complicated way to monitor your heart rate is to watch your level of breathing. Your goal will be to work hard enough so that you are huffing and puffing but able to talk and carry on a conversation for the entire 20 minutes. If you are panting and working so hard that you can barely talk, you need to slow down. If you aren't huffing and puffing, speed up to that point.

If you want to increase your knowledge of the physiology of aerobic exercise beyond the scope of this book to stretch your fitness level and/or to lose weight, look into Covert Bailey's two informative books, *Fit or Fat Woman* (Houghton Mifflin, 1989) and *Fit or Fat* (Houghton Mifflin, 1991).

Finally, use imagery or autogenic messages to reinforce your commitment to well-being and to enhance your performance. See yourself in your mind's eye looking robust, healthy, strong, confident, yet relaxed in whatever form of exercise you are engaging in. Imagine yourself able to go beyond what you thought you were physically capable of doing.

Once "hooked" on fitness, never let it go! Besides the immediate benefit of increased energy and stamina which you need for balancing work with all the other demands of your life, you will derive the emotional and psychological benefits of positive attitude, self-confidence, and self-appreciation. (These show on your face, too, so you give out "vibes" of good health.) If, because of other commitments, you can't commit to the recommended three to five times per week, do what you can do. You will still live a better life as you vent the effects of accumulated stress.

THE DANCE OF WORK

The "dance" of work has many moves, from shouldering a briefcase and sitting for hours bent over a desk to cradling a phone, along with bending, twisting, and reaching. The choreography for many of these "dances" is often awkward, out of sync and physically stressful. The following section will present you with ways to create a pleasing rhythm by performing the movements of work with grace and ease.

Posture

Mirror, mirror on the wall, am I standing/sitting straight and tall? Both our inner beauty and outer beauty are reflected in how we hold and present ourselves.

Any structure, whether a chair, house, bridge, or soaring skyscraper, needs a balanced framework over a solid foundation. The way we sit, stand, and carry ourselves is diagnostic of how effective our "architecture" will be. Poorly engineered buildings tend to sag, lean, and eventually collapse upon themselves. If your body's alignment is not correct it, too, can develop structural problems such as back, leg, knee, and foot pain, shortness of breath and fatigue.

Okay, so you already are starting to squirm and fidget. You've probably heard about posture throughout your life — especially from your parents: "Stand up straight; Don't round your shoulders." But did the value of good posture really ever sink in? Did you ever care? Probably not. And, apparently, hardly anyone else cares either. If you look around at your co-workers or people walking on the street, you'll most likely notice more people with bad posture than with good posture. In fact, how can you recognize really great posture? Look around. Find three people today who, in your opinion, carry themselves in a fabulous, effortless way. Isn't it rather inspiring?

Influences on Posture

There are many things that affect our posture:

Gravity: Gravity, thank goodness, keeps us from floating off into the cosmos, but it is an ever-present force against which we must use energy and awareness if we are to maintain correct posture.

Heredity: What you inherit from your parents will contribute to your body type and the health of your spine. Women who are tall sometimes round their shoulders to compensate for their height. If we are uncomfortable with our breast size, large or small, we often round our shoulders to hide them.

Muscle Strength: It takes strong muscles throughout your body to maintain good posture. Of particular importance are the abdominal, back, shoulder, and chest muscles. Being active throughout your life helps to strengthen and maintain good muscle tone.

Emotional Issues: Your body can often mirror your emotions. Rounded shoulders can be symbolic of guarding or protecting oneself. A slumping back and drooping head may be the result of periodic or chronic bouts of depression.

Motherhood: New mothers sit for hours throughout the day feeding their babies. They are constantly lifting and carrying them. These patterns can lead to a habit of poor posture and strained muscles that the mothers carry back to work.

Body Mechanics: Throughout the day you may frequently lift, carry, and bend. Performing these common movements improperly contributes to poor posture.

Work Habits: We are often surrounded by poor work environments; these, in turn, feed demoralizing work habits. Sitting all day in uncom-

YOUR WELL-WORKING BODY

Young plants and trees often need to be staked to support their stems and trunks. As their roots grow deeper into the soil and their stems or branches extend up into the sunlight, their entire structures lengthen and gain strength. You might want to use this vision of a beautiful tree growing from earth to sky to feel your connectedness to the earth while reaching for the open heavens.

fortable chairs and leaning over a desk presents quite a challenge to maintaining joyful posture. Obviously, you can't quit your job, but you can change the way you sit, develop posture awareness, and do simple exercises to enhance your posture.

Work Shoes: Unfortunately, those flattering high-heeled shoes wreak havoc on our bodies. In high heels, you are actually walking around on tiptoes. If they are worn regularly, your calf muscles can shorten. Your pelvis and body shift forward, causing your back to sway. High heels are fine for occasional wear but not on a regular basis.

How to Stand

First stand in front of a full-length mirror and observe the way you naturally hold yourself. Then, place the fingertips of one hand gently on your breastbone. Now think of lifting your breastbone to the ceiling while relaxing your shoulders gently down and back. As you do so you should notice that your chest and abdomen lengthen and your shoulders relax. They are not pulled back as in a military posture. Breathe freely and allow your abdomen to move.

Next, place one hand on your sacrum, or tailbone. Gently tuck your tailbone downward to create a proper pelvic tilt. It's a subtle movement. Keep your buttocks relaxed; otherwise, you may tend to overcompensate by squeezing your buttocks together. (You know the word for THAT type of person!) You'll notice that as you tuck your tailbone down, your abdominals contract and pull inward. The word "pelvis" means basin in Greek. Think of your pelvis as a bowl that holds all the contents of the pelvis — your uterus, bladder, and other organs. If the bowl is tilted incorrectly its contents will tend to spill out or fall forward. Allow your pelvis to keep its contents in a healthy, upright manner by maintaining the proper pelvic tilt. When you feel you understand the above posture, then move on.

Your chin should be slightly tucked to lengthen the neck. You've seen the Harried Harriet type who is in such a hurry that she leads with her chin as she walks. This shortens the cervical (neck) part of the spine. Or, perhaps you've met Downward Doris who studies the ground as she walks. This rounds the neck.

Now pay attention to the way your feet and legs are supporting your body. Your feet play a vital role in creating a strong foundation. It is helpful to think of the soles of your feet as having three points that need to make contact with the earth: the ball of the big toe, the ball of the little toe, and the ball of the heel. Stand with bare feet on an uncarpeted floor, feet hip distance apart, and see if you can feel these three contact points.

YOUR WELL-WORKING BODY 205

You have now proceeded from your chest and shoulders down to your feet in the process of increasing posture awareness. How are you feeling?

If you've had poor posture all your life, standing erect will feel foreign and probably uncomfortable. Recognize that you are shifting entire muscle groups out of old and destructive habits into a new and exciting mold. You can expect to feel strange at first, but keep it up! If your shoulders have been rounded, it's common to feel discomfort in your back between your shoulder blades. If you experience pain and it persists for more than a few days, consult a professional! If you have had poor posture for, let's

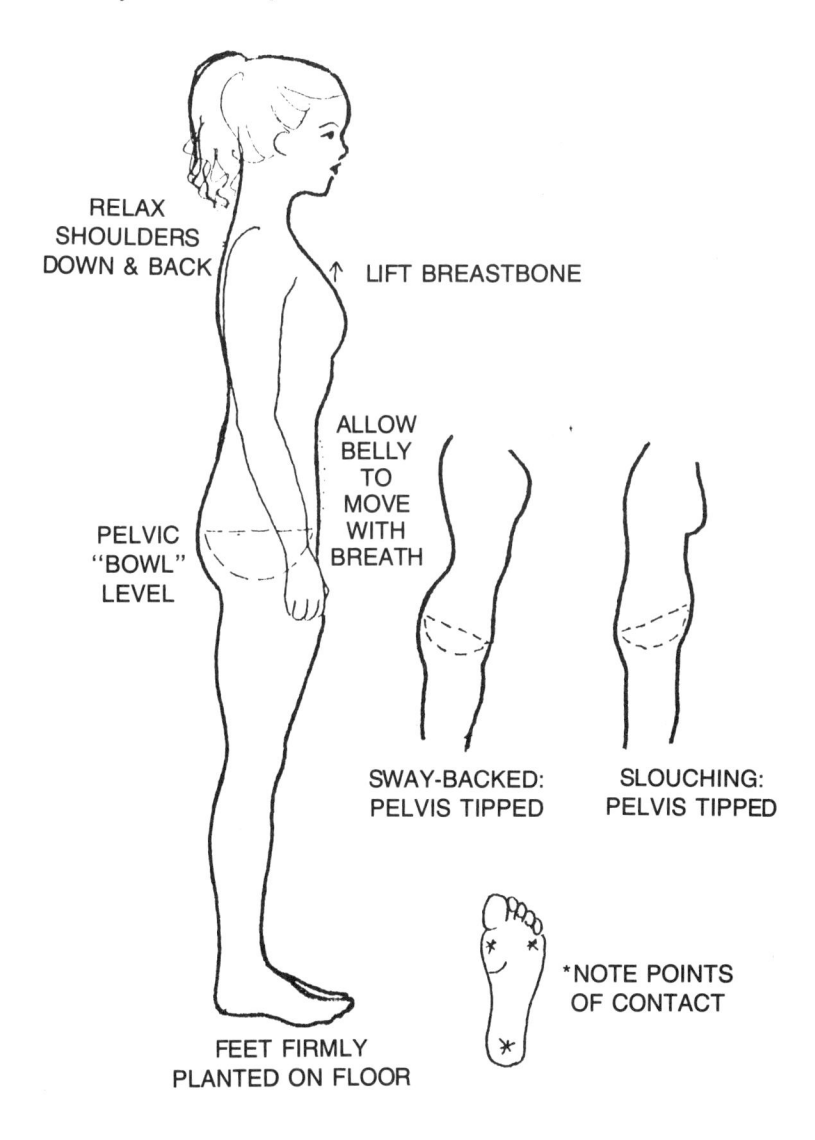

RELAX SHOULDERS DOWN & BACK

↑ **LIFT BREASTBONE**

PELVIC "BOWL" LEVEL

ALLOW BELLY TO MOVE WITH BREATH

SWAY-BACKED: PELVIS TIPPED

SLOUCHING: PELVIS TIPPED

FEET FIRMLY PLANTED ON FLOOR

*****NOTE POINTS OF CONTACT**

say, thirty years, change will come slowly and will require patience and daily awareness to restructure your body and accept the unfamiliar feelings.

Try reversing the entire posture exercise and begin with the placement of your feet; continue to your hips, pelvic tilt, chest lift, shoulders relaxed and down and chin tilted slightly down and under. Throughout your day have a posture check during your varied activities — sitting at a desk, walking, standing. Eventually your posture awareness will become an integral part of you and your actions. You literally connect heaven and earth when you align your stature in a healthy, uplifted way.

How to Sit

Sit on the edge of a straight chair or your office chair. Begin to slump by rounding your back and sitting back on the soft, fleshy part of your buttocks. Whenever we sit it's easy to assume this incorrect position. Now let's see what it's like to sit correctly.

Place your hands on your knees and pull your back up straight so there's a gentle, natural inward curve of your lower spine. Now you're about to have a close encounter with your sitting bones. These bones are the bony knobs at the base of your pelvis. While sitting you can feel them by reaching under the side of the fleshy part of each buttock. Raise your buttock slightly and slide your fingers, palm up, well under you. Gradually lower your weight onto your fingers until you feel a bony protuberance. This is it! Do both sides, and you are "in touch" with your sitting bones. They are called our sitting bones precisely because they are meant to be sat upon to keep us from slumping. Now take your hands out. Still sitting, feel your sitting bones making contact with the chair while bending slightly forward at the hips. Now "walk" your buttocks back one step each and keep your spine straight. Resume an upright position. Feel the difference? Sitting on them maintains a proper pelvic tilt — and your pelvic basin is full, just as it should be.

Sitting on your sitting bones requires the lower back or waist to be pulled inward to maintain the lower spine's natural curve. This action, in turn, requires good strong abdominal and back muscles. Sitting in a good posture will generate strength in these areas. Likewise, strong abdominal and back muscles will facilitate good posture.

Work Moves

Something really exciting is happening to women and their bodies. "According to the latest Women's Sports Foundation survey, 62 percent of American women over age eighteen exercise regularly."[6] We are not

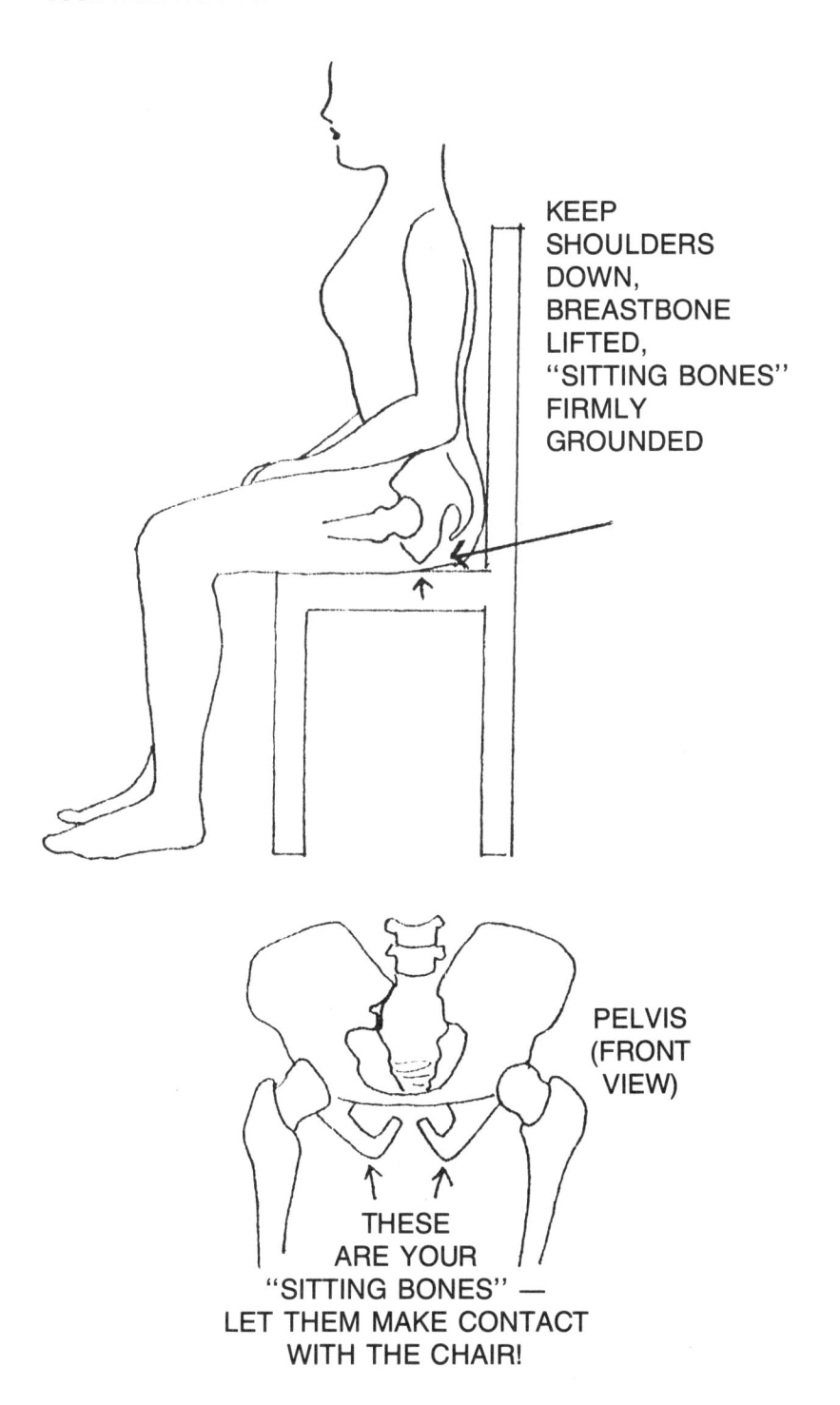

KEEP SHOULDERS DOWN, BREASTBONE LIFTED, "SITTING BONES" FIRMLY GROUNDED

PELVIS (FRONT VIEW)

THESE ARE YOUR "SITTING BONES" — LET THEM MAKE CONTACT WITH THE CHAIR!

certain what percentage of that 62 percent are women who are working full-time. But we do know that the fitness craze of the 80s has caught on; many working women do exercise, either through a fitness program offered by their employer or on their own. It takes time, commitment, organization, and discipline to schedule exercise into an already fully packed workday. But the benefits of feeling so much better in body, mind, and spirit help keep that motivation and dedication strong.

In the Foreword to *The Bodywise Woman* by the Melpomene Institute for Women's Health Research, Billie Jean King so wisely says, in relation to her being physically active, "The sensation of being 'at home' with my body is something I never take for granted."[7] None of us can afford to take our bodies for granted, especially if we are working. We, therefore, have designed an exercise program to help you feel more "at home" with your body throughout your workday.

Refer to Appendix I for safe and simple exercises you can easily do at work. Besides nurturing your body, they will help improve your posture, relieve tension and stress, and increase circulation.

Moves for Pelvic Health

Even though this exercise doesn't relate specifically to the workplace, it's presented here so that more women will be aware of the importance of maintaining well-toned pelvic-floor muscles. Pregnant women usually learn the importance of doing pelvic-floor exercises (nicknamed "The Kegel") from either their caregiver, childbirth education class, or through their pregnancy and birth readings. Like any unused muscle, pelvic-floor muscles become weak if not regularly exercised. Weak pelvic-floor muscles can contribute to "female" problems such as prolapse of the uterus, bladder, rectum, or vagina. Stress incontinence (uncontrollable urination when sneezing, coughing, or exercising) can also occur if pelvic-floor muscles are weak. In extreme cases hysterectomies may need to be done to correct the problem. Fortunately, simple regular exercise of your pelvic-floor muscles can prevent these potential problems from occurring. (Do your women friends a favor and pass this valuable information along to them, especially to those who may not know about it from a pregnancy.)

The "Kegel" Exercise

Each woman has a set of muscles on her pelvic floor that roughly forms a figure eight around the three openings on her pelvic floor (urethra, vagina, anus). These muscles provide support to the bladder, vagina, and rectum. They constantly have to defy gravity. If they are weak, the muscles will begin to sag like everything else — just like an overloaded bookshelf. Besides preventing medical problems, well-toned pelvic-floor muscles are supposed to enhance your sexual experience during lovemaking; thus, the "Kegel" has also been called a "sexercise."

To understand how to exercise these muscles, try to stop the flow of urine the next time you urinate. You will feel a pulling upward and inward of these muscles. These are your pelvic-floor muscles.

When you practice your "Kegel" imagine, as you contract your pelvic-floor muscles, that they are on an elevator ride going up to the first, second, and third floors. Each level up try to increase the muscle tension. When you have pulled up as high as you can, keep them contracted for a count of 5 to 10; then slowly, with control, release back to the beginning. In the beginning there may be a tendency to tighten the thighs and buttocks and raise the shoulders. With practice, eventually you'll be able to just contract the pelvic floor muscles while keeping the rest of your body relaxed.

Try to do 10 a day on a regular basis for the rest of your life. Associating doing this with some other activity can be a helpful reminder. A good time might be during your commute to work or while waiting in grocery lines and so on.

Practicing Good Body Mechanics

Our workday requires us to use our bodies in a variety of ways. In addition to practicing the exercises in Appendix I, make certain you continue to be kind to your body by being aware of:

1. *How to pick up objects without hurting your back:*
   Never bend over with a rounded back or straight legs.
   Always protect your back by bending your knees while bending forward from the hips NOT from the waist, which rounds the back, causing strain.
   Use the strength of your legs and arms to lift, not your back.
2. *How to carry your purse and/or briefcase:*
   Habitually carrying a purse, especially if it's a shoulder purse and/or a briefcase, can strain neck, shoulder, and back muscles. To help prevent problems, avoid always carrying it on the same side — switch sides every so often. If you carry a shoulder purse, you can wear the strap across your body to help displace the weight. (So much for fashion! Start a trend.) When carrying a briefcase, hold it in front of you against your body to help support the weight, especially if you are experiencing neck and shoulder tension.

THE HEAVY BURDEN OF SUCCESS?

3. *How to hold your phone:*
   When using a hand phone, a common posture we use is to cradle the phone with our shoulder, which frees up our hand. Chronic use of this position can strain the neck and shoulder. Instead, be aware of keeping your head centered while holding the phone to your ear with your hand. Also, try to switch sides from time to time. If you must use your hands while talking, obtain a phone cradle or shoulder rest that can be easily attached to the receiver, which helps to eliminate strain. There are two sizes. The smaller one is more esthetically appealing but the larger model offers better support.

Beat the Rush Before It Beats You

The tick-tock of the clock (or more currently, "the blinking of digital numbers") can mean different things to different people. It can be heard as a threat for you to hurry up or as a signal that you have plenty of time. If you know you are usually in a rush and barely have a moment to accomplish things, or you are in doubt about your relationship with "old man time," then perhaps you might want to consider what causes you to feel time-pressured. *The Relaxation and Stress Reduction Workbook* describes six symptoms of poor time management:

1. Rushing.
2. Chronic vacillation between unpleasant alternatives.
3. Fatigue or listlessness with many slack hours of nonproductive activity.
4. Constantly missed deadlines.
5. Insufficient time for rest or personal relationships.
6. The sense of being overwhelmed by demands and details and having to do what you don't want to do most of the time.[8]

If you live your workday experiencing any or all of the above symptoms on an ongoing basis, then it's "high time" for you to examine your rela-

HOW DO YOU FILL YOUR DAY?

tionship with the clock. Chronic rushing and feeling time-pressured is physically stressful. Whether you're literally running to catch the elevator, or sitting in a meeting worrying about running to catch the elevator, the cumulative negative impact on your health is essentially the same. This is a powerful argument in favor of time management for the sake of your body, just as Chapter Three demonstrated how the effective use of time can benefit your emotionality. Refer back to that chapter to review time-management principles and suggestions.

Another dimension of time management is making decisions. The slang term "getting bent out of shape" is a good one. Think of some of the mental gyrations we go through over "Should I" or "Shouldn't I," "If only I did" or "If only I didn't." Heavy-duty major decisions will often require that we get bent out of shape, but most of our day-to-day decisions such as, "Should I smile at her because she never smiles at me?" or "Maybe I shouldn't have said what I did," and so on, are really minor in the scheme of things. Such disproportionate decision-making can damage your health by triggering the stress response and causing unresolved tension in your body. When you find yourself getting stuck over making minor decisions, say to yourself, "Is it really that important to me to spend all this time and energy thinking about it?" Keep a "lighten up" button with you and push it at the first sign of struggle.

CRACKING UP TO PREVENT STRESSING OUT

Can you remember back to the last time you were totally consumed by laughter — a time when something was so hilarious you laughed hysterically? Afterward, your body felt weak from laughing so hard, but your spirits were probably soaring. Humor and laughter are just more tools of many to help you deal with stress.

Tension and stress are no joking matter, but laughter experts find that laughter can give instant relief from stress by allowing you to vent your feelings. It lifts the lid off the steam kettle. And laughing actually has a physiological effect on our bodies by decreasing the production of stress hormones (adrenaline and cortisone). In addition, "after a slight rise in heartrate and blood pressure during the laugh itself, there's an immediate recoil: muscles relax and blood pressure sinks below prelaugh levels; and the brain may release endorphins, the same stress reducers that are triggered by exercise."[9]

The late Norman Cousins, in *Anatomy of an Illness*, wrote about his discovery that long bouts of laughter eased his pain when he was suffering from a painful connective-tissue disease. Another advantage is that laughter is an easy but effective way to give your face, diaphragm, and abdomen a gentle massage. Someone once said that it takes more muscles to make a frown than it does to give a smile.

Probably the best perk of all is that humor allows us to step aside from a stressful situation and re-evaluate it. In other words, it's often our attitude or perspective that creates our stress. "Several philosophers and writers have pointed out that comedy and tragedy are different ways of looking at the same stressful event."[10]

Humor Helpers

Humor and comedy are very personal. What may be hilarious to one person might seem plain stupid to another. Here are some suggestions to help you tickle your funny bone.

1. Keep at work a few of your favorite books of cartoons or jokes. Or make your own book of humor by collecting funny jokes/cartoons from newspapers and magazines. During your break read through them.
2. During stressful times make it a point to watch your favorite funny movies. Make a mental note of the funniest scenes so you can replay them in your mind during times of stress.
3. Find some thread of humor in every stressful situation. Seek out co-workers who have a good sense of humor. Share your stress and look for the humor that may be lurking in the background.
4. Depersonalize your stress by seeing your favorite comedian in your place. Imagine how she/he would handle your situation.
5. Subscribe to *Laughing Matters*, a magazine published quarterly by the Humor Project, which is devoted to offering humorous solutions to stress. See Resources for address.

SCENTS MAKE SENSE

Can you remember what your favorite flower smells like? Are you able to recall what sniffing the fragrance did for you? Besides enjoying the scent, it may have also made you feel good all over. That's because there's more to smells than what meets the nose. Modern science, in fact, is studying the benefits of aroma therapy — the ancient practice of natural herbal medicine. The modern name of aromatherapy was created in the 1920s to describe the practice of using essential oils from plants, flowers, trees, herbs, and bushes for therapeutic results.

Current research is resulting in some interesting findings. One belief is that smell is our basic primal sense. It is our only sensory system that feeds directly into the limbic system of our brain where we process emotions and memories. Recent findings show that certain scents can help to diminish depression, anxiety and aggression.[11] A group of researchers who presented their findings at the American Association for the Advancement of Science reported, ". . . scents can keep people more alert and improve performance of routine tasks."[12] Two studies showed that workers given a task performed 25 percent better when receiving whiffs of peppermint oil or Lily of the Valley as opposed to those who did not receive any fragrance.[13] A large company in Japan is actually able to deliver behavior-altering scents through air-conditioning ducts to reduce stress and increase efficiency among factory and office workers.[14] So, in essence, modern science is now confirming what Egyptians knew 6,000 years ago — that certain scents can be calming and restorative while others may be stimulating and rejuvenating.

In *Aromatherapy For Women*, author Maggie Tisserand says, "If we feel good within ourselves, then the outside pressures never penetrate as deeply or wound as hurtfully as when we are feeling 'low' and vulnerable. For me, using essential oils is not only therapeutic on a physical level, but also on a mental and emotional one."[15]

If the idea of aromatherapy is appealing, you can use essential oils in a variety of ways. Be aware that they are potent and only a drop or two needs to be used to be effective.

For Smelling: Use a few drops on a tissue.
For Massage: Use a few drops in a pure vegetable oil.
For Perfume: Use a minute amount directly on the skin.
For Bathing: Use a few drops added to your bath water.

Every work environment has its own scent and often not the most pleasing ones. To help freshen your "space," you could use light citrus oils like lemon, rosewood, bergamot, or melissa. Out of consideration for your co-workers, first check with them to see if using any of the above scents would bother them. Place a few drops on a tissue or cotton ball and keep it near you.

In general, the following scents are recommended:

To Calm, Soothe and Relax	*To Stimulate, Refresh and Invigorate*
Lemongrass	Peppermint
Lavender	Rosewood
Geranium	Lemon
Rose	Bergamot
Pine	Basil
Tangerine	Rosemary
Ylang-Ylang	Spearmint

Natural essential oil can usually be obtained at health food stores. (For further information, refer to Resources.) Another delightful way to surround yourself with a refreshing scent is to keep a vase filled with your favorite-smelling flower(s). It's easy to take a whiff whenever you feel the need to alter your sense.

FOOD FOR THOUGHT

Not another lecture on diet and nutrition! Well, don't think of it as a lecture; instead, think of the following comments as "food for thought" on foods we eat at work and how they might affect us under stress.

Many car owners like to use high grades of gas to keep their cars in good condition. Applying the same principle to our bodies makes good sense. Food not only is fuel for "running" our body, but it also nourishes it with vital minerals and vitamins. Just as we fertilize our plants to produce beautiful and healthy leaves and flowers, we also need to feed our bodies well to keep them flourishing. Eating poor food could mean that the body may break down and need frequent servicing — just as an uncared-for car does.

Our goal is not to provide you with a specific diet because satisfying one's appetite in a healthy way is very individual, ranging from being a meat eater to being a strict vegetarian, both of which can provide good nutrition. Our purpose is to make you more aware of the impact that our diet has on our bodies, especially in relation to stress. Understanding how what you eat affects your life may encourage you to modify your eating habits.

It's unfortunate that the subject of nutrition often puts people to sleep because the way the foods we eat affect us on a biochemical level can be quite fascinating. It's just that we've heard all our lives about the importance of the four food groups. And did we ever really care? Knowing in your mind what foods are good for your health is one thing. Eating the right foods is another matter. By now most of us know that the general guideline for healthy eating is to eat a high-fiber, high-carbohydrate, and low-fat diet. We ought to eliminate, or at least drastically reduce, caffeine, sugar, alcohol and, of course, smoking. If your diet hasn't been a healthy one, you might consider making some changes.

Changing habits and making new ones are challenging enough, but altering how we eat can be extremely difficult for many people. That's because we eat for many different reasons other than the obvious one of physical hunger. We also eat to feed our emotions. Eating food can be used as a way of dealing with stress. If bored, tired, angry, or frustrated, we may eat. We may seek food for comfort when depressed or eat when we want to celebrate. Our daily life, and certainly our work life, functions around eating rituals of lunch breaks and coffee breaks, whether we are hungry or not. So, changing eating habits may also mean changing your usual responses to handling stress.

Traditionally, the workplace has been a haven for those addicted to sugar, caffeine, and fat. How about the constant flow of coffee and the ever-present greasy doughnut or sweet roll greeting you in the morning? How about all the vending machines filled with soft drinks, candy, and cookies along with other favorite junk food? Although coffee breaks are given to recharge you with stimulants to keep you going, they may not be really effective.

A Sweet Dilemma

How sweet it is! It's rare when someone doesn't enjoy sweets of some kind. It's the love of sweets and their being so readily available that keeps our sweet tooth munching and our body and emotions at risk. It's 3:30 in the afternoon. You are feeling sleepy, and you are craving your favorite candy bar. What's the big deal about having a soft drink along with your candy? Sugar can trick you into thinking it will give you lots of energy because at first it does. In other words, sugar can give you a quick fix but when eaten in great amounts, it can have negative effects. It's true that when eating something sweet your blood sugar goes up, which gives you energy. But, as the old saying goes, "What goes up must come down." When you ingest a lot of sugar your pancreas gets the message to secrete insulin, a hormone that will cause the glucose (sugar) to be absorbed into your body's tissues. Under normal conditions, sugar is used up quickly. Insulin, however, likes to hang around because it takes longer to break down. Therefore, insulin will stay in your blood for several hours, removing too much sugar, thus causing your blood sugar to drop even lower than your previous blood-sugar level before you had the candy bar. This means that after your quick burst of energy, you start to feel really tired, unfocused, and perhaps irritable and depressed. When your blood-sugar levels drop, you start to crave more sugar for another hit. And so goes the see-saw effect of sugar highs and lows. Can you see how the quick fix of sugar can lead to long-term addiction?

Some signs of low blood sugar are hunger with a craving for sweets, fatigue, headaches, anxiety, irritability, and depression, none of which will serve you well in the workplace.

Solutions for the Sweet Dilemma

Grazing. Eating frequently — 4 to 5 small meals rather than 2 to 3 large meals with several hours between them will help to keep your blood-sugar levels more even.

Eating with Awareness. Eat more unrefined, complex carbohydrates, i.e., whole grains, legumes (beans, lentils, peas), nuts, seeds, fruits and vegetables. Complex carbohydrates take longer to break down to supply energy. This gradual conversion of food into fuel occurs over a period of several hours. It helps to maintain a fairly even level of blood sugar, thus avoiding the peaks and valleys of energy flow created by simple carbohydrates (refined foods containing white sugar, white flour, instant foods, etc.). Unrefined, complex carbohydrates also are rich in nutrients, whereas refined foods lack many of their vitamins and minerals. Sugar has no nutritive value.

Read Labels. Packaged food products are labeled with their contents. The ingredients are listed in order of their amount, with the most being first. If the label you read indicates that sugar is in the first few ingredients, then it's most likely high in sugar. You will be surprised how common sugar is in most packaged foods. Juice drinks often have sugar added. There are many juice beverages that are 100 percent juice, but you've got to read the label to find that out.

Bring Your Own Food to Work. Packing your own lunch and/or bringing healthy snacks does involve more time but is well worth the effort. Nuts, seeds, whole-grain crackers, yogurt, fresh fruit, carrots and celery are all good snack foods that usually satisfy a "munchie attack." Carbonated water added to juice helps to reduce its natural sugar content while making it taste more like a soft drink.

Take Turns Providing Snacks. If possible, maybe once a week or once a month, take turns providing snacks for a group of your co-workers. Sharing food makes it a more interesting, supportive, and social event.

Watch for Saboteurs. There's bound to be someone at work who may want to tease you about any new and more healthful eating habits you may assume. Seek to eat with co-workers who will offer support, or at least be non-judgmental, and avoid the ones who may lead you to temptation (not to be confused with serpents!).

Exercise. When craving sweets or caffeine or feeling energy-depleted, instead of "climbing the walls" climb the stairs for a few floors, walk around your office and/or do some of the stretches in Appendix II. Movement stimulates your circulation, relieves tension, increases energy, and makes you feel better all over.

FAT FACTS

It's not uncommon that fats can make up 40-45 percent of an American's diet. The American Heart Association recommends that we reduce our daily fat intake to less than 30 percent of our calories, while other experts feel that 10 percent is even better. The obvious peril of excess fat is the risk of heart disease, the number-one killer of women. And it's now known that too much fat can contribute to breast and colon cancer, may aggravate adult-onset diabetes, and might increase gallstone formation. These reasons alone should be enough to say "no" to fat, but if they aren't enough, fat makes you FAT — which can cause emotional problems in addition to health concerns.

How to Fight Fat

- If you are a meat eater, choose lean cuts and cut off any visible fat before cooking.
- Eat more chicken without the skin (white meat has less fat than dark) and fish.
- If eating dairy products, use low-fat ones.
- Read labels for fat content.
- Avoid greasy, fried foods.
- Eat lots of complex carbohydrates, such as legumes and grains.

Fiber Fitness

Fiber, derived from plant foods, cannot be broken down by our digestive juices. For good health it's essential that our diet has the two types of fiber. Insoluble fiber, such as wheat bran and grains, helps to propel digested food through the intestine more quickly so that there is "less time to deposit chemical impurities and cancer-promoting compounds on the intestinal wall."[16] It also makes stools larger and softer and "the generous amount of water absorbed by the fiber dilutes any potential carcinogens in the intestines or stool itself."[17] Soluble fiber serves the body by helping to lower blood cholesterol, prevents constipation, and helps to stabilize blood sugar levels. Together they help to control weight because high fiber foods:

- need more chewing, which means you will eat slower and less
- swell within your stomach, making you feel full
- are high in nutrients and low in calories
- are used for energy

YOUR WELL-WORKING BODY

Foods high in fiber are found in whole grains, vegetables, fruits, legumes, nuts and seeds.

Caffeine Caution

To coffee lovers, there is nothing greater than the smell of freshly brewed coffee. And it tastes even better. Many of us can barely get our eyes open, let alone focused, without that first cup or two of java. If you are not hypersensitive to caffeine, one or two cups of coffee may not pose a problem.

It's when more cups are taken throughout the day that caffeine can cause trouble. Black teas, colas, and chocolate have caffeine, along with some over-the-counter drugs. Mild amounts of caffeine will make you more alert and able to concentrate. But the more one drinks, the worse one can feel. Caffeine can cause anxiety, increased heart rate, irregular heart rate, high blood pressure, and jittery, shaky feelings.

"A syndrome known as caffeinism occurs in people who drink five or more cups of coffee a day (about 500 mg. of caffeine). The syndrome is very much like anxiety neurosis, and the people affected suffer from nervousness, irritability, agitation, headache, muscle twitching and rapid heartbeat."[18] These symptoms, combined with the normal stress of work, only create more stress.

Adjusting Your Caffeine Intake

- If you decide to eliminate coffee completely, do so slowly so that you don't experience "caffeine withdrawal" symptoms such as headaches. *(If you are really addicted, having to drink several cups a day to function, it would be wise to seek a medical opinion.)*
- Switch to decaffeinated coffee, herbal teas, or roasted grain beverages that taste similar to coffee. Keep them at work.
- Read labels on cola drinks to see if the product contains caffeine. Substitute those without caffeine.

Vitamins and Minerals as Stress Busters

There is a controversy among experts regarding the use of vitamin and mineral supplementation. Those against taking vitamins claim that a well-balanced diet contains all the nutrients needed. Those who advocate taking vitamins believe that even if a diet is nutritionally sound, it could still be lacking in all the necessary vitamins and minerals for the following reasons:

- Fresh fruit and vegetables lose vitamins as they sit out.
- Canned and frozen foods lose some nutrients during processing.
- Stress quickly uses up vitamins and minerals, especially vitamin B complex, vitamin C, and magnesium.[19]

If you decide to take vitamins, it would be wise to consult with your physician or a professional trained in nutrition so that you will be taking the right kinds of vitamins along with the right dosage. Some can be toxic in too high a dosage, and some need to be taken with others to be effective.

Smoking

We are assuming that in this day and age everyone knows the harmful effects of smoking and/or exposure to smoke. We urge you to quit if you are a smoker. There are numerous ways to stop smoking. See Appendix IV for Resources.

Alcohol

Alcohol is obviously not appropriate while working. This includes lunches — business or otherwise — during the workday.

Processed Foods

Our sisters of yesteryear didn't have to worry about reading food labels. They ate an abundance of plant life naturally rich in nutrients and fiber. It seems the more civilized we become, the more refined our foods have become. Highly refined and processed foods, however, are lacking in fiber and essential nutrients. The very terms "refined" and "processed" mean that the original form, which was perfect to begin with, has been altered to a less-than-perfect food. Our fast-paced lifestyle, combined with fast-food meals, encourages the use of processed foods. But, think about it: It doesn't take any longer to toast a whole-grain piece of bread than bread made from processed flour. The same concept applies to whole-grain pastas and rice (brown rice, however, does take longer to cook, but it's well worth the extra time). Be kind to your body by eating foods with awareness, just as Eve did.

Nature's Tonic

To work well, our body needs about eight glasses of water a day. Inadequate water intake will cause dehydration, which can lead to an overall feeling of fatigue. Water helps to prevent constipation and fluid retention (swollen ankles), rids the body of built-up toxins, and helps to maintain proper muscle tone. And, if those aren't enough good reasons, ample water aids in fat control. So start guzzling!

WRAPPING IT UP

How's that old serpent doing? It must be chattering away in your mind about all the things you know you really *should* do and feel so guilty for *not* doing, but you *just* don't have the time for; and why try to start a program when you *really* can't maintain it, but you *know* your lower back hurts, and you could stand to lose 15 pounds?

In case you feel overwhelmed reading about the bodily problems work can create, or in case you have started physical self-care programs before and haven't stuck with them, think of each exercise/tool presented here as a piece of juicy fruit, gradually ripened from a bud into a blossom to motivate you toward either pleasure or pain. Pick the "apples" that look the ripest to you, and begin to nibble on them; you can work up to bigger chunks. For any alteration in behavior to feel successful, you must begin by biting off only what you can chew right now. As you have progressed through this book, you will have found many ways to improve your emotional and spiritual well-being and your physical self on the job. Aim for gradual improvement in each area, trusting that wellness in one area will support and reinforce wellness in the other two. If you are unclear as to which techniques are the "best," choose the ones that seem best for *you*. Listen to where the wise serpent is making the most noise: where your body is most uncomfortable. Remember: an "apple" a day really does keep the doctor away!

CHAPTER NINE
Weeding Your Garden of Eden

Okay, okay. So Eve gets herself kicked out of Eden. She checks the classified ads looking for suitable employment and/or a place to live:

> SCRIBE NEEDED: MUST BE SKILLED WITH STYLUS AND CLAY TABLET. 150 CHARACTERS PER MINUTE. EXPERIENCE NECESSARY.

> RENT-A-TENT: FINEST SKIN DWELLINGS. DESERT SUNSETS. HAUL OWN WATER.

This probably doesn't sound too thrilling after languorous days in the equivalent of Tahiti or some such idyllic place. Eve finds that she must continually adapt in order to survive, dealing with fluctuations in temperature, precipitation, uneven ground, no furniture to speak of, poor office equipment (clay tablets!?), and the presence of aromatic animals — doesn't sound like a desirable work milieu.

Today's gleaming office buildings are habitats with controlled temperature and humidity, artificial lighting, cubicles, work stations, and electronic wonders of all sorts. All of these are, in their own way, attempts to structure a stable, productive environment. However, even the most carefully designed complexes are often not only uncomfortable in their artifice but they also put employees physically at risk. The air, lighting, seating and space accommodations are just a few of the factors which, ironically, can produce the opposite effect of what's intended.

Many work sites are hermetically sealed, providing no access to fresh air. Many offices do not even provide windows to let in daylight; if there are windows, they cannot be opened. Employees often don't know if it's rainy or sunny, and there is an eerie sense that it could just as well be nighttime as daytime.

In the last decade there has been global attention to caring for our planet, Earth. Recycling has become a household word, and air pollution is a vital concern to everyone. This same concern for well-being needs to be applied to our working environment. Where and how we work varies greatly, from the executive suite to the assembly line. Regardless of the type of work we perform, all our jobs impose certain physical stresses upon our bodies, depending on the level of noise, the kind of lighting, the quality of the indoor air, and the kinds of physical movements and demands our work requires.

Many of the potential physical hazards that working women face are beyond the scope of this book. Excellent books have already thoroughly addressed these concerns (See Resources). The major focus of this chapter will be on the physical challenges that we do have control over, such as our posture and movements at work. Because using a video display terminal (VDT) is so much a part of office life, there is a separate section on the potential problems associated with its use. Choosing the correct office chair will also be addressed.

ENVIRONMENTAL DIS-EASE

"It's not that I'm sick of work; it's just that my work is making me sick. Actually, my office is sick, and I caught what it has." This woman is referring to a modern condition known as "sick-building syndrome" or "tight-building syndrome." Many physical symptoms can be present. Common ones, similar to flu-like symptoms, are itchy eyes, sore throat, congestion, wheezing, dry skin, tightness in the chest, headaches, and drowsiness. "Sick-building syndrome" evolved as a result of the energy crisis in the 70s. Because of the great desire to economize on energy use, buildings were hermetically sealed so that windows couldn't be opened, and thick layers of insulation were installed to hold in warm or cool air. Some buildings have made ventilation systems more efficient by having outside vents close automatically when the outdoor temperature moves above or below a certain point. This means that the building's air continues to recirculate without access to fresh air. The indoor air not only becomes stale but continues to recirculate trapped chemicals, molds, and bacteria.

According to an article in *U.S. News & World Report*, studies by the National Institute for Occupational Safety & Health (NIOSH) and the Environmental Protection Agency, as well as university researchers, confirm that buildings can make people ill. "A NIOSH study blames about one-half of the cases on poor ventilation. The other half are a combination of bad air coming in from outside; specific inside sources, such as copy machines and electrical equipment, and microbes such as mold and fungi."[1] Some things that contribute to office air pollution are: free-floating fibers from insulation linings and air ducts, cigarette smoke, chemicals from paints and cleaning materials, adhesives in carpeting, formaldehyde (used in carpeting and particle board), glues (used in furniture and dry wall), office supplies, ozone from copying machines, dust and fungi from dirty air vents, and poorly organized office space. People themselves unknowingly contribute to office air pollution by wearing perfumes, deodorants, and cosmetics, using hair spray at work, and smoking. All these, among other potential contaminants mixed with the carbon dioxide produced by many workers, can create — if the building is not well ventilated and maintained — a severely polluted atmosphere.

Gary Crawford, vice president of Boelter Environmental Consultants and a certified industrial hygienist, explains: "There is rarely only one cause of a sick building; it is usually the result of a very complex situation." He also likes to point out that "many of the physical symptoms of a sick building, such as headache, difficulty breathing, and fatigue are also symptoms of emotional stress and anxiety. In this day and age, most of us at work, regardless of our profession, are confronted by a tremendous amount of stress." He makes his point not to downplay the validity of sick-building syndrome but to illustrate how highly complicated the factors are in diagnosing a building as sick.

ENVIRONMENTAL EASE

For many of us, gone are the good old days when you could simply open a window to allow fresh air to perk you up or to feel the pleasure of a breeze. But whether or not you have the luxury of opening your office window, there are many things you can do if you suspect that you and your office are showing symptoms of sick-building syndrome. First and foremost, seek medical treatment from a qualified medical doctor. (Keep in mind that some physicians may not be familiar with sick-building syndrome.) It's always possible that you could be suffering from an underlying medical condition that's giving you symptoms similar to those caused by a sick building. Once it's established by your doctor that you are suffering as a result of sick-building syndrome, obtain a written diagnosis. In addition:

- Contact the building management and/or personnel department and share your concerns.
- Poll your co-workers to see how many others have symptoms.
- Keep a daily log of your symptoms at work. Note whether they ever subside or stop when away from work.
- If your building is vulnerable to carbon monoxide (being next to a loading dock or where the air intake system is near an alley or street where cars and buses idle, or close to an exhaust pipe, a furnace or chimney), it would be wise for the management to have a carbon monoxide indicator test available in the building. They can be obtained at safety supply stores listed in the Yellow Pages.
- Obtain NIOSH's (National Institute for Occupational Safety & Health) pamphlet "Indoor Air Quality" (1-800-356-4674).

If your complaints are not being taken seriously and/or you wish to remain anonymous, you can contact:

- OSHA (Occupational Safety and Health Administration), a federal government agency that investigates unsafe workplaces. The Washington, D.C. office (202-523-8148) can give you the phone number and address of your regional office. OSHA is required to respond to complaints and will not disclose your name if you request it. They employ trained staff to diagnose sick-building syndrome.
- Contact your local and state health departments.

BEWARE THE CHAIR

A "couch potato" is a comic reflection of someone at home who flops on the couch, assuming the shape of a banana and doesn't do much more than a potato. You may or may not be a "couch potato" at home. But, quite possibly, you could be a "chair potato" at work when it comes to the kinds of positions you are forced to assume when sitting in office chairs.

Nature created us with bodies designed to perform best when standing and moving. We need to use them properly to maintain and enhance their artistic design. But unlike cave women who spent their days roaming the land, we who work in an office spend most of our working hours sitting. We sit not only at work but during the commuting time and then sit once again at home. According to Dr. Herbert Junghanns, a world-renowned spine specialist, "Sitting, no matter in which of the many positions it is performed, is and remains the worst posture for the human body."[2] Throughout long hours of sitting incorrectly, our bodies easily give way to the shape of the chair, potentially causing any number of problems: muscle spasms, tension, fatigue, poor circulation, spinal disc problems, varicose veins, problems with the neck, shoulders, and entire back and even thrombophlebitis, an inflammation of the veins.

Poorly designed office chairs, coupled with bad posture, keep surgeons, osteopaths, chiropractors, and massage therapists in business and you in discomfort and pain. Besides being uncomfortable, an inappropriate chair also creates distractions which can lead to a decrease in productivity. The best device is what's called an "ergonomic" chair, a chair engineered to be compatible with human anatomy in a way that facilitates production.

Typically, office chairs are designed for the average person. But what constitutes being average, and who is average to begin with? If you don't qualify as average, and your chair is not adjustable, you are stuck in a chair meant for Ms. Average. If it's too high it will cause you to have to bend forward to reach your work surface. If your feet can't touch the floor your circulation can be compromised. Too low a chair can strain your back. Too soft a seat cushion doesn't provide enough support, which contributes to low-back problems. If the cushion fabric isn't porous the pelvic area coming in contact with the cushion can't breathe properly. Hours of sitting on such fabric could contribute to bladder infections and vaginitis. Support for the lower back may be inadequate or not adjustable to meet your specific needs, again potentially causing low-back pain.

Even though your office chair may be one of the few things in your work environment that can be individually geared to your needs, it often may be more pleasing to look at than to sit in. Your comfort and well-being begins with a good, ergonomically correct chair.

Sitting Pretty

Silence no more for the sitting majority! Fortunately, our age of increased health awareness, safety, and prevention has ushered in ergonomics — the art of adapting and designing the workplace to meet the needs of its workers. Ergonomics has helped to fine-tune office chairs by combining form and function.

To increase your sitting pleasure and productivity while decreasing discomfort and pain, your hips and knees should be at right angles, and your feet should rest flat on the floor. Your chair should:

- Adjust to both your body and working needs.
- Adjust for height and angle.
- Provide a built-in back support, ideally 4–6 inches above the seat cushion. (If not, obtain a lumbar [lower back] support cushion available in orthopedic supply stores, pharmacies, and mail-order catalogues.)

As far as the chair structure is concerned, there are ergonomic guidelines:

- Seat size should end about 5 inches behind the bend of the knees when you are sitting straight with your spine against the back.
- Seat-cushion material should be porous and breathable (wool and rayon breathe well, whereas plastic and synthetics do not) and should be textured to prevent sliding.
- The chair should allow you to lean back slightly without forcing the seat to come up, which raises your feet off the floor. (Sitting back helps to open up your body, which lengthens the spine and increases circulation.)
- It should have adjustable arm rests to take weight off the neck and shoulders.
- The front edge of the seat should be rounded.
- The base of the chair should provide good stability (5-pronged base is better than 4-pronged), and the casters should not roll too easily or too slowly.
- If working at a VDT it's best to have a chair that's able to tilt forward, which takes pressure off the spine, with a kidney-shaped back rest which fits snugly against the lower back.

The best antidote for prevention of physical problems and/or to relieve discomfort is to be aware of and maintain good posture and to stand up at every opportunity (while talking on the phone or to co-workers). Take a standing, stretching, walking break whenever possible. Practice the exercises in Appendix II.

"TERMINAL ILLNESS" — VIDEO DISPLAY TERMINALS

We all know how the amazing invention and use of computer technology has affected our lives professionally and personally. We benefit from obtaining "magical" instant information and time-saving procedures, but can using computers also lead to long-term health problems? Critics have several concerns for video display terminal users. They believe that long-term use can potentially cause eye strain, postural problems, repetitive motion injuries, physical and psychological stress, and harmful exposure to electromagnetic radiation. According to the pamphlet *VDT Syndrome*, published by the 9 to 5 National Association of Working Women and Service Employees International Union, AFL-CIO, CLC, "The surge of VDT workers suffering severe wrist pain, vision disorders, back strain and stress has prompted various scientific investigations into the health hazards of VDT jobs." The publication goes on to cite a study stating, "VDT work was associated with higher rates of many stress symptoms, such as headaches, and gastrointestinal, musculoskeletal and menstrual problems." Let's take a closer look at some of these concerns.

Using the VDT is extremely vision-demanding. "According to the experts, the most common health complaints by VDT users involve eye problems ranging from general discomfort, burning, tearing, headaches, and tiredness to frequent changes in prescriptions for glasses. Preliminary research from the School of Optometry at the University of California at Berkeley shows that working regularly at a VDT may cause some individuals to need reading glasses prematurely."[3] It's also thought that many people have marginal vision problems that may not always be apparent until further stressed by VDT use.

Eye strain from VDT use can be caused by prolonged staring at the screen and from your eyes having to shift continuously from the screen to material you are using to enter data. The size and sharpness of the letters can contribute to eye strain. Letters that are small and/or fuzzy-looking will be more difficult to read. Any glare from overhead lights or windows, or brightness from painted walls and ceilings or shiny office furniture can cause eye strain. Flickering of a screen's image will also strain the eyes. Postural adjustments to adapt to an inadequate VDT work station can be another challenge for your eyes. Those who wear contact lenses may be prone to dryness of the eyes from the decrease in blinking caused by staring at the screen. Screens that are immovable will challenge those who wear reading glasses or bifocals. Depending on your prescription, you may have to lean forward or back or tilt your head to read the letters properly.

Easing Eye Strain

9 to 5 suggests you get your eyes examined before you begin VDT work by an eye doctor knowledgeable about VDTs. Write down all information regarding your work and the demands made on your vision. Measure the distance from your eyes to objects you look at most frequently — especially the VDT. Note any health symptoms especially relating to your eyes. Obtain yearly follow-up exams if under 40; if over 40, every six months. 9 to 5 also recommends, to prevent unnecessary glare:

- Avoid placing VDT on a light-colored or shiny desk top.
- Nearby walls should not be white or off-white.
- Avoid wearing white-colored tops.
- Place screen at right angle to windows.
- Tilt screen away from reflection, if possible.
- Remove any shiny, reflective objects such as glass-covered pictures behind the VDT.
- Keyboards should have a matte finish.

Other guidelines are:
- Keep lights about half as bright as normally needed for other office duties.
- Diffuse direct window light by using drapes or blinds.
- Shut off light above computer and use adjustable task lighting.
- Obtain diffusing grids for ceiling lights to direct light down.
- Use a glare-reducing screen.
- Place a document holder in such a position that the letters on the screen and on the paper you're working from are about the same size to avoid having to refocus each time your eyes move between screen and paper.
- Vary brightness, contrast, and color if your computer can be adjusted.
- Make certain the screen has no visible flickering and that the letters are sharp, not fuzzy.
- The screen should be placed 16–24 inches from your eyes. If you are farsighted, you may need corrective lenses to prevent blurring. If you wear bifocals, they may need to be adjusted. They are usually designed for a downward viewing angle of 25 degrees, which is greater than the 10–20-degree angle for VDT work.
- Relax your eyes during your 15-minute "eye break" by: alternately focusing on near and distant points; rubbing the palms of your hands together for a minute until they are warmed and then cupping them over your closed eyes for 30–60 seconds — then slowly lower your hands as you gently open your eyes.
- Make certain your VDT screen is cleaned on the outside by you and inside by a qualified technician.

Wrist Watch and More

Hours of key punching can put a tremendous strain on the wrists, arms, shoulders, and back. 9 to 5 states, "Key stroke rates exceeding 12,000 strokes per hour (40 words per minute) are directly related to CTD (cumulative trauma disorder) and other injuries. Productivity, incentives, key strokes monitoring and overtime are major contributing factors."[4] The constant repetitive motion can make one vulnerable to RSI (repetitive strain injury, otherwise referred to as CTD, cumulative trauma disorder). RSI is a physical condition which results from the overuse of muscle tendons causing inflammation, swelling, and pain. According to the Bureau of Labor and Statistics, RSI now accounts for over 50 percent of all reported occupational injuries. This increase in injuries is due to the fact that today's jobs are faster, more streamlined, and increasingly repetitive, compared with yesterday's. Prior to word processors, typists had a variety of skills to perform involving different movements like changing the paper and making margin adjustments. Word processors, however, enable workers to move 40 percent faster. Having no pauses is great for productivity but can be stressful to the worker.

RSI can occur anywhere in our bodies, but our focus will be on where it occurs as a result of VDT use — the wrist, arm, and shoulder. Carpal tunnel syndrome, a common example of RSI, is a condition of the wrist and hand that results from repetitive motion. It results when keyboards are too high or improperly designed, causing the hands and wrists to angle up over the keys with the forearm hanging down. In time, when the wrist is constantly being flexed, the sheaths surrounding the tendons (carpal tunnels) become stretched, inflamed, and swollen. This swelling puts pressure on the median nerve that runs through the carpal tunnel into the hand, causing tingling, numbness, burning, tenderness, and pain. Without intervention, real disability can occur. Grasping, holding, or handling objects can become increasingly difficult and punching the keyboard next to impossible.

If the serpent isn't hissing loudly enough, there are other assaults. The quick flexing of the wrist and fingers can cause pain in the wrist and the back of the hand called tenosynovitis. Constant pressure on the ulnar nerve which also passes through the wrist can irritate the nerve, which can lead to a condition called ulnar neuropathy. There are more. Occupational Cervical Brachial Syndrome is a long name for a painful condition of the shoulder, back, neck, and arm. It's caused by a lack of support for the arms while using the VDT. Also, Thoracic Outlet Syndrome is caused by compression of the nerves between the neck and shoulders. Its symptoms (numbing in the fingers and tingling in the arms) are similar to Carpal Tunnel Syndrome, but the cause and treatment are different. Because of this difference, it's important that a correct diagnosis be made. Not all keyboard users develop RSI, but for those who do develop symptoms it's important for them to seek treatment.

Wrist Rest

The key to keyboard comfort is prevention. Most RSI injuries and, specifically, Carpal Tunnel Syndrome, can be prevented by using intelligent work habits, well-designed work stations, and the conscientious support of the employer.

9 to 5 suggests:
- Keyboard work should comprise no more than one-half of the work on any given day.
- Build in rest breaks — preferably one hour of keyboard work alternated with one hour of another type of work.
- Keyboard should be positioned at a level close to the height of the elbows so the forearms are parallel to the floor. Conventional desks are too high.
- Ideally, the keyboard should adjust to your needs and size. If not, you definitely need a chair that adjusts.
- Arm rests can help support your forearms but should be short enough to allow your chair to move up close to your work space.
- You need to hold your wrists in a neutral position so they aren't bent backward or downward. Ideally, there should be a large enough surface supporting the keyboard to also support your wrists.

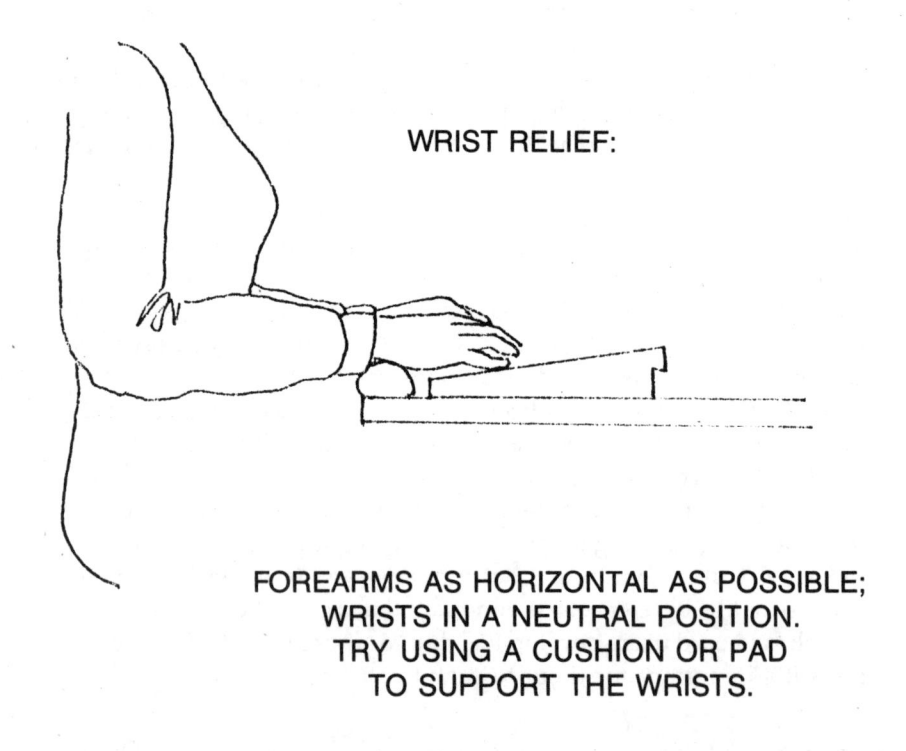

WRIST RELIEF:

FOREARMS AS HORIZONTAL AS POSSIBLE; WRISTS IN A NEUTRAL POSITION. TRY USING A CUSHION OR PAD TO SUPPORT THE WRISTS.

If you should develop RSI symptoms, such as pain, tenderness, numbing, tingling, and so on, definitely analyze your work environment and habits to see how they might be altered; more importantly, seek immediate qualified medical help. Bear in mind the following, from a recent report in the *Journal of the American Medical Association* by Dr. David

M. Rempel, which states that there is not a lot of medical research on RSI: "Many physicians are unable to identify patients working in high-risk environments and are inadequately prepared to treat patients with symptomatic disorders. . . . Medical intervention for the patient with (a disorder) requires not only accurate diagnosis and appropriate therapy, but also direct involvement in changing the patient's work environment."[5] Besides seeing a medical doctor such as your internist or an orthopedic surgeon, you could also consult with a qualified physical therapist or chiropractor.

Postural Problems and the VDT

Working at a VDT station can certainly challenge our posture. The chair can be too high, too low, or too deep. The keyboard may not be the appropriate height. The screen may be too hard to see due to glare, poor lighting, inadequate letters, or eye strain. Any or all of these conditions invite poor posture — slouching, rounding the back and/or shoulders, leaning the neck forward or too far backward. Poor posture in any form will cause any of the neck, shoulder, and back muscles to tense and even spasm, resulting in discomfort ranging from mild to severe.

Emotional Stress

Stress — which NIOSH recognized as one of the top ten occupational dangers — is higher among computer users than among other types of office workers. Certainly any of the physical problems already discussed will also contribute to emotional discomfort. Office computers have turned once varied clerical tasks into assembly-line motions. Hours and hours of this monotonous sameness can play havoc with our emotions. Boredom, apathy, depression, frustration, irritability and anger can have a sandpaper effect on work enjoyment, wearing it down until simple tasks feel like drudgery. Computer technology has also enabled employers to monitor their employees' productivity through electronic surveillance. The computer can monitor keystrokes, errors, rates, time spent on each task and even bathroom breaks. It's easy to understand how this kind of monitoring is both intimidating and stressful. It's unfortunate that in some instances productivity takes precedence over physical and emotional well-being.

Easing Terminal Stress

Prevention, once again, can eliminate or ease many of the potential physical or emotional problems associated with computer use. However, symptoms can be overlooked in the early stages, or not credited as job-related because they develop gradually and may be attributed to a variety of different factors. In general, NIOSH recommends a 15-minute break for every two hours of VDT work with moderate demands and a 15-minute break every hour with intensive use. 9 to 5 recommends alternating one hour of VDT work with one hour of another type of work.

Catching Some Rays? (especially if you are pregnant)

Electromagnetic fields surround computer monitors. The concern is whether or not extremely low frequency (ELF) magnetic fields can cause some forms of cancer and, for women, miscarriages and/or birth defects to babies born to mothers who use VDTs. To the lay person, the information available on the potential harm of ELFs is confusing, to say the least. In 1991 NIOSH released the results of a study they did on 2,430 female telephone operators in eight southeastern states, half of whom used VDTs and half of whom did not. The study concluded that, "The use of VDTs and exposure to the accompanying electromagnetic fields were not associated with an increased risk of spontaneous abortion."[6] It is important to note that the results of this study related only to the problem of miscarriage. NIOSH is still looking into the effect of VDTs on birth, low birth rate, and premature birth, but the results won't be known for another year or so.

Diana Roose, research director for 9 to 5, believes it's important that the NIOSH study was done but points out that it does not close the door on the question of whether VDTs are harmful. Obviously, more definitive studies need to be done regarding potential health risks of working with VDTs. Fortunately 9 to 5 is cooperating with Mount Sinai Medical Center in New York City to study a broad range of health issues for working women, especially the effect of VDTs on pregnancy. Several thousand women will have been studied for several years. The results of the study won't be available for 2-3 years.

Avoiding Rays

Until more is known about VDTs and potential health risks, 9 to 5 suggests that if you are pregnant and working at a VDT, ask for a transfer to a position that doesn't require VDT exposure. If this is impossible, turn off the VDT when it is not in use. All VDT workers, whether pregnant or not, can lessen radiation by keeping at least an arm's-length away. Monitor emissions are stronger at the back and sides, so be certain to keep at least 3-4 feet away from other monitors that may be behind or next to you.

Older monitors are more likely to emit higher levels of electromagnetic radiation. Some are now making VDTs that conform to the Swedish guidelines — some of the strictest ones on electromagnetic emissions in the world. Check with the manufacturer to see which terminals meet these standards. Liquid-crystal display (LCD) and plasma gas screens do not emit electromagnetic radiation, so these are another option. They are found on many laptop and notebook computers and on some larger screens.

YOU'VE COME A LONG WAY?

Sick environments, terrible chairs, VDT perils? Maybe that goatskin tent in the desert and that clay tablet don't sound so bad after all? Nah. Technology worked hard to create artificial Edens; there are just a few more bugs to be worked out, that's all. In the meantime, awareness leads to the incentive to change, both on an individual and societal level. Even if you're not yet in physical discomfort (and let's hope you never are!) remember to take regular mini-breaks, walk around, get some fresh air. While your workplace isn't Biosphere II, bring some plants indoors to improve both the aesthetics as well as the air. Create that tropical Arcadia around you. If Eve can't go to Eden, maybe a little bit of Eden can come to her. And if the Garden has a few weeds and you can't get rid of them yourself, talk to your co-workers and the advocacy groups who can help you with them. Do what you need to do to make your environment the healthiest it can be.

CHAPTER TEN

Hormonal Rites Of Passage At Work

The story of Eden was not written, thank goodness, as one of those deliciously trashy paperbacks replete with meaningful glances, heaving bosoms, and panting desires. (Can't you just picture what the cover of the Good Book would look like if Adam and Eve were the main characters in a drugstore novel?) In leaving out the seamier details, however, the Eve story also leaves out the practical ones: Was Eve subject to the monthly rhythm of her hormones? Did she menstruate? Have cramps? Mere speculation, of course. But, if you follow the story line, Eve was not only ushered out of Paradise with Adam; she was also doomed. From then on, so the tale goes, she would bring forth her children in pain. Is this what some mothers refer to when, after telling their prepubescent daughters what a wonderful transformation is about to take place in their bodies, they tell them it's called "The Curse"?!

The meaning of the female reproductive cycle, throughout history and in all cultures, has been fraught with mystery, taboo, prejudice . . . a good portion of which was imposed by male rulers, shamans, priests, even physicians — as witness the move to bring birth out of the home and the hands of female midwives into hospitals and the hands of male doctors. Isn't it time our society respects a woman's biological rhythm as a natural part of womanhood, that our natural healthy cycles of menstruation, pregnancy, and menopause be thought of as normal and not a disorder or disease — especially not as something "unclean" or to be joked about? At the same time, isn't it our responsibility as women to deal positively with our cycles' hormone fluctuations and transitions, whether cramps, PMS, morning sickness, or hot flashes, rather than blaming the hormones? This chapter will address three health issues that are unique to women at work: PMS, pregnancy, and menopause. It will focus on the potential problems that each of these hormonal passages may present at work, along with self-care suggestions to help women be women at work. In addition, the politics of women's health and family issues will be discussed.

PMS — ON THE JOB

Usually your well-orchestrated body plays a great symphony. But some women complain that for a few days up to two weeks before a period they feel out of tune and downright dissonant. They are referring to having PMS, or premenstrual syndrome. (Some might want to name it "Pretty Miserable Situation.") That's because there are up to 150 different physical and emotional symptoms that women can experience. Common emotional ones are anger, anxiety, depression, irritability, feeling out of control, and withdrawal. Physical ones can be bloating, breast tenderness, insomnia, headaches, fatigue, spaciness, clumsiness and food cravings, especially for chocolate, salt, and sweets. These symptoms range from minor to major reactions and can last from a few days before a period for up to two weeks.

Just what is PMS? Katherine Dalton, M.D., an English physician who has been studying PMS since 1948 and is considered to be a foremost authority on PMS, states: "The term 'Premenstrual Syndrome,' is used to embrace any symptoms or complaints that regularly come just before or during early menstruation but are absent at other times of the cycle. It is a precise definition and means that the symptoms must be present each and every month. Symptoms must occur premenstrually, and there must be a symptom-free phase each cycle. It is the absence of symptoms after menstruation that is so important in this definition."[1] The intensity and symptoms may vary from month to month, but they will always be there.

Having lived within our female bodies, we have all experienced, from time to time, signs of premenstrual changes — occasional cramping, breast tenderness, bloating and irritability, to name a few. It's important not to confuse these periodic premenstrual symptoms with PMS. Remember that for the symptoms to be PMS they must occur every month prior to menstruating, go away once the period begins and then recur sometime within two weeks before the next period.

Even though for the last fifty years PMS has been studied and treated in Europe and England, PMS wasn't fully recognized in the U.S. as a condition until about 1981. And in spite of increased awareness of PMS, researchers still don't agree on exact causes of PMS and why some women experience it while others do not.

PMS has often been thought to be caused by a hormone imbalance. A recent study from the National Institutes of Mental Health in 1991 suggests that PMS may be the result of a cyclic mood disorder that is synchronized with, but not caused by, the menstrual cycle. Other suggested causes include: "Vitamin deficiency, retention of fluids, excess prolactin (a pituitary hormone), stress, psychosomatic causes and chronic yeast infections."[2]

Regardless of the cause(s) of PMS, the symptoms are real and may affect working women. It's been estimated that 40 percent of women have PMS and that 5-7 percent have severe enough symptoms to cause some kind of problem at work.[3]

If you have been diagnosed as having PMS, you might easily identify with the following responses working women with PMS gave when asked how this condition affected them at work:

I am very irritable and find myself unable to cope with the usual pressures.
Feeling scattered.
Everything is bothersome to some degree.
Being mean.
Snapping at people and unable to focus.
Everything bothers me.
My mind just goes totally blank, and I can't deal with things.

PMS is not only a medical concern; it's also a social concern. On the one hand, it's fortunate that finally a label has been put on what many women thought was their own private "weirdness" or "hell" for several days out of each month. But the backlash is that women may be punished at work by not being promoted and by lack of respect if it's known that they have PMS. On the other side of the coin, will legitimate feelings of irritability and anger be dismissed with words like "she must be on the rag" or "feeling a little PMS, dear?" that will only enrage us more?

Lisa, who has had PMS for the past eight years, said, "There's no way I would share my PMS problems with any of my co-workers and, in particular, with my male supervisors, especially in view of the fact that many of the male doctors from whom I sought help didn't recognize PMS as a legitimate condition and would imply that 'it's all in my head.' Well, it is in my head, but in the form of migraine headache every ten days before my period."

Elizabeth states: "I've had PMS symptoms for several years. I've worked in both large and small corporations. The desire for advancement and the competition to secure it was great at all of them, regardless of their size. Because of the struggle to get ahead, I wouldn't share my problem with PMS with my female co-workers for fear that it could be used against me. And if the male doctor from whom I sought help for my symptoms couldn't give me much empathy, how can I expect my male boss to understand?"

Another woman stated she was a teacher and was afraid to reveal her challenge with PMS because she feared getting fired and not being able to get rehired. Margaret, who works in a medical position, said she was able to talk freely with her female supervisor, who was extremely supportive. Janet reports that she works in a medical position. Her PMS symptoms usually involve being irritable, crabby, and very emotional. She chooses not to share details of her PMS with anyone at work. Janet copes by charting her PMS days and makes certain not to schedule any important meetings during those days. To get through her PMS days, she's usually quiet and withdrawn during her workday, but when she gets home she vents her frustration, anger, and irritability on her husband and children.

Turning PMS into a Manageable Situation at Work

Fortunately, women no longer have to suffer silently with PMS symptoms nor feel victimized. A good way to begin dealing with PMS is to begin to reframe your thinking about it. Yes, you dread it; yes, you can't learn to love it; yes, you wish you didn't have it! But, if you do, there are ways to help you cope with it. You can use it to guide yourself to a more fulfilling life.

If you haven't already been diagnosed as having PMS by a medical authority, the first thing you'll want to do is determine if your symptoms are, indeed, related to PMS to rule out any other medical conditions that could mimic PMS. There are several excellent books on PMS that would be well worth reading so you'll be as informed as possible (see Appendix IV). Prior to your medical exam, you'll save time and money by doing thorough research. After reading the recommended books, begin by charting your symptoms in relation to your period for three months and take the results to your appointment. If you do this, your caregiver will be able to see clearly if there is a cyclic nature to your symptoms, which will help her in making a diagnosis.

A host of self-help techniques can help alleviate PMS symptoms. Diet and exercise (not again!!!) are two very important ones. Before you dismay, a PMS diet is actually the epitome of a great, healthy diet that, ideally, everyone should follow. It's similar to what was already discussed in the "Food for Thought" section in Chapter Eight. The good news is that you'll be able to eat often, but the challenging news is that you may have to eliminate some of your favorite foods. A generally agreed-upon PMS diet is as follows:

1. Eat small meals frequently to keep your blood sugar adequate.
2. Eliminate sugar, honey, and artificial sweeteners.
3. Eliminate refined carbohydrates, i.e., breads, crackers, pasta, etc., made from white flour.
4. Eat whole grain and other complex carbohydrates.
5. Eliminate caffeine — no coffee, even decaffeinated; no caffeinated teas; no colas with caffeine; no chocolate. Watch for over-the-counter drugs that may contain caffeine.
6. Adjust salt intake. Some experts feel it only needs to be eliminated if bloating is a symptom.
7. Eliminate alcohol.
8. Enjoy drinking lots of water — at least eight glasses a day.

In addition to diet, exercise regularly. Aerobic exercise seems to be especially beneficial.

Dr. Mary Lang Carney, medical director of the St. Francis Center for Women's Health in Evanston, Illinois, says, "The more self-aware a woman is, the better able she is to care for herself." So, in addition to modifying your eating habits and exercising on a regular basis, you can also consider the following:

1. Mark on your calendar your predicted PMS days so you'll know how to plan your daily events around your symptoms. Schedule your PMS days lightly.
2. Make use of self-affirmation:
   - "I am a unique being with much to offer."
   - "On days I'm feeling 'down,' I know there will be other days I'll be feeling 'up.'"
   - "And this too shall pass."
   - "My monthly cycle is just that. I will have my good days, and I will have my bad days. I'll go easy on myself."
3. Join a PMS support group.
4. Practice your favorite relaxation exercises learned in Chapter Eight.
5. During your PMS days, plan something to nurture yourself. For some women it might be a manicure, pedicure, facial, or massage. For others it could be taking a stroll through a favorite park, setting aside time to sit and listen to music, or watching a special movie. Whatever it is, treat yourself.

Dr. Linda Hughey Holt, chairman of the Department of Obstetrics and Gynecology of Rush Presbyterian North Shore Hospital in Skokie, Illinois, states:

> PMS in its most severe form may be disabling and/or require professional help to treat. While no single treatment works for all women, if self-help measures are not sufficient, women should find a gynecologist, internist, or psychiatrist familiar with medical aspects of PMS treatment (termed "late luteal phase disorder" in psychiatric jargon). PMS sufferers often have low levels of serotonin during the premenstrum. Serotonin is a chemical made in the central nervous system which affects moods, and rapid swings in estrogen and progesterone levels in the premenstrual phase of the cycle affect production of serotonin. Most women do not require medication to control PMS, but for some women hormonal manipulation or agents which increase serotonin levels can have a dramatic beneficial effect.

There is a variety of help available for women with PMS, ranging from self-care to medical care. Using both approaches should enable you to live more in harmony with your cycle.

BEING PREGNANT AT WORK

With more and more women joining the work force, being pregnant on the job is commonplace. It's important for expectant mothers and their employers/employees to view pregnancy as a normal event for which their bodies were magnificently designed, a joyful event, and usually a healthy event. But just as giving birth can be different for every woman, so can the experience of being pregnant at work vary. Much of the experience will depend upon the demands of the particular job and the uniqueness of each pregnancy. Many women feel wonderful throughout pregnancy; others may have minor complaints; and some can experience pregnancy as physically and emotionally stressful. Some women may feel like working until the moment they go into labor; others may want to take a leave of absence a few days to a few weeks before their due date; and a few may need to stop working due to medical reasons. The decision to stop working should be the mother's, along with her caregiver's input (midwife or doctor), and not because of company policy. Obviously, if you are working in any kind of situation where you feel you or your baby may be at risk, no matter how minor, you need to discuss these concerns with both your caregiver and employer to seek a transfer to a safe working environment for you and your baby.

All pregnant women will go through certain physiological changes. The potential side effects of these changes can be minor or major, depending on each woman's unique experience. The following are common changes that occur in pregnancy that may cause some physical and emotional challenges. The list is by no means complete. (Remember that this book's content is focused on the work environment of an office. If you work in any other environment, like a factory or on construction, etc., you would need to take into consideration other factors such as lifting, toxic fumes and so on. If you work at a VDT, see Chapter Nine for some cautions and hints.) These changes are normal and need to be respected by both the mother and her employer. We'd also like to indicate that, fortunately, there is an abundance of valuable information available for pregnant women. No pregnant woman should go through pregnancy, childbirth, and breast feeding uninformed. (See Appendix IV for a list of books and resources.)

First Trimester Changes

A pregnant woman's blood volume increases about 40 percent, and there is tremendous hormonal change. Fatigue and morning sickness are common symptoms during this time, and she may experience them on the job. It's important for newly pregnant women to get extra sleep, either at night and/or a catnap after work. Practicing the relaxation exercises in Chapter Eight will help.

The nausea or "morning sickness" felt typically in the first three months could be due to low blood sugar. Other symptoms of low blood sugar can be headaches and fatigue. The nausea is often more apparent in the morning because the stomach, which is empty, is secreting acid. *The Pregnant Woman's Comfort Guide* by Sherry Lynn Mims Jiménez[4] recommends that after awakening in the morning you first neutralize the acid by eating an apple, soda cracker, or potato (no skin), or by drinking a glass of milk. If you can't bear the thought of food, take two calcium tablets to neutralize the acid, which should give you enough relief within a half hour to enable you to eat something. As already discussed in Chapter Eight, it's important to eat small meals frequently in order to avoid low blood sugar. In pregnancy these small meals should include foods rich in proteins (cheese, eggs, milk, fish, chicken, nuts, tofu, etc., depending on your taste). Chewing or sucking on ice chips may help along with applying a cold cloth or ice pack to the throat.[5] Acupuncture by a licensed professional has been known to help. The hormone change can make women emotionally vulnerable. At times they may feel a little blue without knowing the cause. Kidney function increases, causing frequent urination. During this time and throughout the pregnancy, it's essential for women to practice the Kegel exercise (pelvic-floor exercise described in Chapter Eight) on a daily basis to keep the pelvic-floor muscles well toned.

Changes in Second Trimester

During these next three months your body will begin to "go public" with its pregnancy. Your weight gain will increase, along with the size of your baby and uterus. Your center of gravity shifts as your baby grows bigger, which may affect your balance. Hormonal changes have loosened your joints and softened your ligaments to accommodate your baby. Some women may feel achy, particularly in their hip joints and in the mid- to low-back. Maintaining good posture can help to ease and/or prevent some of these aches and pains. Performing the exercises outlined in Appendix I is essential in preventing and/or easing problems, especially the ones for the back, chest, and shoulders. All the exercises are safe during pregnancy unless otherwise indicated by your caregiver or if they don't feel comfortable to do. Varicose veins, which tend to be hereditary, may also occur. To avoid or relieve them, don't sit with your legs crossed. Take frequent standing and "moving around" breaks to stimulate your circulation. Practice all the leg exercises described in Appendix I several times during your workday.

Changes in the Third Trimester

Many pregnant women agree that pregnancy is one month too long. It's during the third trimester that you might begin to understand this comment. Uterine length is at its highest point, with the uterus pressing up against the diaphragm, perhaps causing shortness of breath. Stretching your arms up overhead and reaching toward the ceiling may help relieve this symptom. The weight of the baby and uterus puts a lot of pressure on the bladder, meaning even more trips to the bathroom. Fatigue and bouts of sleeplessness may also increase. Twinges of sharp pain felt low on either side of the groin may occur, especially upon quick twisting movements. Usually this pain is caused by pulling or spasms of the round ligaments that support the uterus. Moving in the direction of the pain usually helps to ease it. Avoid sudden, twisting movements to help prevent this symptom.

Rights of Pregnant Workers

A working pregnant woman has to make many decisions. Besides choosing a quality caregiver for herself and one for her baby, she also has to decide if she wants to continue to work throughout her pregnancy and/or return to work once she has her baby. Some pregnant workers may be unaware of their rights on the job. The Boston's Women's Health Book Collective wrote the following information on the rights of pregnant workers in their informative (but unfortunately out-of-print) book *Our Jobs, Our Health*. They have generously allowed us to reprint the following information:

> RIGHTS OF PREGNANT WORKERS
>
> In recent years working women have won certain legal rights that protect them from being discriminated against, or treated differently, when they are pregnant. The Federal Civil Rights Act, including the Pregnancy Disability Amendment of 1979, provide certain protections. There are also laws in various states that may be useful.
>
> Employers Must Apply Rules Equally
> - Employers cannot refuse to hire or promote a pregnant woman who can perform the major functions of the job.
> - Employers cannot demote or fire a woman because of pregnancy.
> - Employers cannot refuse to allow a woman to return to work when she has been temporarily absent because of a pregnancy related disability, but then recovers before childbirth.
> - Employers must treat women who cannot do all or part of their tasks because of pregnancy in the same way they treat workers

disabled from doing their regular work by other medical conditions: by providing light work, assistance, modified tasks or leaves.

Pregnancy Disability Must Be Treated Like Any Other Disability Under Insurance Plans

This means that pregnant women:
- must be covered for the same length of time as workers disabled by other medical conditions;
- must be covered for the same types of treatment as workers disabled by other medical conditions — for example office visits;
- must have the same policies with regard to limitations on coverage, deductibles and reimbursements applied to them as are applied to workers disabled by other medical conditions;
- must not be charged more to be covered for pregnancy;
- must not be excluded from coverage or treated differently because of marital status;
- must be judged for eligibility for coverage by the same standards as workers disabled by other medical conditions.

Unemployment Benefits

Women cannot be denied unemployment benefits merely because of pregnancy. To be eligible a woman must be able and willing to work. She cannot be voluntarily unemployed or totally disabled from all work. If a woman is fired or laid off because of pregnancy she is eligible for benefits. If she is on leave because she couldn't do her regular work and her employer didn't provide alternate work, her eligibility is unclear.

Check Your State Law for other Rights You May Have

There may be laws in your state that affect your rights as a pregnant worker. For example, in Massachusetts a woman is entitled to eight weeks maternity leave, which may be paid or unpaid depending on the employer. Her employer must treat requests for leaves for childbearing and child care in the same way he treats requests for leaves for education, travel or other personal reasons.

Enforcing Your Rights

You can enforce your rights through your union, through your employee grievance procedure if there is no union, and/or through the Equal Employment Opportunity Commission. You can also go to the state agency responsible for enforcing discrimination laws. You can get the name of the agency from your state attorney general's office. It usually is best to file grievances with both the EEOC and the state agency at the same time.

Refer to the Resource section to find out how to contact the EEOC and the Boston Women's Health Collective.

THE POLITICS OF WOMEN'S HEALTH AND FAMILY ISSUES

Comparatively speaking, little research has been done specifically on women's health. Recently this has begun to change, but the neglect of this issue borders on the outrageous. The majority of medical research is done on men, the results of which may not apply to women. For example, research on the effects of stress on the body may not take into account female and male hormonal differences. The good news, however, is that for the first time the National Institutes for Health (NIH) is currently conducting a comprehensive study of women's health, the results of which, however, won't be known until the end of this century. Until then, keep yourself as informed as possible, make responsible choices, and practice the self-care techniques learned from this book and others you read. In addition, a strong women's movement to push for changes that benefit women is essential. Women are slowly infiltrating positions of power that can influence change. The more female doctors, lawyers, judges, and politicians we have, the better heard and represented we'll be. In recent elections barely known women candidates have been able to win over their established male opponents.

Elected officials, however, will not solve the problems of the "body politic," such as the issue of the treatment of women at work based solely on their reproductive anatomy. Eve's legacy to us is our female bodies. Being a woman is truly an amazing experience. We are able to conceive and bear life's children, to nurse, nurture, and raise them. We are expected to balance a home/family life with the demands of our work and, with what's left over, pursue a personal life. Our commitment and professionalism are suspect because of our biology. We are denied upper-level and key management positions because we might value our children more than our work! This insane proposition is bad under any circumstances, but, if you are also a woman of color and/or a single mother, you have a double or triple whammy to contend with.

Birth and life are sacred and vital to the well-being of our nation, yet society/corporations are remiss in providing services and policies to support these values. So much is expected of women, yet so little aid has been offered to help working mothers (and fathers) ease the challenge of juggling so many different roles while meeting the variety of demands. Little time is left for self-care.

This book focuses on women's needs, but the issue of working fathers/families cannot be excluded. The core of dealing with the underlying causes of the moral, emotional, physical, and spiritual decay which seem to be eroding the quality of life for all people, regardless of race, gender, or age, is rooted in the family. Quality family life must take precedence if our country is to feel whole. In this day and age when going into space and exploring the cosmos is no longer news, when computer technology skills often challenge our comprehension, and when our nation is capable of mobilizing the armed forces to wage a technological war out of science fiction — it's truly incomprehensible that the country does not make available quality prenatal care for all pregnant women and a consistent, enforced corporate policy for parental/family leave. President George Bush vetoed the Family and Medical Leave Act of 1992. If the bill had passed, it would have required employers with fifty or more workers to grant up to twelve weeks of unpaid leave for a birth or adoption or for personal or family illness (e.g., to take care of a sick child, spouse, or parent).

A number of states have enacted some type of leave policy ranging from six weeks to a year but, in many cases, just for state employees. Many private businesses voluntarily offer parental leave. The Families and Work Institute, a not-for-profit research and consulting firm that explores a range of work and family issues, recently published a book, *Beyond The Parental Leave Debate*. According to this book, research done in four states showed that companies both large and small did not incur substantial costs when complying with parental-leave legislation. According to Laurie Kane, research assistant at the Families and Work Institute, 25 states and the District of Columbia have enacted some form of parental-leave legislation. To find out if your state has a parental-leave policy, contact your state's General Services phone number in the government listings in your phone directory, or you can call the Families and Work Institute at 212-465-2044. An article in *Self* magazine noted that about 60 percent of employees in medium and large companies and 85 percent of employees in small companies have jobs that provide no maternity benefits at all,[6] — a sad statistic. Maternity issues aside, what about childcare? In 1990, 66.7 percent of mothers with children under 18 were working, and almost 54 percent of mothers with children under three were employed.[7] "Of nearly six million employers, only 6,000 currently provide some sort of childcare assistance."[8] The policy of quality childcare for working women/families is of great importance. Future generations of workers should not come into the work force handicapped in some way because today's workers are ignored. Use your right to vote. Electing politicians who are aware of and support women's needs and interests is one way every woman can help bring about much-needed change. See Resources (Appendix IV) for a list of organizations devoted to women's issues and family matters.

"THE CHANGE OF LIFE" AT WORK

Gail Sheehy, who has helped lead us through many of life's passages, recently wrote an article titled "The Silent Passage: Menopause." (She has since written a book with the same title.) In the article she comments, "Over the next few years the boardrooms of America are going to light up with hot flashes."[9] Indeed, it is a fact that the baby boomers of post-World War II are now "booming" into menopause. We are more fortunate than our mothers and grandmothers who had to enter this hormonal passage alone, with little or no support. Until recently, valid recognition of "going through the change of life" was not easily given; instead of understanding and support, jokes were often made (and still are).

Fortunately, the veil of mystery surrounding menopause is at last being lifted; the subject is "coming out of the closet." Women are talking about this final hormonal passage, valuable information is being printed, and scientific research is being done.

Menopause is defined as a woman's last period. It doesn't happen all at once but over a period of years while a woman's estrogen production decreases. The average age of menopause is around fifty, give or take a few years. Besides the famous hot flashes associated with menopause, there can be several other emotional and physical symptoms — irritability, sleeplessness, fatigue, decreased sexual desire, and forgetfulness, to name a few. Just as in being pregnant, some women may feel very little, if any, menopausal symptoms while others experience many.

Historically, menopause has been looked upon negatively by our society. It's been viewed by women and culture as a stage of loss — besides losing the ability to conceive, women were (and still are) afraid of losing sex appeal, power, and youth. Gail Sheehy asks, ". . . is it any wonder that today's women approach fifty under a shadow of archetypal fears of being transformed, all at once, into Old Women?"[10]

Fortunately, myths are being replaced with truths, and new perspectives restore fresh meaning to menopause. Sheehy refers to menopause as a stage of *coalescence*, explaining that it's a time in which women can find a new zest for life. She describes this stage as ". . . discarding the shell of the reproductive self — who came into being in adolescence — and coming out the other side to *coalescence*." She goes on to say, "It is a time when all the wisdom a woman has gathered from fifty years of experience in living comes together. Now that she is not subjected to the culture's definition of woman as primarily a sexual object and breeder, a full unity of her feminine and masculine sides is possible. Today's 'coalescents' are mapping out a whole new stage of life for which evolution never provided."[11]

And what a value this new stage can provide for our work force! When asked if menopause has an effect on working women, Diana Roose, research consultant for 9 to 5, answered: "Research consistently shows that older women, as compared to others, are more productive, more stable and have less absenteeism." She believes that menopause should have little bearing on women at work. (Ageism, however, is another story. Older people, both men and women, are discriminated against in the work force.) A five-year study examining the health of 2,500 midlife women showed that three-fourths of the women felt either relieved or neutral about menopause, while only three percent viewed it negatively.[12] The more value we place on our self-worth, the more gracefully we'll be able to move through yet another passage of our womanhood, whether at home or on the job.

Menopause and Your Physical Health

There are some real health concerns that can potentially affect all postmenopausal women, whether they are working or not. According to the National Osteoporosis Foundation, one third to one half of all postmenopausal women will be affected by osteoporosis — a condition of porous and weak bones which makes a woman vulnerable to bone fractures.[13] Of equal concern is heart disease. It's estimated that one out of two women will die of heart disease.[14] On a brighter note, much can be done to prevent and/or control both osteoporosis and heart disease. Medically, hormonal therapy can be considered. The decision of whether or not to use hormonal replacement is a complicated one involving the consideration of many medical factors along with weighing the risks and benefits. Besides seeking medical advice from an expert, it's recommended that you also consult with the National Women's Health Network and the Boston Women's Health Book Collective for the latest update on hormonal therapy (see Appendix IV).

Physically, you can strengthen your bones and body through diet and exercise. It's essential to supplement your diet with calcium. Besides eating foods high in calcium (green, leafy vegetables and dairy products to name a few sources), most medical experts recommend taking between 1,200 and 1,500 milligrams of calcium daily. Combining calcium with magnesium helps make the absorption of calcium more effective. Be certain to check with your caregiver regarding the right dosage for your body.

Weight-bearing exercise is necessary to keep both muscles and bones strong. Weight-bearing exercise includes walking, jogging, and biking (not swimming). A strengthening exercise class where light hand and leg weights are used, or working out on weight machines, will also do the trick. Aerobic exercise, as discussed in Chapter Eight, will keep your cardiovascular system healthy.

Maidenhood, motherhood, menopause-hood . . . the female body marks time during this earthly sojourn with a life rhythm as well as a monthly one. Fertility coincides with the majority of a woman's working years, when perhaps she labors not only for her own enjoyment but also to feed and clothe her nestlings. Menopause coincides with her generative years, when her identity and maturity become truly her own. Biology is hardly destiny when it comes to working women; the question is, can destiny be shaped by biology? Can the ability of women to understand cycles, to allow a new creation to gestate within themselves, to physically provide nourishment in order to sustain life — can these become translatable metaphors for the business world, balancing the masculine, testosterone-oriented work models with the feminine wisdom that our bodies teach us? Can we integrate creative nurturing into the hunt, the chase, the territorialism, the competition, the displays of power, the conquest — and still honor our own boundaries and needs? Can women learn to appreciate and harness their hormonal cycles to add to the creative possibilities of a job? The understanding that being a "daughter of Eve" is not a curse, but a privilege, heightens the wonder of a woman's miraculous body. Out of respect for that body comes care, responsible management, and willingness to listen to its ebb and flow. The power of hormonal passages in a healthy, happy woman can lend rich variety to an experience of working that is the exclusive privilege of the female. As each woman learns to work with and capitalize on the high and low points of all her hormonal cycles, she contributes to the day when women will not be discriminated against, feeling accursed and in emotional pain, because of our chemistry.

THE WHOLE PICTURE

Hormones. Life stages. Body. Feelings. Spirit. Reflect on the times in your life when you felt present, fully alive, vigorous, healthy, serene. Think of the moments when time seems to stand still. Paradoxically, during a matter of seconds, minutes, hours, your linear existence can vanish, you lose track of time, and are completely one with yourself — the experience of eternity. Whether alone or with someone else, these glimpses of everlasting peace deepen your longing for wholeness, for heaven on earth. Some of these experiences may have occurred while you were at work, others not. A full-time job probably occupies the majority of your waking hours and uses the best of your talents. Therefore, your job should be an oasis of health and happiness, not a sea of numbness or an island of pain.

Here's a metaphor: Three frogs are sitting on a log, not knowing what to do. They sit and sit. Finally, one decides to jump off the log. How many are left?

If you answered, "Two," guess again. There are still three frogs on the log because one frog only *decided* to jump. Deciding is an important step, but it is not sufficient to get you where you want to go. *Jumping* gets the frog off the log!

The vicissitudes of life and work can intrude and distract from the desire for wholeness. It is entirely possible — we have all been there — to *decide* to make constructive changes, but the inertia brought on by daily realities keeps us on a comfortable but compromising log. There is a core experience of basic happiness that is attainable through the unity of emotional, spiritual, and physical wellness. This celestial self IS the Promised Land, able to keep you buoyant and healthy through normal events, to rely on a resilient cushion in the aftermath of trauma, and to achieve bliss beyond periods of mere contentment.

The legacy of Eve is the longing to return to Eden; this longing impels and motivates. The often-present aches, sorrows, confinements, and trade-offs of spending the majority of your life at work are the sweet serpents, turning up the volume on your longing. Go for it; never limit your vision of what a fertile and nurturing Garden you can have. Be good to yourself on all levels, be good to others, and you can hold heaven in your heart. But don't just *decide* to jump. JUMP! Begin today to incorporate even one new skill or technique into your workday. Commitment *and* practice will start you on your journey and keep you on the road until you reach your destination.

A toast to you women who are reclaiming your heavenly heritage: Here's to a long and happy life, and to the ongoing and gradual emergence of ecstasy as you play your part in creating a healthier self at work and a more balanced world for all of us. *A votre santé!*

NOTE

Karen and Kathy offer "Serpents and Apples" seminars and workshops to businesses and groups of individuals. These workshops are designed to help women create wellness at work.

For further information contact:
New Win Publishing (908) 735-9701.

APPENDIX I

Self-Massage Techniques

When doing self-massage, never exert pressure to the point of pain. If you discover a few tender spots in your muscles, hold the pressure and breathe freely. Allow the tension to go out with your breath and to dissolve under the warmth of your touch. Each of the following massage techniques can be practiced for at least a minute and can be repeated as often as desired. Try them all, and then use the ones that seem to work best for you.

TO RELIEVE TENSION AND HEADACHES (Take eyeglasses off.)

Massage your temples (a slight indentation located on either side of your eyes) with forefinger and middle finger held together. Slowly make a small circular motion, or just hold a constant pressure — whichever feels better to you.

Press your fingers across your eyebrows; make little circles around your entire forehead and into your hairline.

Place the pad of each thumb where your eyebrow meets the bridge of your nose. Begin to exert gentle pressure up against the bone of your eye socket (not down toward your eye).

Place each thumb at the back of your head on either side of the long bony ridge just behind your ear lobes. Make little circular movements up and against the bony ridge. Instead of your thumbs you could use your fingers.

Warm the palms of your hands by rubbing them together for about one minute. Gently cup them over your closed eyes and feel the warmth of your hands relax your eyes. Hold them there until the warmth dissipates (about one minute). Slowly lower your hands as you gently open your eyes.

Massage your entire scalp with your fingertips, using a firm circular motion.

Using your forefinger and middle finger, make small circular movements on either side of your neck from your shoulders up to and past the hairline.

Press the pad of the thumb of your right hand into the web of skin between your thumb and forefinger of your left hand. You have to press fairly deeply until you feel a tenderness. Hold for about one minute and repeat on the other side. (DO NOT DO THIS IF YOU ARE PREGNANT.) This technique can be particularly helpful to relieve a headache and is even more effective if someone could do both hands for you at the same time.

TO RELIEVE JAW TENSION

When angry, tense, or frustrated we often grit our teeth together, which tenses our jaw (masseter or chewing muscle).

To locate your jaw muscle, close your mouth and gently bite down. Place your hands on either side of your cheeks. You'll feel your jaw muscles contract. Then relax your jaw by parting your teeth. Gently massage those muscles by making little circles with a finger or hold finger pressure into the muscle; release and repeat until you've done the entire muscle.

TO RELIEVE SHOULDER TENSION

Use your right hand to squeeze, knead, and lift the muscles of your left shoulder. Repeat on other side.

Place the index finger of your right hand on the middle-top of your left shoulder. Begin to press directly downward until you feel a tender spot. Hold the pressure for about one minute or until the tenderness fades away.

TO RELIEVE ARM FATIGUE:

Squeeze and knead the entire length of each arm.

TO RELIEVE HAND AND FINGER TENSION

Using the thumb of your right hand, knead the entire palm of your left hand. Repeat on other hand.

Squeeze and knead each finger; gently lengthen each finger by pulling lightly.

Gently bend downward entire hand at wrist; gently extend or bend hand backward. Do both hands.

TO RELIEVE LOWER BACK TENSION

Place your thumbs on either side of your spine at your lower back. Press the pads of your thumbs evenly downward and inward toward your pelvis. Hold for several seconds; slowly release; move your thumbs away about one inch and press downward and inward for seconds. Repeat this procedure until you have "walked" your thumbs out to your hip bones.

Make little circles with your thumb or fingers into your lower back muscles on each side.

APPENDIX II
Work Moves

Practicing these exercises slowly allows you to feel how your body is benefiting from them. Breathe freely — never hold your breath. As you do these movements, experience your breath as a filtering system. Upon inhaling, breathe in energy and calmness. Upon exhaling, breathe out any fatigue and tension. View these exercises as nourishing movements that add physical grace to you and the way in which you perform your work.

All the exercises can be performed while sitting at your desk or standing up. They can be done in work clothes, and no special equipment is needed. Ideally, practice them on a daily basis — especially during breaks and at any time you feel discomfort.

MOVES FOR THE BACK

Pelvic Tilt Against the Wall

Directions: Find a wall to stand against. Walk your feet about 12–18 inches away from the wall, feet hip distance apart. Bend your knees slightly. Gently press your waist against the wall so that your lower back is flat to the wall. You should be able to feel your abdominal muscles and navel pull inward. If you find it difficult to press your waist to the wall, bend your knees more. Hold this position for 30–60 seconds. It may feel so good you'll want to hold it longer.

Benefits: Relaxes the lower back muscles.

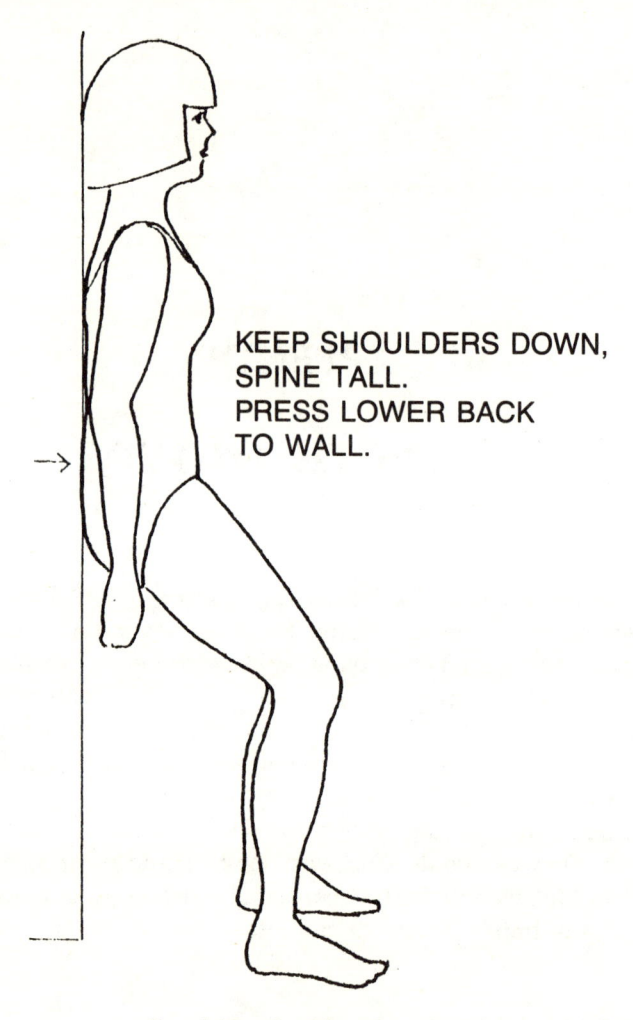

KEEP SHOULDERS DOWN,
SPINE TALL.
PRESS LOWER BACK
TO WALL.

Reaching Overhead

Directions: Sit with a straight spine on the edge of your chair. Place your hands on your knees and adjust your pelvic tilt until you are aware that you are sitting directly over your sitting bones. As you inhale, stretch your arms out to the sides of your body. With palms facing upward, raise your arms overhead in a smooth motion. Continue to breathe as you reach your arms toward the ceiling for at least 10 seconds (the longer the better), and then slowly relax your arms back down to your side. Be careful not to slouch — keep your back straight. Repeat 5–10 more times.

Benefits: Lengthens the spine and gently tones the abdominal and back muscles.

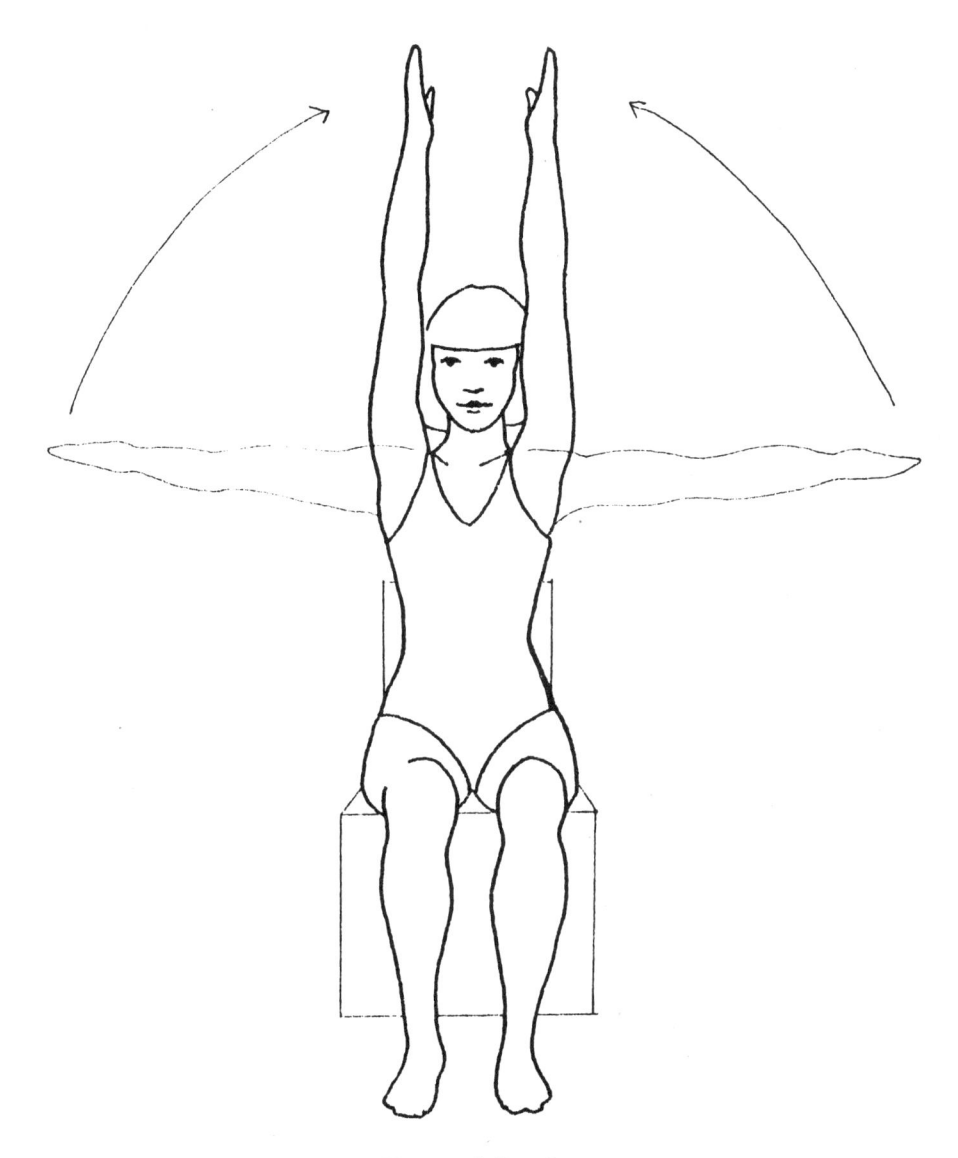

Forward Bend

Directions: Sit near the edge of your chair, on your sitting bones, with feet at least hip distance apart or further. Place your hands underneath your thighs about four inches or so behind your knees. Bending from your hips (not the waist) while keeping your spine straight, lean over and onto your thighs. Keep your neck and head in a straight line with your spine.

Benefits: Relaxes lower back muscles and lengthens the spine.

KEEP SPINE (AXIS) TALL AND STRAIGHT THROUGHOUT EXERCISE

BEND FROM THE HIPS TO PROTECT BACK, STRENGTHEN ABDOMINAL MUSCLES

WHERE ARE THOSE "SITTING BONES"?

FEET ARE HIP DISTANCE APART

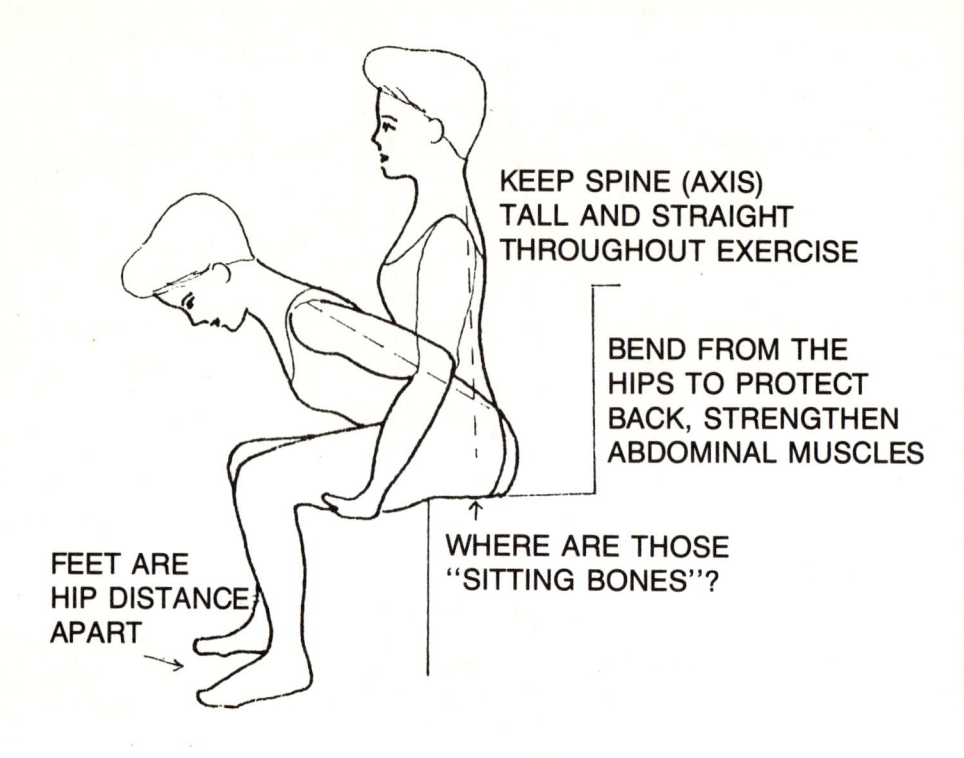

Gentle Spinal Twist

Directions: Sit near edge of chair on your sitting bones with feet on floor, hip distance apart, and your spine straight. Gently twist (with a straight spine) to your right. Place your right hand on back of chair as you place your left hand on your right thigh, turning as though you want to look behind you. Breathe continuously as you stay there for a few seconds and repeat on the other side.

Benefits: Lengthens the spine while keeping it flexible.

MOVES FOR THE NECK AND HEAD

Ear To Shoulder

Directions: Sit or stand with a straight spine.

(1) Slowly lower your right ear toward your right shoulder. Keep your shoulder down. Continue to breathe as you hold it for several seconds. Feel the opposite side of your neck and shoulder lengthen. Slowly return to center and repeat on other side.

(2) Slowly turn your head to the right and hold for 5 seconds. Slowly return to center and repeat on other side.

APPENDIX II — WORK MOVES   261

KEEP SHOULDERS
OPEN AND DOWN,
SPINE TALL

FEET ARE
HIP DISTANCE
APART

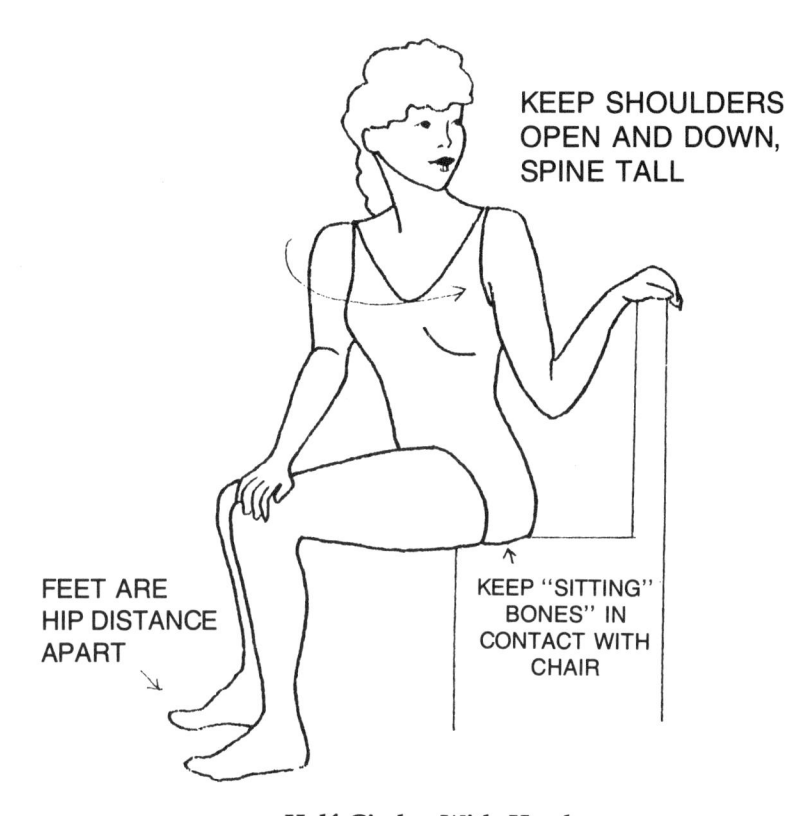

KEEP "SITTING"
BONES" IN
CONTACT WITH
CHAIR

Half Circles With Head

(3) Slowly make a half-circle with your head by first lowering your ear to the right. Then bring your chin down toward your chest; then slowly roll your left ear toward your left shoulder. Then reverse the action. Repeat several times, but in very slow motion. (Do not make a full circle which allows the chin to point up toward ceiling; that action can strain your neck.)

Benefits: Increases circulation and relieves neck tension.

MOVES FOR EYES

General Eye Exercises

Directions: Slowly and gently:

(1) Gaze softly at a distance far away from you for a minute or so (preferably look out a window at something pleasing to you).

(2) Look to the right and then to the left, without moving your head.

(3) Look up at the ceiling and then down to the floor.
(4) Roll your eyes in a complete circle in each direction.

Benefits: Strengthens and relaxes your eyes.

General Relaxation for the Eyes

Directions: Quickly rub the palms of your hands together until they are quite warm (for about 60 seconds). Close your eyes (take glasses off) and gently cup the warmed palms of your hands over your eyes for a minute or so. Feel the soothing warmth of your hands penetrate your eyes. Slowly lower your hands as you gently open your eyes.

Benefits: Relaxes your eyes.

MOVES FOR THE SHOULDERS AND CHEST

Shoulder Shrugs

(May be done standing or sitting on the edge of a chair with back straight.)

Directions: Round your shoulders forward to an exaggerated slump. Then pull your shoulders back to an exaggerated military posture. Now relax them about halfway in between. Keeping them there, inhale and shrug your shoulders up. Exhale and push them deeply down. Relax to center. Repeat the shrugging/pushing down 5–10 times.

Benefits: Increases flexibility and relieves tension in the shoulders; increases general awareness of shoulders and their proper posture.

Shoulder Rotation

Directions: Inhale and roll your shoulders forward and up. Exhale and roll them back and down so as to make a complete circle. Then reverse the circle. Do at least 5 times in each direction.

Benefits: Increases flexibility in the shoulders. The latter action of rolling the shoulders back and down is more important; this movement opens the chest, which helps to counteract rounded shoulders.

Chest Opener #1

(May be done standing or sitting.)

Directions: Raise your arms at your sides, elbows bent at a right angle, palms facing forward. Point your fingertips to the ceiling. Keep your elbows even with your shoulders. Gently and slowly squeeze your shoulders back and toward each

APPENDIX II — WORK MOVES 263

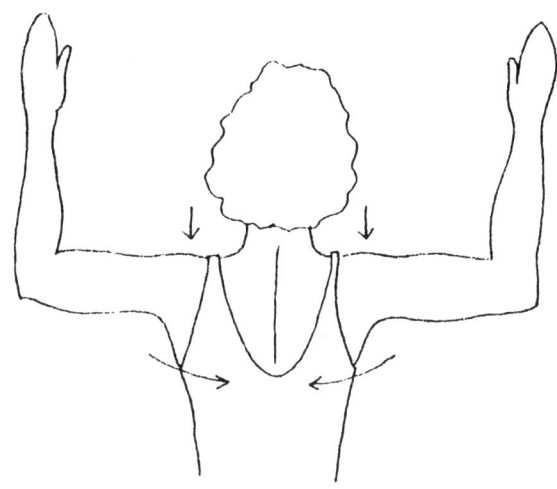

GENTLY SQUEEZE SHOULDER BLADES TOWARD EACH OTHER. KEEP SPINE TALL, SHOULDERS DOWN.

other and feel your chest open. Hold for 5–10 seconds and then release. Repeat 10 times.

Benefits: Opens the chest by stretching the pectoral muscles. Strengthens the upper back muscles. Counteracts rounding of the shoulders.

Chest Opener #2
(Do standing.)

Directions: Hold your hands behind your back. Straighten your elbows. Expand your chest. Squeeze your shoulders back and together and relax your shoulders down. If your chest muscles are extremely tight, it will be difficult or impossible to straighten your arms. In that case, hold a towel as illustrated.

Benefits: Same as above.

MOVES FOR THE ARMS, HANDS AND FINGERS

(May be done standing or sitting.)

Arm Extensions

Directions: With good posture slowly raise both your arms halfway up from your sides, keeping them about 2 inches lower

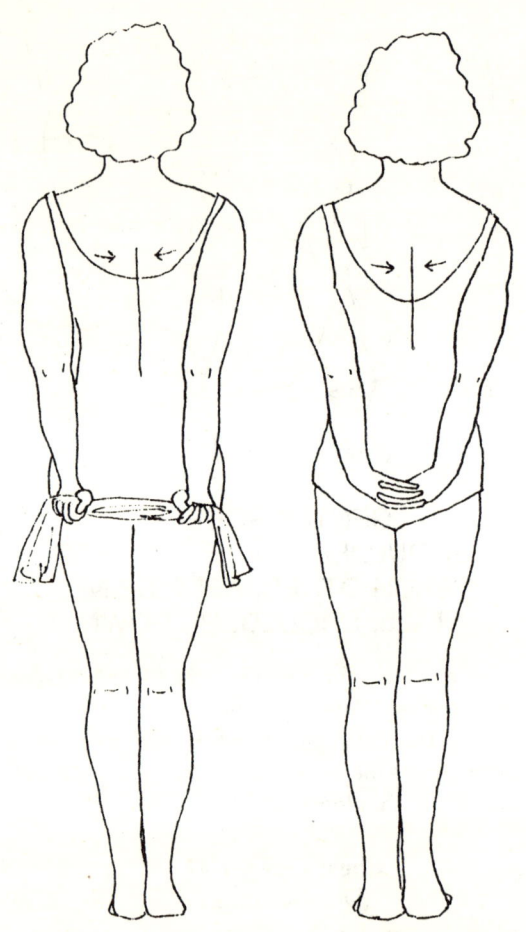

1. LESS FLEXIBLE   **2. GREATER FLEXIBILITY**

than your shoulders. Begin to extend the heel of your palm as you straighten your fingers to the ceiling. Feel all the muscles in your arm contract. Hold for 10 seconds and then lower down. Repeat as often as needed.

Benefits: Strengthens arm muscles and increases circulation.

Hand Rolls and Waves

Directions: Make circles with both your hands several times in each direction. Wave (flex and extend) your hand slowly up and down and then from side to side.

Benefits: Increases circulation; keeps joints, wrists flexible.

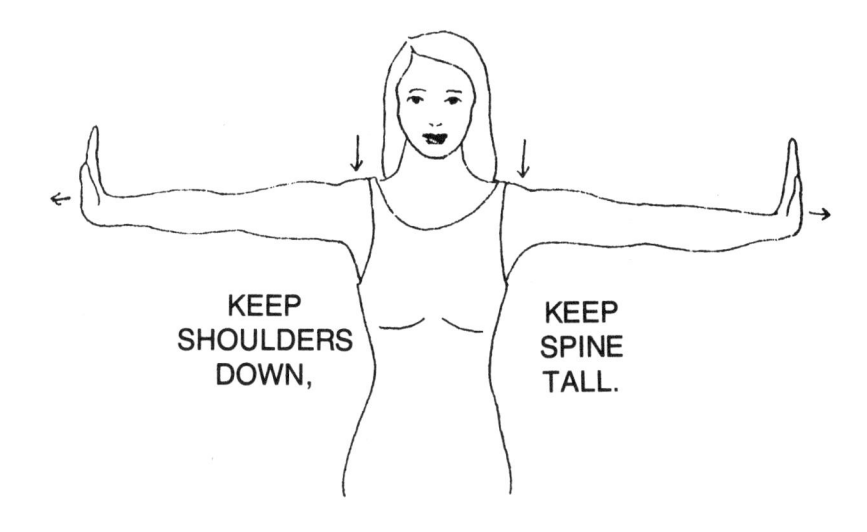

KEEP SHOULDERS DOWN, KEEP SPINE TALL.

Hand Squeeze

Directions: Make fists with your hands and then extend all your fingers. Repeat several times and then gently shake them.

Benefits: Increases circulation to your hands, relieves tension, and keeps finger joints flexible.

MOVES FOR THE LEGS, ANKLES AND FEET

Thigh Exercise

Directions: Sit with your back to the back of your chair on your sitting bones and with a straight spine. Straighten your right leg and squeeze your thigh muscles. Hold for several seconds and slowly lower. Repeat on other side.

Benefits: Strengthens thigh muscles and increases circulation.

Ankle Rolls and Pointing and Flexing the Toes

Directions: Make circles with your feet several times in each direction. Point your toes and then extend your heels several times.

Benefits: Increases circulation; keeps ankle joints flexible.

APPENDIX III
Affirmation and Question Cards

TO THE READER

If you care to use the small cards provided here, cut them out and transfer one question/affirmation to each card. (See pp. 135–137 for directions on using them.) Or use heavier paper, such as card stock, to make your own.

Daily Questions

1. Who am I, really?
2. Is my work today truly meaningful to me?
3. What do I need right now for inner peace?
4. What is keeping me from complete happiness on the job?
5. What can I find right now to be grateful for?
6. Am I compromising my values in any way at work?
7. Is any fear keeping me from living a fulfilling life?
8. Who loves me deeply?
9. What have I done today to make life a little better for someone else?
10. What do I need to do to trust that the rest of my workday will be just fine?
11. Do I believe that everything happens for a reason?
12. Can I trust my Higher Power to provide all that I need today?
13. What is my purpose in life?
14. Is my work in keeping with my life's purpose?
15. Who at work accepts me unconditionally?
16. At work, whom do I admire and respect as a highly developed person?
17. With whom could I establish a supportive spiritual connection?
18. If I found out I had three days left to live, what would I do?
19. When I am on my deathbed and look back on my life, what will I tell myself about my work?
20. What would make me saddest of all about myself, and why?

Daily Affirmations

1. My life and work have a higher purpose.
2. I am loved unconditionally by my Higher Power and myself.
3. I am capable of loving unconditionally.
4. I am able to accept misfortune and allow my Higher Power to help me rise above it.
5. I am able to be open and honest with myself.
6. I live in keeping with my values.
7. I am living fully in the present moment.
8. I approach each problem with acceptance and deal with it wisely.
9. I am making a positive contribution in my work or career.
10. I am grateful for this day and desire to make the most of it.
11. I am becoming healthier both on and off the job.
12. I want the best for myself and everyone else.
13. I am able to focus on what's really important right now.
14. I am an important part of the universe.
15. I am able to give up trying to control everything.
16. I am being true to myself each day.
17. I am able to learn from my mistakes.
18. There is so much more to my life than my job.
19. I am able to open my heart more and more to the goodness of life.
20. I am of immense value, even when I'm doing nothing.

Question Cards

Instructions: Cut out the Affirmation and Question Cards along the solid lines. Keep at work or in your purse. See pp. 128–129 for suggestions on using these cards. If additional cards are needed, please feel free to photocopy.

Affirmation Cards

Instructions: Cut out the Affirmation and Question Cards along the solid lines. Keep at work or in your purse. See pp. 128–129 for suggestions on using these cards. If additional cards are needed, please feel free to photocopy.

APPENDIX IV
Resources and Further Reading

CAREER CHANGES

Organizations

Bernard Haldane Associates

A national career marketing firm, the oldest and largest in the U.S.; offices in most major cities. Offers complete services: one-on-one counseling to help the client become clear on what she/he loves to do and is suited for; resume writing; interviewing skills; seminars; obtaining interviews in the unadvertised job market; networking; creating ideal career positions; salary negotiations. Client pays the fee. (If you live in or near a large city, check your phone book for a listing; Bernard Haldane Associates also advertise in the Sunday Classified Section of newspapers, in the "Jobs" pages.)

Books

Bolles, Richard. *What Color Is Your Parachute?* Berkeley, CA: Ten Speed Press, 1991 (Revised).
Catalyst Group Staff. *Marketing Yourself.* New York: Bantam, 1981.
———. *What To Do With The Rest Of Your Life.* New York: Simon & Schuster, 1981.
Chapman, Jack. *How To Make $1000 A Minute: Negotiating Your Salaries and Raises.* Berkeley, CA: Ten Speed Press, 1991 (Revised).

Germann, Richard and Peter Arnold. *Job And Career Building*. Berkeley, CA: Ten Speed Press, 1982.

Jackson, Tom. *Guerilla Tactics in the New Job Market*. New York: Bantam, 1991.

_____. *Mastering the Hidden Job Market: How to Create New Opportunities in a World of Uncertainty and Change*. New York: Random House, 1992.

Sinetar, Marsha. *Do What You Love, The Money Will Follow: Discovering Your Right Livelihood*. New York: Dell Books, 1989.

CODEPENDENCE, ADDICTION, AND COMPULSIVITY ISSUES

Support Groups

Codependents Anonymous (CODA)
P.O. Box 33577
Phoenix, AZ 85067-3577
(602) 277-7991

This can be a very helpful program for those who exhibit characteristics associated with codependence: over-responsibility, rescuing, controlling, people-pleasing, protecting others from the consequences of their actions, etc. The format of meetings is based on that of other Twelve-Step groups such as Alcoholics Anonymous. This is a self-help program.

Adult Children of Alcoholics (ACA and ACOA)
P.O. Box 3216
2522 W. Sepulveda Boulevard
Suite 200
Torrance, CA 90505
(213) 534-1815

For those who grew up in homes where alcoholism or other addictions existed, and therefore act out in their workplace the same patterns of dysfunction as they did in their families. Also a Twelve-Step self-help group.

Books

Beattie, Melody. *Beyond Codependency*. San Francisco: Harper/Hazelden, 1989.

_____. *Codependent No More*. San Francisco: Harper/Hazelden, 1987.

_____. Codependent's Guide to the Twelve Steps. New York: Prentice Hall Press, 1990.

Schaef, Anne Wilson. *Co-Dependence: Misunderstood — Mistreated.* San Francisco: Harper & Row, 1986.
Woititz, Janet G., Ed.D., & Garner, Alan, M.A. *Life Skills For Adult Children.* Deerfield Beach, FL: Health Communications, Inc., 1990.

EMOTIONAL NEEDS/RELAXATION/STRESS MANAGEMENT

Books

Borysenko, Joan. *Minding The Body, Mending The Mind.* Reading, MA: Addison Wesley Publishing Co., 1987.
Fassel, Diane. *Working Ourselves to Death: The High Cost of Workaholism, The Rewards of Recovery.* San Francisco: Harper San Francisco, 1990.
Goldhar, Harriet Lerner. *Dance of Anger.* New York: Harper & Row, 1985.
_____. *Dance of Intimacy.* New York: Harper & Row, 1989.
Gordon, Thomas. *Leader Effectiveness Training.* New York: Bantam, 1984.
Schaef, Anne Wilson. *Meditations For Women Who Do Too Much.* San Francisco: Harper San Francisco, 1990.
Seligman, Martin, Ph.D. *Learned Optimism.* New York: Knopf, 1991.
Stern, Ellen Sue. *Running On Empty: Meditations for Indispensable Women.* New York: Bantam/Doubleday/Dell, 1992.
Tubesing, Donald. *Kicking Your Stress Habits.* Duluth, MN: Whole Person Press, 1981.
_____ and Nancy Loving Tubesing. *Seeking Your Healthy Balance.* Duluth, MN: Whole Person Press, 1983.
Tassi, Nina. *Urgency Addiction.* Dallas, TX: Taylor Publishing Co., 1991.
Woodman, Marion. *To Be a Woman: The Birth of the Conscious Feminine.* Los Angeles: J.P. Tarcher; New York: St. Martin's Press, Distributor, 1990.

Support Group

Emotions Anonymous (EA)
P.O. Box 4245
St. Paul, MN 55104
(612) 647-9712

A twelve-step self-help group, modeled on Alcoholics Anonymous, to help people overcome a variety of emotional difficulties which interfere with their healthy functioning, such as anger, depression, grief, anxiety. There are "lifetime" members and "crisis" members.

ENLIGHTENMENT ABOUT YOUR WORKPLACE — HOW THE SYSTEM WORKS

Books

Lareau, William. *Conduct Expected: The Unwritten Rules for a Successful Business Career*. Clinton, NJ: New Win Publishing, 1985.

Schaef, Anne Wilson and Diane Fassel. *The Addictive Organization*. San Francisco: Harper & Row, 1988.

EXECUTIVE NEEDS

Books

Densen, David W., Ph.D. *Worksite Wellness*. Paramus, NJ: Prentice Hall Information Services, 1987.

Organizations

National Association for Female Executives
127 W. 24th St.
New York, NY 10011
(212) 645-0776

Provides discount programs, venture capital loans, and a national profile of successful executive females.

Women of the Nineties
7336 S. Oglesvy Ave.
Chicago, IL 60649-3412
(312) 374-3550

A Chicago Metropolitan network of the National Association for Female Executives. A network for career and self-employed women seeking procurement and technical assistance opportunities.

HEALTH HAZARDS AT WORK

Federal Government Agencies

Environmental Protection Agency
401 M St. SW
Washington, DC 20460
(202) 260-2090

Conducts research and provides information on indoor air quality; regulates a variety of pollutants found in the workplace.

NIOSH (National Institute for Occupational Safety and Health)
4676 Columbia Pkwy.
Cincinnati, OH 45226
(513) 533-8326
(800) 356-4674

Conducts health-hazard evaluations at worksites, does research, and publishes information.

OSHA (Occupational Safety and Health Administration)
200 Constitution Ave. NW
N 3641
Washington, DC 20210
(202) 523-6091

Sets workplace standards and enforces them.

Private Organizations

9 to 5 National Association of Working Women
614 Superior Ave. NW
Cleveland, OH 44113
(216) 566-9308

All working women should know about this valuable resource. 9 to 5 does advocacy, lobbying, and research on women and work. For membership and/or to obtain their informative publications on the subject of safety in the workplace, contact above address. For any job-related problem call their National Job Problem Hotline at (800) 522-0925. They can offer advice on just about any problem at work, ranging from VDT's to sexual harassment.

COSH Groups
(Committee/Coalition/Council on Occupational Safety and Health)
To locate your nearest COSH group, contact NYCOSH at (212) 627-3900.

Several cities have COSH groups. They are private and not to be confused with government agencies. The groups are composed of workers, unions, and health advocates to help employees and unions in occupational health and safety concerns.

Books

Makower, Joel. *Office Hazards: How Your Job Can Make You Sick*. Washington, DC: Tilden Press, 1981.

Stellman, Jeanne, Ph.D. and Mary Sue Henifin, M.P.H. *Office Work Can Be Dangerous To Your Health*. New York: Pantheon Books, 1983.

Turning Things Around: A Woman's Occupational and Environmental Health Resource Guide by the National Women's Health Network (202) 347-1140.

HUMOR

The Humor Project, Inc.
Dr. Joel Goodman, Director
110 Spring St.
Saratoga Springs, NY 12866
(518) 587-8770

Provides programs and consultation on the power of humor and creativity to businesses, professionals, educators, managers, parents, and others. Besides selling books on humor they publish a quarterly magazine, *Laughing Matters*. To subscribe and/or for further information, contact the above address.

LEGAL, ECONOMIC, HEALTH, AND POLITICAL ISSUES

Organizations

Boston Women's Health Collective
P.O. Box 192
Somerville, MA 02144
(617) 625-0271

Comprehensive women's health information center which provides materials relating to occupational issues.

Equal Rights Advocates
1370 Mission St.
San Francisco, CA 94103
(415) 621-0505

Offers legal advice on employment issues.

APPENDIX IV — RESOURCES AND FURTHER READING 279

Families and Work Institute
330 7th Ave.
New York, NY 10001
(212) 465-2044

A not-for-profit research and consulting firm which explores a range of work and family issues throughout the life cycle of women.

Feminist Majority Foundation
1600 Wilson Blvd. #704
Arlington, VA 22209
(703) 522-2214

Leading feminist think tank specializing in the development of creative new strategies to empower women through action.

Institute for Women's Policy Research
1400 20th St., NW
Washington, DC 20036
(202) 785-5100

Studies economic issues concerning women.

National Committee on Pay Equity
1126 16th St. NW
Washington, DC 20036
(202) 331-7343

Researches and lobbies on issues of women's salaries.

National Women's Health Network
1325 G. St. NW
Washington, DC 20005
(202) 347-1140

Offers consumer advocacy and is a clearinghouse on all women's health issues. If they don't know the answer to your question, they will get it for you. They have published an excellent book, *Turning Things Around: A Woman's Occupational and Environmental Health Resource Guide*. To purchase, contact the above address.

National Women's Law Center
1616 P. St. NW
Washington, DC 20036
(202) 328-5169

Lawyers will handle cases/lawsuits on issues that relate to women.

National Women's Political Caucus
1275 K St. NW
Suite 750
Washington, DC 20005-4051
(202) 898-1100

The only bipartisan group that supports progressive women candidates.

New Ways to Work
149 9th St.
San Francisco, CA 94103
(415) 552-1000

Helps companies and individuals plan flexible hours and creative work situations.

NOW (National Organization for Women)
1000 16th St. NW
Washington, DC 20036
(202) 331-0066

Works to bring women into full participation in the mainstream of American society.

Public Citizen
2000 P. St. NW
Suite 605
Washington, DC 20036

A not-for-profit organization founded by Ralph Nader in 1971. Focuses on consumer rights, corporate and government accountability.

Wider Opportunities for Women
1325 G St. NW
Washington, DC 20005
(202) 638-3143

National advocacy and employment group.

Women's Legal Defense Fund
1875 Connecticut Ave. NW
Washington, DC 20009
(202) 9986-2600

Represents women filing lawsuits, does advocacy and lobbying.

MENOPAUSE

Books

Conway, Sally, *Menopause: Help and Hope for This Passage*. Grand Rapids, MI: Pyranee Books, 1990.

Gillespie, Clark. *Hormones, Hot Flashes, and Mood Swings*. New York: Harper & Row, 1989.

Kahn, Ada P. and Linda Hughy Holt, M.D. *Midlife Health*. New York: Facts on File Publication, 1987.

Sheehy, Gail. *Silent Passage*. New York: Random House, 1992.

Newsletter

Menopause News
2074 Union Street
San Francisco, CA 94123
(415) 567-2368

A bimonthly newsletter that provides up-to-date information on medical and psychological effects of menopause. To subscribe, contact above address.

OLDER WORKING WOMEN

American Association of Retired Persons (AARP)
1909 K St. NW
Washington, DC 20049
(202) 872-4700

Offers membership, services, information, and advocacy for issues concerning people over age 50. Contact above address for your local chapter.

Older Women's League
730 11th St. NW
Washington, DC 20001
(202) 783-6686

Advocacy group for older women, especially regarding benefits and career opportunities.

Books

Doress, Paula Brown, Diana Laskin-Siegal and the Midlife and Older Women Book Project. *Ourselves, Growing Older*. New York: Simon & Schuster, 1987.

A superb book on women as they age. Refer to its excellent resource section for a comprehensive list of books and organizations related to aging women.

PHYSICAL NEEDS

Aromatherapy

For books, refer to the bibliography. For products, your local health food store may carry them. Other resources are:

Altar Bazaar
P.O. Box 897
Oxford, NY 13830

Aura Cacia
P.O. Box 3157
Santa Rosa, CA 95402

Weleda, Inc.
841 South Main St.
P.O. Box 769
Spring Valley, NY 10977
(914) 356-4134

Exercise

Alter, Judy. *Stretch and Strengthen*. Boston: Houghton Mifflin Co., 1986.
Tobias, Maxine and Mary Stewart. *Stretch and Relax*. Los Angeles: The Body Press, 1985.

Massage

Dauning, George. *The Massage Book*. New York: Random House, 1972.
Hudson, Clare Maxwell. *The Complete Book of Massage*. New York: Random House, 1988.

Organizations

American Massage Therapy Association
(312) 761-AMTH

Provides referrals to certified massage therapists in your area.

PMS

Organizations

Madison Pharmacy Associates (MPA)
429 Gammon Place
P.O. Box 9641
Madison, WI 53715

Since 1982 MPA has specialized in PMS management, consultation and education. MPA has 24-hour phone consultation. Publishes an excellent newsletter, *PMS Access*. To subscribe, contact above address.

Books

Bender, Stephanie. *PMS: A Positive Program to Gain Control*. Tucson, AZ: Body Press, 1986.
Dalton, Katharina. *Once a Month*. Claremont, CA: Hunter House, Inc., 1990.
Halas, Celia, Ph.D. *Relief From Premenstrual Syndrome*. New York: Frederick Fell Publishers, 1984.
Harrison, Michele, M.D. *Self-Help for Premenstrual Syndrome*. Revised. New York: Random House, 1985.
Lark, Susan, M.D. *Premenstrual Syndrome Self-Help Book: A Woman's Guide to Feeling Good All Month*. Los Angeles: Forman Publishing Co., 1984.

PREGNANCY AND BREASTFEEDING

Organizations

Bradley Method (American Academy of Husband-Coached Childbirth)
P.O. Box 5224
Sherman Oaks, CA 91493
(213) 788-6662

ASPO/Lamaze
1840 Wilson Blvd., Suite 204
Arlington, VA 22201
(800) 368-4404

Offers advocacy for safe childbirth and training in the Lamaze Method of childbirth.

ICEA (International Childbirth Education Association)
P.O. Box 20048
Minneapolis, MN 55420-0048
(612) 854-8660

Offers advocacy and training in safe childbirth. Provides extensive mail order catalogues offering books, tapes, movies relating to pregnancy, birth, and breastfeeding.

LaLeche League
9616 Menneapolis Ave.
Franklin Park, IL 60130-8209
(312) 455-7730 (or check your phone book for local listings)

Advocacy for breastfeeding, mail-order catalogues and phone consultation for breastfeeding mothers.

Books

Cain, Kathleen. *Partners In Birth*. New York: Warner Books, 1990.
Eisenberg, Arlene, Heidi Eisenberg Murkoff, and Sandee Eisenberg Hathaway, R.N., B.S.N. *What to Expect When You're Expecting*. New York: Workman Publishing Co., 1984.
Huggins, Kathleen. *The Nursing Mother's Companion*. Boston: Harvard Common Press, 1986.
Lieberman, Adrienne. *Easing Labor Pain* (Revised). Boston: Harvard Common Press, 1992.
Mason, Diane and Diane Ingersoll. *Breastfeeding and the Working Mother*. New York: St. Martin's Press, 1986.

IF YOU HAVE LEGAL QUESTIONS REGARDING PREGNANCY AND WORK, CALL: 9 to 5 National Association of Working Women (800) 522-0925.

SEXUAL HARASSMENT

Organizations

9 to 5 Hotline for advice on sexual harassment at work
(800) 522-0925

U.S. Equal Employment Opportunity Commission (EEOC)
(800) USA-EEOC

A federal agency that creates and enforces policy around issues of discrimination and sexual harassment. Call above number to get advice/help on filing a complaint.

Books

Breakwell, Glynis. *The Quiet Rebel: How to Survive As a Woman and Business Person.* New York: Grove Press, 1985.

Neville, Kathleen. *Corporate Attractions: An Inside Account of Sexual Harassment with the New Sexual Rules for Men and Women on the Job.* Washington, DC: Acropolis Books, 1990.

Powell, Elizabeth. *Talking Back to Sexual Pressure.* Minneapolis, MN: Compcare Publishers, 1991.

Webb, Susan. *Step Forward: Sexual Harassment in the Workplace.* New York: Mastermedia, 1991.

SMOKING

ASH (Action on Smoking and Health)
2013 H St. NW
Washington, DC 20006
(202) 659-4310

A national organization concerned with regulation and policy regarding smoking.

Also, contact your local chapter of the American Cancer Society and the American Lung Association for literature and information on stop-smoking groups.

SPIRITUAL NEEDS

Organizations

Career Enterprises
225 W. Ohio St., Suite 525
Chicago, IL 60610
(312) 670-4370

Offers a course, *Contribution, Leadership and Grace* for individuals who have answered the most fundamental questions about career direction and are ready to expand their contribution both inside and outside work, and to express their spirituality more fully in their everyday life. For networking on spirituality and work, contact Robin Sheerer or Marsha Haake at the above address.

Books

Giles, Mary E., editor. *The Feminist Mystic*. New York: The Crossroad Publishing Co., 1982.

Hamilton-Merritt, Jane. *A Meditator's Diary*. New York: Harper & Row, 1976.

Huyghe, Rene. *Art and the Spirit of Man*. New York: Harry N. Abrams, Inc., 1962.

Luks, Allan. *The Healing Power of Doing Good*. New York: Fawcett Columbine, 1991.

Schaef, Anne Wilson. *Meditations for Women Who Do Too Much*. San Francisco: Harper San Francisco, 1990.

Stern, Ellen Sue. *Running on Empty: Meditations for Indispensable Women*. New York: Bantam/Doubleday/Dell, 1992.

Wollf-Solin, Mary. *No Other Light: Points of Convergence in Psychology and Spirituality*. New York: Crossroad, 1986.

Zukav, Gary. *The Seat of the Soul*. New York: Simon & Schuster, 1989.

WORKING MOTHERS

Brothers, Joyce. *The Successful Woman: How You Can Have a Career, Husband and a Family and Not Feel Guilty About It*. New York: Simon & Schuster, 1988.

Ferguson, Trudi and Joan S. Dunphy. *Answers to the Mommy Track: How Wives and Mothers in Business Reach the Top and Balance Their Lives*. New Horizon Press, 1991.

Gerson, Kathleen. *Hard Choices: How Women Decide About Work, Career, and Motherhood*. California: University of California Press, 1985.

Grollman, Earl A. *The Working Parent Dilemma: How to Balance the Responsibilities of Children and Careers*. Massachusetts: Beacon Press, 1986.

PRODUCTS

Time Management

The Franklin Day Planner
(800) 654-1776

Comes with its own set of tapes to instruct the user in the product; seminars also available to provide training.

The Ultimate Organizer
order through:
  Productivity Plus, Inc.
  375 E. Elliot Rd., Suite #6
  Chandler, AZ 85225-1129
  (800) 872-0232

Comes with a workbook to train the user; some distributors offer seminars.

Music

Many women have favorite classical pieces, such as Pachelbel's "Canon in D," which soothe and center them. There is also a wealth of contemporary music which is conducive to visualization, generally found in the "New Age" sections of music stores. (If the term "New Age" is a turn-off, don't rule out the music. Try it out. Ask in a store to listen to the two asterisked tapes listed below; they are very different from each other. If you like either one, the clerk can help you locate similar tapes by the same or other artists.)

*Brian Eno: "Music for Airports"
*Herb Ernst: "Dreamflight III"
 Ray Lynch: "Deep Breakfast"
 R. Carlos Nakai: "Spirit Horses"
 Vangelis: "Opera Sauvage"
 Andreas Vollenweider: "Behind the Garden . . ."
 George Winston: "Autumn"

You may also wish to try a musical subliminal tape. These tapes contain inaudible affirmations/hypnotic suggestions. The theory is that your subconscious mind picks up these positive affirmations. Some women report that subliminal tapes are an effective aid to relaxation, quitting smoking, losing weight, increasing productivity, a more satisfying sex life, etc. There are tapes which address a variety of such problems. However, other women report that they don't find the tapes help with their behavior, but the music is wonderful. If you'd like to experiment, try the music side of the tape "Serenity: Recovery Subliminal Audio." Order it through Adventures in Cassettes, P.O. Box 11041, Minneapolis, MN 55411.

Catalogues

These catalogues contains books, tapes, and other products for self-care: relaxation, stress management, and personal growth.

A Head for Books (516) 741-2155
Avery Publishing Group
120 Old Broadway
Garden City Park, NY 11040

Pacific Spirit (800) 634-9057
Whole Life Products
1334 Pacific Ave.
Forest Grove, OR 97116

Red Rose Collection (800) 451-5683
P.O. Box 280141
San Francisco, CA 94128-0140

Rudra Press (800) 876-7798
P.O. Box 1973
Cambridge, MA 02238

The Self-Care Catalogue (800) 345-4021
5850 Shellmound St.
P.O. Box 8813
Emeryville, CA 94662-0813

Whole Person Associates
1702 E. Jefferson
Duluth, MN 55812

Notes

CHAPTER ONE

1. Anne Wilson Schaef, *When Society Becomes An Addict* (San Francisco: Harper & Row, 1987), p. 15.
2. Carol Kleiman and Laurie Cohen, "Spotlight on Sexual Harassment Moves Victims to Break Silence," *Chicago Tribune*, Oct. 10, 1991.
3. *Ibid.*

CHAPTER FOUR

1. James Gleick, *Chaos: Making A New Science* (New York: Penguin Books, 1987), p. 8.
2. Laurie Goering and Carol Kleiman, "Fighting Harassment Pays, Experts Say," *Chicago Tribune*, Oct. 29, 1991.

CHAPTER FIVE

1. Adapted and reprinted with permission from *Structured Exercises in Stress Management, Volume 20,* Nancy Loving Tubesing and Donald A. Tubesing, Editors, (c) Whole Person Press, PO Box 3151, Duluth, MN 55803, (218) 728-6807, pp. 77–80.

CHAPTER SEVEN

1. Anne Wilson Schaef, *Co-Dependence* (San Francisco: Harper & Row, 1986), pp. 75, 80–83, 85.
2. Isabel Briggs Myers and Peter B. Myers, *Gifts Differing* (Palo Alto, CA: Consulting Psychologists Press, 1980), p. 54.
3. Deepak Chopra, M.D., *Quantum Healing* (New York: Bantam Books, 1989), p. 238. (In this book, Dr. Chopra examines physiology and quantum mechanics,

and ancient healing practices involving meditation, to build a case for the healing power of consciousness.)
4. Adelaide Gardner, *Meditation* (Wheaton, IL: The Theosophical Publishing House, 1986).
5. Denise Denniston and Peter McWilliams, *The Transcendental Meditation Book* (Allen Park, MI: Three Rivers Press, 1975), p. 75.
6. Kenneth Woodward et al., "Talking to God," *Newsweek* (Jan. 6, 1992), p. 39.
7. Denniston & McWilliams, *Ibid*.

CHAPTER EIGHT

1. Martha Davis, Elizabeth Robbins Eshelman and Matthew McKay, *The Relaxation and Stress Reduction Workbook*, 3rd Ed. (Oakland, CA: New Harbinger Publications, 1988), p. 3.
2. Swami Rama, Rudolph Ballatine, M.D., and Alan Hymes, M.D., *Science of Breath* (Honesdale, PA: The Himalayan International Institute of Yoga Science and Philosophy, 1979), pp. 40–41.
3. Davis, *et al.*, *The Relaxation and Stress Reduction Workbook* (Oakland, CA: New Harbinger Publications, 1988), p. 27.
4. Adrienne Lieberman, *Easing Labor Pain* (New York: Doubleday, 1987, also Harvard Common Press, 1992), p. 66.
5. Ashley Montague, *Touching* (New York: Harper & Row Publishers, 1978), p. 1.
6. Staff researchers of the Melpomene Institute for Women's Health Research, *The Bodywise Woman* (New York: Prentice Hall Press, 1990), p. XIII.
7. *Ibid*.
8. Davis, *et al.*, *The Relaxation and Stress Reduction Workbook* (Oakland, CA: New Harbinger Publications, 1988), p. 155.
9. Stephen Lally, "Laugh Your Stress Away," *Prevention* magazine, No. 6 (June 1991), p. 43.
10. *Ibid*.
11. Christine Sparta, "Perfect Scents," *Ladies Home Journal* (September 1991), p. 149.
12. C. Kallan, "Probing the Power of Common Scents," *Prevention* magazine (October 1990), p. 41.
13. *Ibid*.
14. J. Stone, "Scents and Sensibility," *Discover* magazine (December 1989), p. 26.
15. Maggie Tisserand, *Aromatherapy For Women* (Rochester, Vermont: Healing Arts Press, 1985), p. 23.
16. Robert Pritikin, *The New Pritikin Program* (New York: Simon and Schuster, 1990), p. 103.
17. *Ibid*.
18. Padus Emrika and Editors of *Prevention* magazine, *Your Emotions and Your Health* (Emmaus, PA: Rodale Press, Inc., 1986), pp. 384–385.
19. Padus Emrika, *et al.*, pp. 15–16.

CHAPTER NINE

1. Amy Saltzman, Joanne Silbermen, "When Each Day is a Sick Day," *U.S. News & World Report* (Mar. 13, 1989), p. 66.
2. Herbert Junghanns, *Normal Biomechanical Stresses on Spinal Function*, English Language Edition, Edited by Hans J. Hager (Rockville, MD: Aspen Publishers, 1990), p. 224.
3. F. Scandura and K. Wollmer, "Can a Computer Be Dangerous to Your Health? *Working Woman* (May 1991), 16:106.
4. National Association of Working Women, *Computer Health & Safety Pamphlet* (238 W. Madison Ave., Suite 804, Milwaukee, WI 53203), p. 4.
5. Jon Van, "Carpal Syndrome Reports Rise Sharply," *Chicago Tribune* (Feb. 12, 1992).
6. Teresa M. Schnore, Barbara Grajewski, Richard W. Hornung, Michale Thun, Grace England, William Murry, William Halperin, David Conover, "Video Display Terminals and the Risk of Spontaneous Abortion," *New England Journal of Medicine* (Mar. 18, 1991), 324: 727-733.

CHAPTER TEN

1. Katherine Dalton, M.D., *Once a Month* (Hunter House, CA: 1990), p. 17.
2. Madison Pharmacy Associates (booklet), "Premenstrual Syndrome — The Odds are Almost Even" (429 Gammon Place, P.O. Box 9641, Madison, WI 53715).
3. *Washington Post* (December 10, 1989).
4. Sherry Lynn Jimènez Mims, *The Pregnant Woman's Comfort Guide* (Englewood Cliffs, NJ: Prentice Hall, Inc., 1983), p. 93.
5. *Ibid.*
6. Anne Field, "Women and Work" (*Self* magazine, January 1992), p. 99.
7. *Trendlines, Childbirth Forum* (8044 Montgomery Rd., Suite 450, Cincinnati, OH 45236), p. 7.
8. Judith Nolte, "Is Your Workplace Friendly?" *American Baby* (February 1991), p. 3.
9. Gail Sheehy, "The Silent Passage: Menopause," *Vanity Fair* (October 1991), p. 224.
10. *Ibid.*, p. 252.
11. *Ibid.*, p. 262.
12. Jean Seligman, Deborah Witherspoon, Nadine Joseph and Lauren Picker, "Not Past Their Prime," *Newsweek* (Aug. 6, 1990), p. 6.
13. Sheehy, p. 260.
14. *Ibid.*, p. 262.

Bibliography

Ballatine, Rudolph, M.D. *Diet And Nutrition*. Honesdale, PA: The Himalayan International Institute, 1978.

Benson, Herbert, M.D. *Beyond the Relaxation Response*. New York: Berkely Books, 1985.

———. *The Relaxation Response*. New York: William Morrow and Co., 1986.

Bond, James T., Ellen Galinsky, Michele Lord, Graham L. Staines, and Karen R. Braun. *Beyond the Parental Leave Debate*. New York: Families and Work Institute, 1991.

Braiker, Harriet B. *The Type E Woman: How To Overcome The Stress of Being Everything to Everybody*. New York: Dodd, Mead & Co., 1986.

Briles, Judith. *Woman to Woman: From Sabotage to Support*. New Jersey: New Horizons Press, 1987.

Brothers, Joyce. *The Successful Woman: How You Can Have a Career, a Husband and a Family and Not Feel Guilty About It*. New York: Simon & Schuster, 1988.

Carrington, Patricia, Ph.D. *Freedom in Meditation*. Garden City, NY: Anchor Press, 1977.

Cousins, Norman. *Anatomy of an Illness*. New York: W. W. Norton & Co., 1979.

Dalton, Katharina. *Once A Month*. Claremont, CA: Hunter House Inc., 1990.

Davis, Martha and Elizabeth Robbins Eshelman, and Matthew McKay. *The Relaxation and Stress Reduction Workbook*, (3rd edition). California: New Harbinger Publications, 1988.

Denniston, Denise and Peter McWilliams. *The Transcendental Meditation Book*. Allen Park, MI: Three Rivers Press, 1975.

Donkin, Scott W. *Sitting On The Job*. Boston: Houston Mifflin, 1987.

Faelten, Sharon, David Diamond, and the Editors of *Prevention Magazine*. *Take Control of Your Life*. Emmaus, PA: Rodale Press, 1988.

Gardner, Adelaide. *Meditation*. Wheaton, IL: The Theosophica Publishing House, 1968.

Gawain, Shakti. *Creative Visualization*. New York: Bantam Books, 1982.

———. *Meditations*. San Raphael, CA: New World Library, 1991.

Jiménez, Sherry Lynn Mims. *The Pregnant Woman's Comfort Guide*. Englewood Cliffs, NJ: Prentice-Hall, 1983.

Kahn, Ada P. and Linda Hughey Holt, M.D. *Midlife Health*. New York: Facts on File Publications, 1987.

Lieberman, Adrienne. *Easing Labor Pain* (Revised Edition). Boston: Harvard Common Press, 1992.

Makower, Joel. *Office Hazards: How Your Job Can Make You Sick*. Washington, DC: Tilden Press, 1981.

Mills, Gary K. *Quiet Moments*. California: Media Health Publications, 1986.

Nuernberger, Phil. *Freedom From Stress*. Honesdale, PA: Himalayan International Institute of Yoga Science and Philosophy, 1981.

Ornish, Dean M.D. *Stress, Diet, and Your Heart*. New York: Holt, Rinehart and Winston, 1982.

Padus, Emrika. *The Complete Guide to Your Emotions and Your Health*. Emmaus, PA: Rodale Press, 1986.

Patel, Chandra, Dr. *The Complete Guide to Stress Management*. New York: Plenum Press, 1991.

Pelletier, Kenneth. *Mind as Healer, Mind as Slayer*. New York: Dell, 1976.

Pritikin, Robert. *The New Pritikin Program*, New York: Simon & Schuster, 1990.

Rama, Swami, Rudolph Ballatine, M.D. and Alan Hymes, M.D. *Science of Breath*. Honesdale, PA: The Himalayan International Institute of Yoga Science and Philosophy, 1979.

Selye, Hans. *Stress Without Distress*. Philadelphia; J.B. Lippincott Co., 1974.

_____. *The Stress of Life*. New York: McGraw-Hill, 1956.

Sharon, Michael, Dr. *Complete Nutrition*. London: PRION, 1989.

Siegel, Bernie, M.D. *Love Medicine and Miracles*. New York: Harper & Row, 1986.

Smith, Lendon, M.D. *Dr. Lendon Smith's Low-Stress Diet*. New York: McGraw-Hill Book Co., 1985.

Stellman, Jeanne, Ph.D. and Mary Sue Henifin, M.P.H. *Office Work Can Be Dangerous To Your Health*. New York: Pantheon Books, 1983.

Tisserand, Maggie. *Aromatherapy For Women*. Rochester, VT: Healing Arts Press, 1988.

Tisserand, Robert. *Aromatherapy to Heal and Tend the Body*. Santa Fe, NM: Lotus Press, 1988.

Tubesing, Donald. *Kicking Your Stress Habits*. Duluth, MN: Whole Person Associates, 1991.

_____ and Nancy Loving Tubesing. *Seeking Your Healthy Balance*. Duluth, MN: Whole Person Associates, 1983.

Tubesing, Nancy Loving and Donald A. Tubesing, Editors. *Structured Exercises In Stress Management*, Vol. 2. Duluth, MN: Whole Person Press, 1984.

Vischer, Jacqueline. *Environmental Quality In Offices*. New York: Van Nostrand Reinhold, 1989.

Index

A

AA; *see* Alcoholics Anonymous
Abundance, concensus and, 88
ACA; *see* Adult Children of Alcoholics
Accountability, 27, 40
ACOA; *see* Adult Children of Alcoholics
Action on Smoking and Health (ASH), 305
Active listening, 40, 102-107
Addiction, resources and further reading on, 294-295
Adolescent Narcissistic Personality Disorder, 122
Adrenalin high, 83, 117
Adrenalin
  effect of laughter on, 212
  release of, stress and, 176-177
Adult Children of Alcoholics (ACA; ACOA), 294
Aerobic exercise
  low-impact, in management of stress, 199-201
  osteoporosis and, 251
  premenstrual syndrome and, 241
Affiliation, 87
Affirmation, internal, reinforcement of self-esteem and, 34-35
Affirmation cards, spiritual wellness and, 136-137, 141,281-291
Ageism, 22, 250
Aggression, passive, 25-26
Air pollution, office, 224-226
Alcohol, 220
Alcoholics Anonymous (AA), 115
Alienation, 123
Alliances, 26
Altar Bazaar, 302
Alternate nostril breathing in management of stress,184-185
Altruism, spiritual wellness and, 170-173

Ambitions, self-knowledge and, 58-60
American Academy of Husband-Coached Childbirth, 303
American Association of Retired Persons (AARP), 301
American Massage Therapy Association, 303
Anatomy of an Illness, 212
Ankles, exercises for, 265
Annie Hall, 10
Anxiety neurosis, caffeinism and, 219
Arm extensions, 263-264
Arm fatigue, self-massage to relieve, 255
Arms, exercises for, 263-265
Aromatherapy
  resources and further reading on, 302
  scents and, 213-215
Aromatherapy For Women, 214
Art, spiritual wellness and, 139-140
ASH; *see* Action on Smoking and Health
ASPO/Lamaze, 304
Assertion skills, communication and, 110
Atonement, prayer and, 147
Aura Cacia, 302
Authority, appropriate, 69-73
Autogenic messages
  reinforcement of self-worth and, 34-35
  relaxation and, 191
Awareness
  breathing with, in management of stress, 179-183
  eating with, 217

B

Babysitter, 60-65, 248
Back
  exercises for, 257-260
  lower, tension in, self-massage to relieve, 255
  picking up objects without hurting, 209
Bailey, Covert, 201

INDEX

Beginner's meditation, spiritual wellness and, 142-144
Benson, Herbert, 189
Bernard Haldane Associates, 95, 293
Beyond the Parental Leave Debate, 248
Beyond the Relaxation Response, 189
Bly, Robert, 116-117
Body mechanics
  good, in workplace, 209-210
  posture and, 202
Bodywise Woman, 208
Boelter Environmental Consultants, 225
Bolen, Jean Shinoda, 150
Bonding, 87-88
Boston Women's Health Collective, 245, 247, 250, 298
Boundaries, emotional, restructuring, 73-76
Bradley Method, 303
Breastfeeding, resources and further reading on, 303-304
Breath
  cleansing, in management of stress, 179-180, 184
  complete, in management of stress, 184
  countdown, relaxation and, 191
Breath meditation, spiritual wellness and, 142-144, 145-147
Breathing
  alternate nostril, in management of stress, 184-185
  with awareness, in management of stress, 179-183
  chest, vs. abdominal breathing, 181
  conscious, in management of stress, 183-184
  deep, 38
  diaphragmatic, in management of stress, 180-183
  escape-hatch, relaxation and, 191
  level of, low-impact aerobics and, 200-201
  physiology of, in management of stress, 180-181
  rhythm of, stress management and, 146-147
  while exercising, 257
Briefcase, carrying, good body mechanics and, 209, 210
Burnout, 122
Bush, George, 248
Butterfly Effect, 69

C
Caffeine, effects of, 219
Caffeinism, 219
Calcium supplements, osteoporosis and, 250
Career changes, resources and further reading on, 293-294
Career consultants, independent, job search and, 94
Career Enterprises, 165, 306
Career marketing firms, job search and, 93-94
Career vs. home, 60-65
Carney, Mary Lang, 242
Carpal tunnel syndrome, video display terminals and, 231
Catecholamines, release of, stress and, 176-177
Celebrations, spiritual wellness and, 132, 166-170
Chair, ergonomic, 227
Chair potato, 226-228
Chaos, science of, 68
Chauvinism, 22
Chest, exercises for, 262-263
Chest breathing vs. abdominal breathing, 181
Childcare, 60-65, 248
Childhood, self-esteem and, 5
Children, well-being of, 60-65
Choices of emotional priorities, 12-18
Civil Rights Act of 1964, sexual harassment and, 29
Classified ads, job search and, 94
Cleansing breath
  to clear tension away, relaxation and, 190
  in management of stress, 179-180, 184
CODA; *see* Codependents Anonymous
Codependence
  generosity and, 171
  resources and further reading on, 294-295
Codependents Anonymous (CODA), 115, 294
Collegial structure of company, 20
Comfort, using positive imagery to transform tension into, visualization and, 193-194
Committee/Coalition/Council on Occupational Safety and Health (COSH) groups, 297

Communication, 97-110
 assertion skills and, 110
 buying time and, 104
 content and, 102, 104
 dysfunctional, 97-101
 emotional process and, 102, 104
 feedback and, 102, 104
 feelings and, 102
 I-statements and, 108-109
 learning to listen and, 102-107
 paraphrasing and, 104, 105-106
 in relationships, spiritual wellness and, 157-160
 you-statements and, 109
Communication skills, 102-110
Communion, spiritual wellness and, 141, 145-146
Community in relationships, spiritual wellness and,161-162
Complete breath in management of stress, 184
Compromises, 41
Compulsivity issues, resources and further reading on, 294-295
Concensus, 88
Concentration
 meditation and, 141-142
 in moment, spiritual wellness and, 141-142
 object, spiritual wellness and, 141
Conflict
 emotional, full-time job and, 12-18
 inner, resolving, 49-65
Conscious breathing in management of stress, 183-184
Contemplation, meditation and, 140-141
Contemplation rooms, on-site, 164-165
Content, communication and, 102, 104
Contingency search firms, job search and, 93
Contribution, Leadership and Grace, 165
Contrition, prayer and, 147
Cortisol, release of, stress and, 177
Cortisone, effect of laughter on, 212
COSH groups; *see* Committee/Coalition/Council on Occupational Safety and Health groups
Couch potato, 226-228
Countdown breath, relaxation and, 191
Cousins, Norman, 212
CTD; *see* Cumulative trauma syndrome
Culpability, 27
Cumulative trauma syndrome (CTD), video display terminals and, 230

D
Dalton, Katherine, 239
Day By Day, 137
Deep breathing, 38
Defenses
 defending, 76-80
 inappropriate, 25-26
 too few, 77
 too many, 77-80
Desires, self-knowledge and, 58-50
Dialogues, inner, reinforcement of self-esteem and,36-38
Diaphragmatic breathing in management of stress,180-183
Diet
 and nutrition, 215-217
 osteoporosis and, 250-251
 premenstrual syndrome and, 241
Discontent, 113-127
Discrimination, institutionalized, in dysfunctional hierarchies, 21-22
Domestic discord, reducing, 60-65
Domestic tasks, responsibility for, 13
Dominance, 87
Donation, spiritual wellness and, 132, 170-173
Dreams, self-knowledge and, 58-60
Dysfunctional communication, 97-101
Dysfunctional hierarchies, 19-22, 72
 abuse of power in, 20-21
 disparity of expectations in, 21
 institutionalized discrimination in, 21-22
 use of guilt and shame to control members' behavior in,21
Dysfunctional relationships, 22-28

E
E.A; *see* Emotions Anonymous
Ear to shoulder exercise, 260-261
Easing Labor Pain, 192
Eating with awareness, 217
Economic issues, resources and further reading on, 298-300
EEOC; *see* Equal Employment Opportunity Commission
Electromagnetic fields, video display terminals and,234
ELF magnetic fields; *see* Extremely low frequency magnetic fields
Elitism, 22
Emotional baggage in workplace, 4-8
Emotional conflict
 behavioral manifestations of, 18
 childcare and, 17

INDEX

early warning signals of, 17-18
feelings associated with, 17
full-time job and, 12-18
physical symptoms of, 17
Emotional health
  of employer, 18-19
  responsibility for, 39-40
Emotional issues, posture and, 202
Emotional needs, resources and further reading on, 295
Emotional pain, 7
Emotional priorities, choices of, 12-18
Emotional process, communication and, 102, 104
Emotional rewards of work, 4
Emotional self at work, 1-110
Emotional zone, 22-23
Emotions, eating and, 215-216
Emotions Anonymous (EA), 295
Employer, emotional and mental health of, 18-19
Employment agencies, job search and, 93
Empowerment, concensus and, 88
Endorphins, 126
  aerobic exercise and, 199
  laughter and, 212
Energy Breaks, 196-197
Enlightenment about workplace, resources and further reading on, 296
Environmental dis-ease, 224-225
Environmental ease, 225-226
Environmental Protection Agency, 225, 296-297
Equal Employment Opportunity Commission (EEOC), 22, 89, 90, 247, 305
Equal Rights Advocates, 298
Ergonomic chair, 227
Ergonomics, 227-228
Escape-hatch breathing, relaxation and, 191
Essential oils, aromatherapy and, 214-215
Executive needs, resources and further reading on, 296
Exercises
  aerobic; see Aerobic exercise
  as alternative to eating sweets, 217
  for the arms, hands and fingers, 263-265
  for the back, 257-260
  breathing during, 257
  for the eyes, 261-262
  Kegel, 208-209
  for the legs, ankles and feet, 265
  for the neck and head, 260-261

for pelvic health, 208
posture and, 206-208
premenstrual syndrome and, 241
resources and further reading on, 302
for the shoulders and chest, 262-263
that can be done at work, 257-265
for thighs, 265
weight-bearing, osteoporosis and, 250-251
Expectations, disparity of, in dysfunctional hierarchies, 21
Extortion, sexual harassment and, 29
Extremely low frequency (ELF) magnetic fields, video display terminals and, 234-235
Eye strain, video display terminals and, 229-230
Eyes
  exercises for, 261-262
  relaxation for, 262

F
Families and Work Institute, 248, 299
Family and Medical Leave Act of 1992, 248
Family issues, politics of, 247-248
Family leave, 248
Fat in diet, 218-221
Feedback, communication and, 102, 104
Feelings
  associated with emotional conflict, 17
  communication and, 102
  Gut voice as, 10-12, 36-38
  in workplace, 2-3
Feet, exercises for, 265
Female reproductive cycle, hormones and, 237-252
Feminist Majority Foundation, 299
Fiber in diet, 218-219
Fight or flight response, 25-26, 176-179, 199
Fingers
  exercises for, 263-265
  tension in, self-massage to relieve, 255
Fit or Fat, 201
Fit or Fat Woman, 201
Fitness center, on-site, 199-200
Flexing the toes, 265
Foods, processed, 220
Forward bend, 259-260
Franklin Day Planner, 57-58, 307
Functional hierarchies, 68-86

G

Gardner, Adelaid, 140-141
Gentle spinal twist, 260
Giving, spiritual wellness and, 132, 170-173
Goddesses in Every Woman, 150
Gordon, Thomas, 102
Gossip, 24
Gratitude, prayer and, 147
Gravity, posture and, 202
Grazing, blood-sugar levels and, 217
Group norms, 126
Gut voice, conversation between Little Voice and, 10-12, 36-38

H

Half circles with head, 261
Hand rolls and waves, 264
Hand squeeze, 265
Hands
  exercises for, 263-265
  tension in, self-massage to relieve, 255
Head
  half circles with, 261
  and neck, exercises for, 260-261
Headaches, self-massage to relieve, 253-254
Headhunters, job search and, 93
Health
  emotional, responsibility for, 39-40
  physical, 175-221
  women's, politics of, 247-248
Health hazards at work, resources and further reading on, 296-298
Health issues, resources and further reading on, 298-300
Healthy snacks at work, 217
Heart rate, low-impact aerobics and, 200-201
Heredity, posture and, 202
Hill, Anita, 28
Holt, Linda Hughey, 242
Home vs. career, 60-65
Hormones
  female reproductive cycle and, 237-252
  release of, stress and, 176-177
Humor
  resources and further reading on, 298
  stress and, 212-213
Humor Project, Inc., 213, 298

I

ICEA; *see* International Childbirth Education Association
Imagery, positive, use of, to transform tension into comfort, visualization and, 193-194
Independent career consultants, job search and, 94
Indoor Air Quality, 226
Industrial Revolution, 116-117
Inner conflicts, resolving, 49-65
Inner dialogues, reinforcement of self-esteem and, 36-38
Insoluble fiber, 218
Inspiration, spiritual wellness and, 134-135
Institute for Women's Policy Research, 299
Institutionalized discrimination in dysfunctional hierarchies, 21-22
Interiority, spiritual wellness and, 132
Internal affirmation, reinforcement of self-esteem and, 34-35
International Childbirth Education Association (ICEA), 304
Intimacy, inappropriate, at work, 23-25
I-statements, communication and, 90, 108-109

J

Jacobson, Edmund, 186
Jaw tension, self-massage to relieve, 254
Jiménez, Sherry Lynn Mims, 244
Job description, 39-40
Jobs, changing, 92-95
Junghanns, Herbert, 227

K

Keep It Simple, 137
Kegel exercises, 208-209
King, Billy Jean, 208

L

Labels of food products, reading, 217
LaLeche League, 304
Language of spiritual experience, 126
Laughing Matters, 213
Laughter, stress and, 212-213
Laziness, 27-28
LCD screens; *see* Liquid-crystal display screens
Leader Effectiveness Training, 102

INDEX

Leadership, balanced, 69-74
Legal issues, resources and further reading on, 298-300
Legs, exercises for, 265
Lieberman, Adrienne, 192
Liquid-crystal display (LCD) screens for video display terminals, 235
Listening, active, 40, 102-107
Little Voice (L.V.), conversation between Gut voice and, 10-12, 36-38
Location, spiritual wellness and, 132, 163-166
Lower back tension, self-massage to relieve, 255
Low-impact aerobic program in management of stress, 199-201
Lunch, bringing, to work, 217
L.V.; *see* Little Voice

M

Madison Pharmacy Associates (MPA), 303
Magic thinking, childhood and, 5
Magnetic fields, extremely low frequency, video display terminals and, 234-235
Mail marketing firms, job search and, 94
Mantra meditation, spiritual wellness and, 144-145
Marriage, health of, well-being of children and, 63-65
Martyrs, 27-28, 171
Massage, 196-199
  classic Swedish, 196
  on-site massage, 196, 198
  resources and further reading on, 302
  sports, 196
  therapeutic, 196
Massage chair, 197-198
Meditation
  beginner's, spiritual wellness and, 142-144
  breath, spiritual wellness and, 142-144, 145-147
  concentration and, 140-142
  contemplation and, 140-141
  mantra, spiritual wellness and, 144-145
  spiritual wellness and, 140-147
Meditation: A Practical Study, 140-141
Meditations for Women Who Do Too Much, 137
Menopause
  dealing with, at work, 249-250
  resources and further reading on, 301
Menopause News, 301
Men's Movement, 116-117, 118
Mental health of employer, 18-19
Mental inspiration, spiritual wellness and, 134-135
Mentor in relationships, spiritual wellness and, 160-161
Minerals and vitamins in management of stress, 219-220
Miscarriage, video display terminals and, 234
Monastic vacations, spiritual wellness and, 165
Montague, Ashley, 196
Moods, 46-47
Morning sickness, pregnancy and, 244
Motherhood, posture and, 202
Mothers, working; *see* Working mothers
MPA; *see* Madison Pharmacy Associates
Muscle strength, posture and, 202
Music
  resources and further reading on, 307
  spiritual wellness and, 138-139

N

Nadi Shodhanam, 184
National Association for Female Executives, 296
National Committee on Pay Equity, 299
National Institute for Occupational Safety and Health (NIOSH), 225, 226, 233, 234, 297
National Institutes for Health (NIH), 247
National Organization for Women (NOW), 300
National Osteoporosis Foundation, 250
National Women's Health Network, 250, 299
National Women's Law Center, 299-300
National Women's Political Caucus, 300
Nausea, pregnancy and, 244
Neck and head, exercises for, 260-261
Negative self-talk, 10-12
Negative stressor, 176
New Ways to Work, 300
NIH; *see* National Institutes for Health
9 to 5 National Association of Working Women, 229, 232, 234, 235, 250, 297, 304, 305

NIOSH; *see* National Institute for Occupational Safety and Health
Noradrenaline, release of, stress and, 176-177
Norms, group, 126
NOW; *see* National Organization for Women
Nutrition and diet, 215-217
NYCOSH, 297

O
OA; *see* Overeaters Anonymous
Object concentration, spiritual wellness and, 141
Occupational cervical brachial syndrome, video display terminals and, 231
Occupational Safety and Health Administration (OSHA), 226,297
Office air pollution, 224-226
Office chairs, 226-228
Office politics, 19
Older Women's League, 301
Older working women, resources and further reading on, 301-302
On Site Enterprises, 198
On-site fitness center, 199-200
On-site massage, 196, 198
OSHA; *see* Occupational Safety and Health Administration
Our Jobs, Our Health, 245
Outward Bound, 116
Overachiever, 27-28, 81, 83-85, 117
Overeaters Anonymous (OA), 115, 137
Over-responsibility, 27-28, 81, 83-85, 117

P
Pain, emotional, 7
Paraphrasing, communication and, 104, 105-106
Parental leave, 248
Passive aggression, 25-26
Passive relaxation, 187
Pelvic tilt against the wall, 257
Pelvic-floor muscles, exercises for, 208-209
Perfectionism, 41
Personal power, 87
Personal responsibility for emotional health, 39-40
Personal space, 22
Petition, prayer and, 147
Phone, holding, good body mechanics and, 210

Physical health, 175-221
Physical needs, resources and further reading on, 302-303
Physical space, 22
Physical survival, feelings and, 2-3
Plasma gas screens for video display terminals, 235
Playing the game, 72, 124
PMA; *see* Positive Mental Attitude
PMS; *see* Premenstrual syndrome
Pocket-sized inspiration daily books, spiritual wellness and,137-138
Poetry, spiritual wellness and, 138-139
Pointing and flexing the toes, 265
Political issues, resources and further reading on,298-300
Politics
  power without, 87-95
  of women's health and family issues, 247-248
Positive imagery, use of, to transform tension into comfort, visualization and, 193-194
Positive Mental Attitude (PMA), 46-47
Positive self-talk, reinforcement of self-esteem and,34-35
Positive stressor, 176
Postural problems, video display terminals and, 233
Posture, 201-202
  abdominal breathing and, 182
  exercise and, 206-208
  influences on, 202-204
  sitting and, 206, 207
  standing and, 204-206
Power
  abuse of, in dysfunctional hierarchies, 20-21, 124
  personal, 87
  without politics, 87-95
Power over, 87
Praise, prayer and, 147
Prayer
  attitudes of, 147
  brief restorative, 148-149
  from other cultures, 149
  spiritual wellness and, 147-149
Pregnancy
  dealing with, at work, 243-247
  first trimester changes in, 243-244
  morning sickness and, 244
  nausea and, 244
  resources and further reading on, 303-304

INDEX 301

rights of workers during, 245-247
second trimester changes in, 244
third trimester changes in, 245
unemployment benefits and, 246
video display terminals and, 234-235
Pregnant Woman's Comfort Guide, 244
Premenstrual syndrome (PMS), 46-47, 238-242
  dealing with, at work, 241-242
  diet and, 241
  exercise and, 241
  resources and further reading on, 303
Priorities
  emotional, choices of, 12-18
  juggling, 50-56
Prioritizing needs and limits, reinforcement of self-worth and, 39-45
Process, emotional, communication and, 102, 104
Processed foods, 220
Progressive relaxation, 186-187
Progressive Relaxation, 186
Protestant work ethic, 116-117
Public Citizen, 300
Purse, carrying, good body mechanics and, 209, 210
Pyramid structure of company, 20, 124

Q
Question cards, spiritual wellness and, 135-137, 141, 269-279

R
Racism, 22
Radiation filter for video display terminals, 235
Reaching overhead, 258-259
Recycling, 224
Reflection, spiritual wellness and, 127, 132, 133-140, 141
Relationship, spiritual wellness and, 132, 156-162
Relaxation
  autogenic suggestions and, 191
  cleansing breath to clear tension away and, 190
  countdown breath and, 191
  escape-hatch breathing and, 191
  for eyes, 262
  passive, 187
  progressive, 186-187
  resources and further reading on, 295
  script for, 188
  spiritual wellness and, 185-189

techniques of, to use at work, 190-192
tensing parts of body and, 190-191
visualization and, 192-195
yawn and stretch, 192
Relaxation and Stress Reduction Workbook, 211
Relaxation response, 189
Relaxation Response, 189
Religious writings, spiritual wellness and, 137
Rempel, David M., 232-233
Repetitive strain injury (RSI), video display terminals and, 230-233
Rescuers, generosity and, 171
Responsibility, 80-86
  inappropriate, 26-28
  personal, for emotional health, 39-40
Resume and secretarial services, job search and, 94
Retained search firms, job search and, 93
Retreats, spiritual wellness and, 165
Rewards, emotional, of work, 4
Rights of pregnant workers, 245-247
Rituals, spiritual wellness and, 167-170
RSI; *see* Repetitive strain injury
Rumor mill, 24

S
Sacred writings, spiritual wellness and, 137
Scapegoating, 40
Scents, aromatherapy and, 213-215
Schaef, Anne Wilson, 137
Schedule, rigid, of work, 123-124
Secretarial services, job search and, 94
Self, learned feelings about, 8-10
Self-analysis, 8-18
Self-esteem, 8-10
  autogenic messages and, 34-35
  childhood and, 5
  file of written compliments and, 35-36
  inner dialogues and, 36-38
  personal responsibility and, 38-39
  positive mental attitude and, 46-47
  prioritizing needs and limits and, 41-45
  reinforcement of, 33-47
  in workplace, 4-8
Self-knowledge, ambitions and, 58-60
Self-massage, 199, 253-255
Self-talk
  negative, 10-12
  positive, reinforcement of self-esteem and, 34-35
Sexual harassment, 19, 28-31

Civil Rights Act of l964 and, 29
damaging effects of, on individual, 30
extortion and, 29
resources and further reading on, 305
settling, 89-91
Sheehy, Gail, 249
Shiatsu, 196
Shoes, work, posture and, 204
Shoulder rotation, 262
Shoulder shrugs, 262
Shoulders
  and chest, exercises for, 262-263
  tension in, self-massage to relieve, 254
Sick-building syndrome, 224-226
Sitting, posture and, 206, 207
Smoking
  harmful effects of, 220
  resources and further reading on, 305
Social zone, 22
Soluble fiber, 218
Soul, spiritual wellness and, 114
Spiritual buddy system, 156-162
Spiritual desire, 154
Spiritual growth, commitment to, 154-156
Spiritual needs, resources and further reading on, 306
Spiritual self at work, 111-252
Spiritual wellness, 114, 129-173
  affirmation cards and, 136-137, 141, 281-291
  altruism and, 170-173
  art and, 139-140
  beginner's meditation and, 142-144
  breath meditation and, 145-147
  celebrations and, 132, 166-170
  communion and, 141, 145-146
  concentration and, 141-142
  donation and, 132, 170-173
  giving and, 132, 170-173
  inspiration and, 134-135
  interiority and, 133
  location and, 132, 163-166
  mantra meditation and, 144-145
  meditation and, 140-147
  mentors and, 160-161
  music and, 138-139
  pocket-sized inspiration daily books and, 137-138
  poetry and, 138-139
  prayer and, 147-149
  question cards and, 135-137, 141, 269-279
  questionnaire for, 119-121

  reflection and, 127, 132, 133-140, 141
  relationships and, 132, 156-162
  religious writings and, 137
  rituals and, 167-170
  sacred writings and, 137
  soul and, 114
  spiritual support and, 159-160
  support community and, 161-162
  symbols and, 166-167
  visualization and, 149-156
Sports massage, 196
Standing, posture and, 204-206
Stress, 176-179
  abdominal breathing in management of, 180-183
  alternate nostril breathing in management of, 184-185
  breathing techniques in management of, 179-185
  cleansing breath in management of, 179-180, 184
  complete breath in management of, 184
  conscious breathing in management of, 183-184
  definition of, 176
  diaphragmatic breathing in management of, 180-183
  different ways of responding to, 178-179
  low-impact aerobic program in management of, 199-201
  managing, 179-185
  negative, 176
  positive, 176
  video display terminals and, 233-234
Stress incontinence, pelvic-floor muscle exercises and, 208-209
Stress management
  breathing rhythm and, 146-147
  resources and further reading on, 295
Stress response, 176-179
Stressor, 176
Support groups for single parents, 63
Swedish massage, classic, 196
Swedish standards for video display terminals, 235
Sweets, blood-sugar level and, 216-217
Symbols, spiritual wellness and, 166-167

T
Telephone game, 97
Tenosynovitis, video display terminals and, 231
Tensing body, relaxation and, 190-191

INDEX

Tension
  physical, visualization in easing, 194
  self-massage to relieve, 253-254
  using positive imagery to transform, into comfort, visualization and, 193-194
The Silent Passage: Menopause, 249
Therapeutic massage, 196
Thigh exercise, 265
Thomas, Clarence, 28
Thoracic outlet syndrome, video display terminals and, 231
Tight-building syndrome, 224-226
Time management, 56-58, 210-212
  resources and further reading on, 307
Tisserand, Maggie, 214
Toes, pointing and flexing, 265
Touching, 196
Toughlove, 63
Triangles, 26

U

Ulnar neuropathy, video display terminals and, 231
Ultimate Organizer, 57-58, 307
Underachiever, 81-83
Under-responsibility, 81-83
Unemployment benefits, pregnancy and, 246

V

VDT; see Video display terminal
VDT Syndrome, 229
Video display terminal (VDT), 228-235
  add-on screen and, 235
  cumulative trauma disorder and, 230
  electromagnetic fields and, 234
  emotional stress and, 233-234
  extremely low frequency magnetic fields and, 234
  eye strain and, 229-230
  liquid-crystal display screen and, 235
  plasma gas screen and, 235
  postural problems and, 233
  pregnancy and, 234-235
  radiation filter and, 235
  repetitive strain injury and, 230-233
  Swedish standards of, 235
  wrist strain and, 230-233
Visualization
  in easing physical tension, 194
  extinguishing brush fire as, 194
  images and, 151-152
  inner guide and, 151-153

inner sanctuary and, 153-156
mental movies and, 192-193
relaxation and, 192-195
spiritual wellness and, 145, 146, 149-156
to use at work, 194-195
using positive imagery to transform tension into comfort and, 193-194
Vitamins and minerals in management of stress, 219-220
Vocational guidance, job search and, 94

W

Water, importance of, in diet, 220-221
Weight-bearing exercises, osteoporosis and, 250-251
Weleda, Inc., 302
White noise, mantra meditation and, 145
Wider Opportunities for Women, 300
Wishes, self-knowledge and, 58-60
Women Employed, 28
Women of the Nineties, 296
Women's health and family issues, politics of, 247-248
Women's Legal Defense Fund, 300
Work habits, posture and, 202-204
Work shoes, posture and, 204
Workaholism, 5-6, 7, 27-28, 41, 81, 83-85, 117, 133
Working mothers
  reducing domestic discord and, 60-65
  resources and further reading on, 306-307
Workplace, 1-31
  definition of, 23
  emotions in, 1-110
  enlightenment about, resources and further reading on, 296
  feelings in, 2-3
  good body mechanics in, 209-210
  learned feelings about, 8
Wrist rest, video display terminals and, 231-233
Wrist strain, video display terminals and, 230-233

Y

Yawn and stretch relaxation, 192
Yoga breathing techniques in management of stress, 184
You-statements, communication and, 109